World Cinema

4: IRELAND

The **World Cinema** series

General editor and publisher:
Matthew Stevens

The **World Cinema** series provides historical and appreciative surveys of the cinema of various countries. The following titles are published or in preparation:

1: Poland
Frank Bren
ISBN 0 948911 46 8

2: Sweden
Brian McIlroy
ISBN 0 948911 48 4

3: Holland
Phillip Bergson
ISBN 0 948911 50 6
in preparation

4: Ireland
Brian McIlroy
ISBN 0 948911 51 4

5: India
ISBN 0 948911 57 3
in preparation

6: Hungary
ISBN 0 948911 71 9
in preparation

World Cinema
4: IRELAND

Brian McIlroy

flicks books

British Library Cataloguing in Publication Data

McIlroy, Brian, *1959-*
   World cinema 4 : Ireland.
   1. Irish cinema films, to 1987
   I. Title
   791.43'09415

   ISBN 0-948911-51-4
   ISBN 1-871311-01-2 (Pb)

cover still: Geraldine Page in her role as Maurya in Ronan O'Leary's 1987 film version of *Riders to the Sea*. Still photograph by Wolfgang Suschitzky bsc, reproduced with thanks.

cover design: Barry Walsh

First published in 1989 by
Flicks Books
29 Bradford Road
Trowbridge
Wiltshire BA14 9AN

Typeset in 10 on 11 point and 9 on 10 point Palatino by Quill Auto Graphics, Banbury.

Printed and bound in Great Britain by Dotesios Printers Ltd., Bradford-on-Avon.

For Dad, Mum, Barbara and Michael

Contents

Acknowledgements

The author owes a great debt to the time and generosity of many people and organisations. In particular, he would like to thank all those who kindly agreed to be interviewed: Grace Carley, David Collins, Cyril Cusack, George Fleischmann, Neil Jordan, Louis Marcus, Robert Monks, Michael Open, Morgan O'Sullivan, Thaddeus O'Sullivan, Bob Quinn, David Shaw-Smith and Niall Toibín.

Informal conversations and written communication with the following were also exceedingly helpful: Patrick Carey, Sean Corcoran, Brian Ferran, David Hannon, John Hunt, Marie Jackson, David Kavanagh, John Mac Mahon, Bill Miskelly, Jim Mulkerns, Liam O'Leary, Helena Sheehan and Cheryl Herr.

For factual information, stills and general interest and support we must also thank the following: Tim Booth, Breffni Byrne, Vincent Corcoran, Catherine and David Hammond, Aidan Hickey, Kieran Hickey, Irish Film Institute, Margaret Jones (Film Corporation of Ireland), Martin Mahon (Yellow Asylum), Trish McAdam, Tom McArdle, George Morrison, Northern Ireland Tourist Board, Helen O'Donoghue and Joe Lee (Cityvision), Colm O Laoghaire, Ronan O'Leary, Brenda Rowan, Donald Taylor Black and Siobhán Twomey.

Particular thanks go to Ronan O'Leary and Wolfgang Suschitzky for the use of the cover still.

Help from librarians and their staff at the following institutions was invaluable: The National Library of Ireland; Belfast City Public Library; Linen Hall Library, Belfast; Trinity College, Dublin; University College, Dublin; University College, Cork; University College, Galway; Saint Patrick's College, Maynooth; National Institute of Higher Education, Dublin; The New University of Ulster at Coleraine; The Queen's University of Belfast; The Public Record Office of Northern Ireland; British Film Institute.

Personal thanks are due to Janice Fiamengo, Graham Huggan, Peter Wilkins, Eve Shamash and Rhoda Hanafi.

Introduction:
Unapproved roads –Irish film culture

Unapproved roads are signposted at the border which divides Northern Ireland and Éire. In recent times they have become mythologised as the illegal routes along which terrorists have escaped the clutches of the security forces in the North.

During the research for this book, I have often felt that I was being labelled as one of those shady individuals who stalk unknown paths for dubious purposes. By not viewing the notion of film and Ireland with some disdain, I was guilty, it seemed, of not heeding 'good' advice from the doyens of Irish culture, particularly in literature and theatre.

The cinema in Ireland has a long and impressive history that has not been championed, partly because it has been politically convenient not to do so and partly because of pure neglect. No conspiracy hysteria is intended here, only the recognition that to play down the national history of an art form is equal to saying that we do not wish to encourage that art form. And in the area of film, governments both north and south of the border have been decidedly ambivalent — and not just for financial reasons.

The closure of the Irish Film Board in June 1987 is a case in point. After many years of campaigning to establish an award-giving body and after only five years of (successful) operation on miniscule budgets, the Taoiseach, Charles Haughey, pulled the plug with the rather lame suggestion that the activities of the Film Board could be covered by the Arts Council with the latter's increased funding from the National Lottery. How this will work is unclear.

Equally uncertain when I was travelling around Ireland conducting interviews was the effect this closure would have on the projected Irish Film Centre in Eustace Street, Dublin, to be run by the Irish Film Institute. One can only hope along with its director, David Kavanagh, that the new centre will have so many diverse activities that it will weather any future economic or government dictates.

A noticeable and encouraging feature stemming from the Film Board has been the creation of a number of production companies both north and south of the border. Of these, Aisling in Belfast (*The End of the World Man*) and Strongbow in Dublin (*Eat The Peach*) are the best known.

Furthermore, the arrival in Dublin of a $3 million American project on the production of classical animation films in Ireland augurs well for the future. Over two hundred young Irish people are being trained in the techniques necessary to make feature-length animated films at the Sullivan Bluth studios. *An American Tail* (1987) was produced in Hollywood by animation genius Don Bluth in association with Steven Spielberg and used twenty-six Irish people as part of the production team. Now Bluth and Irish American Morris Sullivan have moved their entire operation to Dublin and soon, they claim, Ireland could become the world centre for classical animation.

Another encouraging sign was the purchase of the Ardmore studios by a consortium consisting of MTM Enterprises, Dublin-based Tara Productions and the National Development Corporation. Now refurbished, Ardmore is run by the ebullient Morgan O'Sullivan, who hopes to attract a major television series to Ireland while upgrading the facilities at the studios.

O'Sullivan, one of those interviewed for the book, quite rightly raises the issue of visual literacy in Ireland. We have placed too much emphasis on the written word, its codes and conventions, and too little on how to criticise television and film in a constructive way. The situation in schools should be changing now that there has been established in England and Wales a Modern Communications and Film Studies 'O' level and Communication Studies and Film Studies 'A' level.

In Ireland undergraduate courses in media studies are taught at the National Institute of Higher Education in Dublin and at the University of Ulster at Coleraine. The Irish Film Institute has helped introduce media studies units into the school and college curricula. Significantly, serious film study has not made any solid entrance into the traditional universities of Ireland. Given the general malaise in university staffing in the 1980s, it is unlikely this deficiency will be corrected in the near future.

With this historical lack of interest by Irish universities, colleges and libraries, added to the general problems of films disappearing, disintegrating or simply being withdrawn from distribution, a film historian must rely on a great deal of written material to fill in the gaps on particular productions. But here, too, we are ill-served. As Kevin Rockett states in his book, *Cinema and Ireland* (1987), there is no accessible and central Irish film documentation centre.

One beacon in this darkness has been Liam O'Leary, Ireland's foremost film historian, who started his own archives many years ago. He has written that he has divided his indexed material on over one thousand films as follows:
(1) films made in Ireland by Irish and foreign directors;
(2) films made abroad by Irish people;
(3) films with an Irish content or theme;

(4) films based on Irish literary works. O'Leary's archive, which includes the Robert O'Doherty Collection (some three hundred boxes of pressbooks from the 1920s), has been donated to the National Library of Ireland and was being catalogued in 1987. O'Leary is currently writing a major history of the early cinema in Ireland.

One of the key questions raised by most cinéphiles is: what constitutes an Irish film? It seems sensible to adopt a liberal policy here, for although a director may be Irish his financial backing and subject matter may not be. Since this book is concerned essentially with Irish film culture, I believe one should consider not only films directed by Irish people on Ireland but also films directed by foreigners on Ireland, provided their images have been regarded as influential. Attention must be paid, for example, to Robert Flaherty's *Man of Aran* and John Ford's *The Quiet Man*.

Similarly it seems peripheral to discuss Irish-born directors such as Rex Ingram and Irish-American actors such as James Cagney because most of their films were made outside Ireland on non-Irish topics. The bulk of this book therefore considers films made in Ireland on Irish subjects whether or not directed by Irish men or women. As a general survey, my text also touches upon many aspects of Irish society, including censorship and governmental artistic policy.

In compiling a national film history, one is tempted to adopt a long shot theory, a contextualising process which links films directly with their social and political era. This approach has been taken up forcefully by Kevin Rockett, Luke Gibbons and John Hill in their book, *Cinema and Ireland*. However, since Flicks Books are attempting to compile a complete Irish filmography, it seems to me sensible for the present to be cautious and place emphasis on individual directors and films. I believe more accurate and wide-ranging assessments will be possible at a later stage.

By including thirteen interviews with Irish film personalities — feature and documentary film directors, cameramen, producers, actors and administrators — the reader may make up his or her own mind about the state of Irish cinema as at June 1987 when the majority of these conversations took place. The inclusion of only one woman is regrettable, although perhaps someone will write a volume on Irish women and film, including the work of directors Marie Jackson and Pat Murphy, and actress Brid Brennan. The selected filmographies and bibliography also attest to the level of interest in cinema and Ireland.

Several other areas of future research are all too apparent - biographical and critical works on Sidney Olcott, Brian Desmond Hurst, Richard Hayward and Donovan Pedelty; George Bernard Shaw as screenwriter; and British and German war films on Ireland. John Ford's many 'Irish' films need a thorough re-examination and the contribution of John Huston, including his last completed film, *The Dead*, requires urgent evaluation.

More attention needs to be paid to star study: since Ireland has always had no shortage of excellent stage actors, it is not surprising that many of them have been sought after for international film roles — Cyril Cusack, Ray McAnally, Brid Brennan, Donal McCann, Niall Toibín and Stephen Rea to name but a few. In tracing these particular artists, a writer may be able to reflect on what it is that makes their Irishness so marketable in the often heady world of film production. For example, what are the similarities and differences in McAnally's portrayal of the bishop in *The Mission* and of Billy the Beast in *No Surrender*? Is his perceived Irishness used to solidify or to challenge stereotyping?

Naturally, the role of television has become increasingly important to independent film-makers. Channel 4 has recently commissioned eight films from independents, each depicting different aspects of Ireland, to be screened in 1988. Radio Telefís Éireann, BBC Belfast and Ulster Television have all played their part over the years in producing filmed documentaries. Much of this work has gone unrecorded, although there are some reverred individuals such as John Mac Mahon at Radio Telefís Éireann and David Hannon at Ulster Television who have and are compiling inventories of their respective collections. One can only hope the rumour that BBC Belfast has thrown out all pre-1967 material is unfounded.

In 1984 Ulster Television made a six-programme series on the history of the cinema in Ireland, which was subsequently shown on Channel 4. It attracted a great deal of criticism from *Film Directions* magazine in the North and Kevin Rockett in the South for not contextualising the films and for not seeking out the distribution and exhibition patterns of certain Irish-made films. The simple fact of the matter, however, is that it is exceedingly difficult to find out accurately how, for example, Richard Hayward's Northern Irish comedies in the 1930s were distributed and under what financial arrangements. Obviously more energetic research and ingenuity are required.

One of my aims in writing this book has been to balance activities north and south of the border. Contrary to the imprecise description they often receive from the world media, the Protestants in the North are *Irish* (as well as British) people who wish to retain a link with Great Britain for economic and social as well as political reasons. Cultural reasons for the separation of North and South are not so obvious. In my estimation, the cultural differences between Galway and Dublin are greater than those between Dublin and Belfast. Yet it is perversely true that the presence of the Protestants in Ireland has stimulated film production in the area of *difference*.

This 'otherness', however, is often unsubtly explored in Irish films as the non-Catholic. It is not hard to criticise the liberal *Willie Reilly and His Colleen Bawn* (1920) for lack of analysis of the 'problem', but one may equally criticise many subsequent films for taking the easiest option — for example, the Black and Tans 'bashing' in Tom Cooper's *The Dawn* (1936).

Significantly, there seems to be a lack of films dealing with the Civil War when Catholic nationalist killed Catholic nationalist, as if this area would open too many old wounds. More serious, perhaps, is the tendency to transfer the fall guy from the English and Scottish Black and Tans to the present-day RUC (Royal Ulster Constabulary) and UDR (Ulster Defence Regiment) in Northern Ireland. Films such as *Angel* and *Cal* can be read, as John Hill has provocatively argued in *Cinema and Ireland*, as unfortunately contributing to the blurring of the real contemporary issues.

I believe it is dangerous to try to fit any tight theoretical framework onto the haphazard and unique collection of films on Ireland. But if I were to take up Hill's dissatisfaction with these two films it would be on the grounds that both in their construction tend towards the depiction of the Protestant community in Northern Ireland in military terms, as if there were only Catholic civilians. To dress Protestants mainly in the uniforms of the RUC and the UDR is to strip them of their Irishness, to give them a transitory military identity that ties them to the Black and Tans. After all, it is easier to categorize a person in uniform, whether with an Orangeman's bowler hat, white gloves and sash, or with the dark attire and grey armoured car of the RUC, bristling with machine guns, than to confront the Protestant civilian ideology. But you cannot force a United Ireland without first uniting the minds of divergent peoples.

Even the interesting 'Protestant' film, *Ascendancy*, resorts to a number of military clichés. Perhaps future Irish films can attack these stereotypes, just as Louis Marcus found that in his remaking of a film on Patrick Pearse, he could no longer applaud a romantic nationalist ideology. One can only hope that such revisionism will help to span the divides that threaten to become unbridgeable in the North today.

The Protestant and Catholic directors of Field Day, an organisation promoting a new approach to old Irish problems, would appear to be part of this vanguard. However, I know that the company has to date not won the hearts and minds of both Belfast communities, whatever success they are having in the North-West. Hampered by a lack of resources, to suggest the company embark on a film programme in addition to their pamphleteering and theatrical activities may only invite ridicule but this is exactly what is needed. Cultural activity can and does educate and this is why it is imperative that governments in both the North and the South (as well as private corporations) should pay attention and encourage with more substance than rhetoric film production throughout the island of Ireland.

Brian McIlroy
Belfast
August 1988

1: Golden offerings —
colonial Ireland 1896-1921

The Palace Theatre, Cork, which Dan Lowrey opened in 1897.

Dan Lowrey

The chronology of Irish cinema begins with a shrewd businessman and entertainer of lowly origin — Dan Lowrey.

Born in 1823 in Roscrea, Co. Tipperary, at the age of six Lowrey and his family emigrated to Leeds, England, where his father found work in the textile industry. In his adopted country, young Dan Lowrey began to make a name for himself as a singer and comedian. Perhaps because he was illiterate, Lowrey worked hard at his dramatic and verbal skills.

Early Irish cinema

Lowrey returned to Ireland in his forties after building up some capital by running The Nightingale, a 'musical tavern' in Liverpool. His first purchase was The Alhambra, a music hall in North Street, Belfast in the early 1870s. Lowrey also looked southwards, opening up The Star of Erin Music Hall in Dublin in 1879. It was at this hall on 20 April 1896 that films (or moving images) were screened in Ireland to a paying public for the first time.

According to Matthew Murtagh and Eugene Watters in their affectionate history of Lowrey's Dublin music hall, the audience was sadly disappointed. Lights flashed on and off and the moving images of prize-fighters and acrobats were barely visible. By October, however, Lowrey had acquired better projection equipment and screened a revamped Lumière programme. Among the films shown was the famous *L'Arrivée d'un Train en Gare de la Ciotat/Arrival of a Train*, whose shot of a train roaring towards the camera shocked and thrilled audiences.

In November this programme was shown at Lowrey's Empire Theatre of

Varieties in Belfast, which had opened in Victoria Street in 1894. This may have been the first exhibition of films in that city, although claims that a screening of moving pictures took place at a business in Belfast's High Street, a few months before Lowrey's presentation, still have to be established.

It is believed that a cinematograph demonstration was given by the Royal Dublin Society in Leinster House, possibly just after Lowrey's first projection attempt in April and after the visit of Georges Promio, the French brothers' cameraman, who came to Ireland in 1896 to record scenes in Belfast, Lisburn, Kingstown (now Dun Laoghaire) and Dublin.

Certainly in 1897 interest in film had taken root: William Nicholl gave a lecture on the electric cinematograph to the Belfast Natural History and Philosophical Society; Robert Paul came from England to present his Animatographe at Belfast's Grand Opera House; and Dan Lowrey expanded his activities to Cork, opening up the Palace Theatre of Varieties in King Street at which was billed Professor Jolly's "Cinematographe". This programme included street scenes in Dublin and footage of the 13th Hussars marching through the capital.

Documenting Irish scenes

One of the more significant local efforts is documented by George Morrison in his brief history of Irish cinema in *Ireland: A Cultural Encyclopaedia*. He records the endeavours of a Dr R A Mitchell, who must have had a strong physique and will to capture on film a yacht race taking place on Belfast Lough in 1898. Mitchell lived near Holywood (County Down, not California!), from where one can look out on the waterway.

More traditionally, it comes as no surprise to learn that when Queen Victoria visited Ireland in 1900, her trip was filmed

L'Arrivée d'un Train en Gare de la Ciotat

and shown in numerous vaudeville houses. But most important that year was the establishment of a company to exhibit and distribute films: the Irish Animated Pictures Company Ltd.

In 1904, as an offshoot from the company, the projectionist Louis de Clerq made a film of his own: *Life on the Great Southern and Western Railway*. This film can be regarded as the first notable Irish documentary, despite the fact that the director was Belgian. 1904 also brought the formation of a production company, the Irish Animated Photo Co., which filmed the consecration of the Roman Catholic Cathedral at Armagh that year. Other films produced in Ireland at this time included footage of semi-official events such as the Dublin Horse Show and boat regattas.

Some intriguing questions about early Irish film material have been raised by Liam O'Leary in a recent *Irish Times* article. Ireland's foremost film historian mentions a recording of Patrick Pearse in 1903 and Robert Paul's 1908 film which drew attention to the Aranmore Whaling Company, *Whaling Ashore and Afloat*. In his monumental history of the cinema, Georges Sadoul mentions the highly political but lost film, also believed to have been directed by Robert Paul, *A Cattle Drive in Galway* (1908).

Film researcher Anthony Slide has ferreted out what must be the first fiction film devoted to an Irish topic, *Irish Wives and English Husbands* (1907). The English director, Arthur Melbourne-Cooper, came over ostensibly to film a travelogue, *London to Killarney*, but he seems to have got carried away as he persuaded a Killarney girl, Kate O'Connor, to star in his comic drama. It must have been a very loose fiction film if, as Slide tells us, it was cut from the travelogue.

In the absence of a film archive in Ireland, films of this type and era either have disappeared altogether or can be found only in private or foreign collections. Sadly, the filming of Patrick Pearse's oration at the funeral of O'Donovan Rossa in 1915 has not survived.

Lucien Bull

If films have regularly emigrated from Ireland so have talented, and later often famous, people. A prime example in this early period is inventor Lucien Bull.

Born George Lucien in Dublin in 1876, Bull was educated at Belvedere College, and at the University of Paris, where he lived and worked most of his life, although

Whaling Ashore and Afloat

he frequently visited Ireland. In 1904 Bull invented the techniques of ultra-rapid and slow-motion photography. Given Ireland's tendency to incorporate anything of importance, however tenuous its connection with the old country, it is surprising that Bull has not become more widely known. Perhaps it is because his interests were so diverse: in 1911 he worked successfully on cinematography of Brownian motion; he experimented with chronophotography of ballistic phenomena in 1919; and in 1952 he recorded cinematic images at one million images per second. He was awarded the CBE and made an officer of the Legion of Honour.

Military historians seem to have given Bull more prominence, as in 1915 he established an apparatus which calculated the distance of enemy guns by the level of gunfire sound. Lucien Bull died in Paris in August 1972.

Film pioneers

Entrepreneurs and film pioneers saw the first fifteen years of this century as an extremely fruitful one. One of the leading lights was James T Jameson whose activities involved screenings in the Pavilion, Dun Laoghaire and Rathmines Town Hall, as well as in selected Irish towns. We have extant pictures of A D Coon's travelling cinema vehicle which looks like an adapted railway carriage, as well as pictures of Ralph and Gaynor Coon operating the projectors for their father's business.

Thus variety halls began to ease the way towards purpose-built cinemas, the most notable in 1907 and 1908 being the Royal Hippodrome and St George's Hall in Belfast and the Queen's Theatre in Dublin. Sometimes these occasional picture-houses ran foul of the authorities: when the Irish Animated Picture Company presented the Johnson-Jeffries "fight" in

4

August 1910, it provoked the severe censure of both the Archbishop and the Lord Mayor of Dublin. However, they were unable to prevent the screenings.

James Joyce and the Volta cinema

It often shocks literary purists that James Joyce, the famous author of *Ulysses* and *Finnegans Wake*, was responsible for Ireland's first cinema: the Volta in Dublin. And although it lasted less than a year, the cinema set a precedent for future enterprises.

Richard Ellmann's biography of Joyce dwells with much humour on the circumstances surrounding this particularly significant incident in Irish film history. In September 1909 Joyce had returned to Trieste. Picking up on a loose remark by his sister Eva — that it was surprising Dublin had not a single cinema while the smaller Trieste had several — Joyce immediately set about thinking how he could capitalise on the deficiency and doubtless bring some infamy to his name.

Through an intermediary he arranged a meeting with four businessmen who had connections with the cinema scene in Trieste. Joyce seemed to impress them, perhaps because of his internationally tantalising statement that he knew of a city with 500 000 people that had not one cinema. Eventually admitting that the city in question was Dublin, he supported his argument by pointing out on a map that, in addition, neither Belfast nor Cork had a custom-built cinema and that therefore Ireland was a market for the taking if they moved quickly.

Joyce set off for Dublin after signing an agreement that he would receive ten per cent of the cinema's profits. By the end of October he had located a suitable building in Mary Street, just off the major Sackville Street (now O'Connell Street). When his

James Joyce in 1902

Italian partners arrived they toured Belfast and Cork to consider the possibilities of opening in those cities, but finally they settled on Dublin.

One of the Italian businessmen, a bicycle-shop owner from Trieste, Francesco Novak, was put in charge of the cinema when Joyce left Dublin. Joyce's father, forever acerbic, labelled one of the businessmen, leather merchant Giovanni Rebez, as "the hairy mechanic with the liontamer's coat" which doubtlessly appealed to his son's theatrical imagination. An Italian projectionist was employed and Joyce interviewed and chose other employees who were Irish.

Once a proper licence had been obtained, the cinema opened on 20 December 1909 and attracted good, though rather superficial, reviews. Its programme included *Bewitched Castle*, *The First Paris Orphanage* and *The Tragic Story of Beatrice Cenci*. The admission prices were 6d, 4d and 2d and a continuous performance was scheduled from 5 pm to 10 pm. A small string orchestra provided entertainment in the afternoon.

The *Bioscope* of 23 December announced that a branch of the International Cinematograph Society Volta was opening in Dublin. Unfortunately, scanty details remain about this organisation, but it was probably blarney by Joyce's businessmen. The announcement stated that they had twenty-three "film-producing factories" in Europe and would specialise in Dublin in "opera film" after French and Italian houses. Joyce seemed then to be on the crest of a wave. In fact he was so enthusiastic about the enterprise that he sent posters of the first screening to his brother Stanislaus in Trieste to convince the former's creditors that good news was just around the corner. The trouble with Joyce and the Volta was that corners never seemed to straighten.

Why Joyce and his partners expected Novak, a bicycle-shop proprietor after all, to succeed in Dublin is not clear; in any event, business deteriorated with Novak's diet of mostly Italian films which were regarded, strangely, as anti-Catholic. Lenny Collinge, an apprentice electrician at the Volta, remembered that the audience consisted mostly of working-class people looking for warmth and shelter.

1909 Cinematograph Act

The state's attitude to the cinema is perhaps best understood by the fact that 1909 also saw the passing of a Cinematograph Act by the British Parliament. This demanded that all cinemas be issued with licences from their local authority.

Although ostensibly this ensured that buildings complied with fire regulations, it also served as a means of censorship. Searching through the Excises Licences Book in Dublin for the years 1909-10, one can discover the granting of a licence on 19 January 1910 to James Joyce, Cinematograph Manager, for "music only and not at all on Sunday".

After seven months of operation the Volta closed down and was sold to the Provincial Theatre Company. Collinge moved to the Grafton Theatre which opened in 1911, following the opening of the Sackville Theatre in 1910: these two theatres became the major picture-houses in Dublin.

Sidney Olcott and the Kalem Company

A village with only a guest house, pub and shop in South-West Ireland became an unlikely centre of film activity between 1910 and 1914.

The man behind this move to the country and to Beaufort village was Sidney Olcott, a Canadian whose mother was born in Dublin; born Alcott, Sidney was renamed after the stage Irishman, Chauncey Olcott.

Olcott worked for the Florida-based Kalem Company which flourished between 1907 and 1915. One day in Hollywood, Olcott was presented by his manager, Frank J Marion, with an offer he could hardly refuse. Marion took out a map of the world, spread it out flat and told Olcott he could go anywhere he liked to make his films. Olcott, so the story has it, pointed immediately to Ireland and set off with his leading lady, Gene Gauntier, and his cameraman, George Hollister.

And so in the summer of 1910 in Beaufort, near Killarney, Olcott made the ten-minute film, *The Lad from Old Ireland*. In this short, Irish emigrant Terry makes a fortune in the United States and returns to the 'old sod' to rescue his love, Aileen, from eviction before they are married. Another one-reeler made at this time was *The Irish Honeymoon*, which Olcott put together by filming various Irish locations such as Blarney Castle and Killarney lakes.

The Lad from Old Ireland was released on 23 November 1910, after some shots were made in New York, and *The Irish Honeymoon* some four months later. Both received good reviews from the *Moving Picture World* which emphasized the fact that here for the first time was an American production company going outside the United States to make films.

Purely on the success of *The Lad from Old Ireland* in the American market, Olcott arrived the next summer with more technicians. After staying just a few days in Killarney, they moved to Beaufort in search of some devastating scenery. The first film they made was *Rory O'More* from the novel of the same name by Samuel Lover, in which a young Irish revolutionary is tried and sentenced but escapes from the British noose and brings his mother and sweetheart to America. Jack Clark, Gene Gauntier and Robert Vignola star.

That summer Olcott and his team produced a further seventeen films whose titles are somewhat endearing: *You'll Remember Ellen*, *Shaun the Post*, *The Fishermaid of Ballydavid*, *The Girl of Glenbeigh* and *Gipsies in Ireland*.

The choice of *Rory O'More* gives us some insight into the character of Sidney Olcott. It is clear that he favoured the Irish struggle against the British and this may be confirmed by the title of another 1911 film — *Ireland the Oppressed*. This partisan approach did not go unnoticed and representations were made to Olcott's company to resist controversial material in order to avoid an unceremonial despatch back to America. Olcott decided to compromise by making adaptations of Dion Boucicault's plays, including *Arrah-na-Pogue*, released on 21 November 1911 in three reels and starring Jack Clark, Gene Gauntier and Olcott himself. A significant feature of this film was the four-piece orchestral score composed by Walter

Rory O'More

Cleveland Simon for the Kalem Company. This was the first American picture to have a musical score specifically written for it.

Kalem bought the rights to the Boucicault plays and an extant letter from Marion to Olcott indicates that the cost for both European and American exclusive rights to *The Shaughraun* (1912) was US$500. We may assume, therefore, that similar deals, although less costly for non-exclusive rights, were settled for other films such as *The Colleen Bawn* (1911). This film stars Gene Gauntier as Eily O'Connor, the colleen, and Jack Clark as Myles na gCoppaleen; it was released in three reels on 16 October 1911. Olcott himself plays the disabled Danny, a part for which he won much praise in *The Moving Picture World*.

Olcott's film was the second version of Boucicault's play made that year; the other was produced by the Yankee Film Company. However, Olcott's film was the most sought after and was reissued in February 1914. This reissue was accompanied with a literal spread of Irish-American sentimentalism regarding the "ould sod". Olcott's company brought over several tons of Irish soil and distributed it in 4' square trays, so that cinema-goers could actually stand in the "magic stuff"!

The filming of *The Colleen Bawn* in 1911 was interrupted for a week by a typically Irish story. One day the Olcott group attended the local church, only to hear the priest criticise the film-makers for degrading the Irish by filming in the churchyard and thereby despoiling consecrated ground; he was also upset at the locals dressed-up in English uniforms. Somewhat taken aback, Olcott sought the assistance of the American consul who had a quiet word with the area bishop who, in turn, suggested that the parish priest apologise. Apparently the priest's original remarks were prompted by complaints from local traders that visitors were ignoring the shops and following the filming instead. This incident may have prompted Olcott's interest in religious figures in his making of *The Franciscan Friars of Killarney* which was released on 29 November 1911.

Agnes Mapes, one of the young Kalem staff, wrote to her New York brother about the 'Irish' experience. Published in *The Moving Picture World* in July 1911, the following excerpt gives a sense of the feeling of paradise which seems to have infected the Kalem Company:

"We came out here Wednesday. Sid found it too far from Killarney proper to run in and out for our locations, so here we are installed in a really and truly country house, by courtesy called a hotel, but in truth an old-fashioned house and an Irish one at that....A long, low stone, whitewashed and strawroofed cabin or cottage in the center, a divided door, stonepaved floor, big open fireplace, peat burning, iron kettles hanging on the crane, cooking the dinner or boiling water, the Irish terrier Barney in the corner of fireplace, a big bench side of wall, hams and bacon hanging overhead and the bar on the side, the daughters acting as barmaids. In the evenings the lads and lassies come in to dance and Miss O'Sullivan, the proprietor's daughter plays the accordion for them to dance. Mind you the room is a small one, and when the square dance is on we all hug the wall....The boys have worked like beavers since we have been here. In fact we all have. Putting up costumes, getting things in order. The stage in the field was built this morning. The boys are now building an outside bathroom. We are certainly making the Irish open their eyes."

The Kalem group returned to Beaufort in the summer of 1912 and made a version of Boucicault's *The Shaughraun*. In December Stephen Bush in *The Moving Picture World* awarded the film many superlatives, if only to argue that the art of film could stand equally beside that of the novel and the play. Bush particularly complimented the advantage of the "moving studio" to give "a perspective of real nature" and he praised the realistic interiors of Irish huts and cottages.

The Colleen Bawn

8

Olcott had progressively been venturing into three-reel films which meant a running time of at least thirty minutes. In many other ways these films advanced the art of film production: firstly, the practice of location filming; secondly, the professional attitude towards the shooting script — Gauntier and Olcott often worked into the small hours to ensure the script was ready for the next day's filming; thirdly, the use of the local population for crowd and bit parts as a way of becoming involved with the community.

Gauntier on Olcott

Gene Gauntier has given a perceptive and colourful account of Olcott at work:

"He was medium height, deep chested, with slender sensitive hands, ruddy skin, and a small well shaped head of close cropped curly hair....He was interested in philosophy and psychic phenomena, and was himself psychic to an uncanny degree. It was impossible to keep anything from Olcott. He knew what was going on through some sixth sense. Consciously, or unconsciously, he used the power of suggestion, or even hypnotism, on his actors. He would stare straight into our eyes with those large blue orbs of his and never shift his glance as he explained the situation or action. No one thought of questioning his instructions or of refusing, no matter how difficult, to do the stunt he demanded. He was Irish and possessed all the sparkle and sentiment of that emotional race....He would work like a Trojan, giving all his strength and vitality....Shouts, threats, sarcasm, cajoling, petting, he would try each in turn. But after the scene was over it was always the same — an arm thrown over the shoulder, compliments, enthusiasm".

1912 proved to be the last trip to Ireland under the auspices of the Kalem Company because trouble was brewing at home.

Earlier in the summer in Egypt and Palestine Olcott had made *From the Manger to the Cross*. This film raised eyebrows in certain quarters, including Ireland, because Gene Gauntier, who had been married to Jack Clark during the previous Irish filming, was now divorced and yet she played the Virgin Mary. To avoid specific personal criticism the Kalem Company released this film without cast or crew credits. Olcott, Gauntier and Clark resigned in protest. Marion had in fact written to Olcott releasing him, though offering to keep him at a reduced salary — apparently because of growing competition, diminishing sales and the threat of government lawsuits.

A few days before Christmas 1912 the Gene Gauntier Feature Players Company was publicised in the variety press. Gauntier, Olcott and Clark were the main members. The company was referred to by some as "the Gee-Gees" and eventually "the O'Gees". They set sail for Ireland and Beaufort where they made *For Ireland's Sake*, released in January 1914 and *Come Back to Erin*, released in March. Olcott broke away from the company earlier that year and formed Sid Films; he travelled with his new leading lady and future wife, Valentine Grant, back to Beaufort for the fifth and last time.

Robert Emmet, Ireland's Martyr was Olcott's next production. This naturally caused some comment and censure by the British authorities who successfully prevented its showing at the Rotunda in Dublin in 1915. The British military argued that the film would have a debilitating effect on war recruitment. It made no difference that Emmet was played by the English actor Jack Melville. Olcott's sympathies for the Nationalist and Republican causes can be gauged by his allowing his prop guns to be used by the Irish volunteers in their march through Killarney. Furthermore, Pat O'Malley, the

Kalem actor, was given honorary status by the volunteers during his time in the country.

Olcott talked of creating a permanent studio in Beaufort but the war intervened and he pursued other projects in the United States. But there is a touching end to the story of Olcott's period in Ireland. After Valentine Grant died in March 1949 and shortly before his death nine months later, Olcott sent Annie O'Sullivan, his hostess in Beaufort, a gold bracelet which had belonged to his wife. His Irish days had obviously been of special importance.

Ireland's first colour film

This early period also saw the first shooting of a colour film in Ireland. This is believed to have been in 1911 when a newsreel was made covering the post-coronation visit of George V, along with other events such as boat-racing and horse shows. These events may have been those shown at the first colour film screening on April Fool's Day 1912 at the Grand Opera House in Belfast.

The enthusiasm for film production ran in tandem with Olcott's activities: the *Bioscope* of 4 April 1912 carried the news that W H Huish, a manager of the Provincial Cinematograph Company in Dublin, wanted to show more Irish films because "Why should not Ireland produce films! We have seen some of the finest scenery in the world, and a wealth of legendary lore, which would form admirable subject matter". Huish had his eye on the American market in particular.

Some of this legendary lore is drawn upon for *The Life of St Patrick* (1913), produced by J Theobald Walsh for the American Photo Historic Film Company, and about which we know little. According to the *Bioscope* of 20 February that year, Dublin picture-house proprietors were gathering to discuss projected plans to deal with the hazards of

exhibition - overcrowding, the risks of fire and charges for British imports and distribution.

It should be remembered that going to the cinema at this time was cheap, novel and often therapeutic; yet there are stories of police regularly breaking up violence outside cinemas as cinéphiles converged to gain entry. By 1914 the police had to monitor some fourteen cinemas in Dublin alone. Often there were disturbances which the police did not have to break up. One example occurred in March 1914 when a British army recruitment film was exhibited at a picture house in Sackville Street, Dublin. A number of the audience hissed at the film, cheered the German Emperor and sang "Who Fears to Speak of '98?"; one gentleman stood up and declared on behalf of "Irish citizens" that it was a disgrace that the British Government should sink to a film screening to lure young Irishmen to fight for the English. The audience also contained English soldiers and Irish people who objected vocally to the protests. The cinema management were able to restore order.

If the Irish police were finding cinema-going a social problem, then it was not long until it threatened to become a political hot potato. Thomas J Clarke, signer of the Independence Proclamation, wrote to journalist John Devoy, a Fenian exile in New York, on 18 June 1913 about the link between film exhibition and political activism: "The Cinematograph picture showing in various towns (Pilgrimage Procession, etc.) will count for much in getting the project [the struggle for Independence] before the minds of the younger element." And a week later he wrote: "The march was very imposing, inspiring. Went off with military precision all the way to the graveside. Jameson, Cinematograph Man, there, took pictures, these have been exhibited twice or thrice nightly since (22nd inst.), in Rotunda and

Rathmines. No pictures he has ever shown (and he has been 14 years in the business) ever received such tremendous applause. The old round room appeared to shake. The pictures are grand."

Ireland — A Nation

One picture the British authorities did not find so grand was the five-reel *Ireland — A Nation* (1914), made partly at Kew Studios in Twickenham by Walter MacNamara. Differing sources label MacNamara American, Irish and Canadian. Cheryl Herr in *Joyce's Anatomy of Culture* (1986) mentions that the scenario and the principal direction of scenes filmed in Ireland were the responsibility of Irish actor-manager P J Bourke.

According to his son, Seamus de Burca, Bourke was commissioned by MacNamara to write the scenario and to take care of the locations, costumes and most of the direction. MacNamara was to pay Bourke £3 a day, a very large sum at the time, but the American did not seem to honour his obligations as there was a court case in which Bourke sued MacNamara, presumably in the latter's absence.

What is particularly interesting about this production is not so much the dramatisation of historical events and figures but the efforts of the directors to make social and political headway through the art of film. In an interview in 1914 MacNamara made his own sentiments quite clear by describing a photograph in his possession:

"Here is a fort built by Oliver Cromwell. To this day no real son of the ould sod passes it without spitting — that's the only way he can adequately express his feelings for the builder....I look upon the screen as the instrument for solving in the near future many social problems, of bringing classes nearer each other so that the one may see the other's viewpoint".

This noble aim did not impress the British authorities who detained MacNamara temporarily for importing guns which were to be employed as props. His speeches in favour of an independent Ireland — one, MacNamara boasts, was delivered at Clapham Common to thousands of people — were undoubtedly regarded as too partisan. However, it was the time of the Home Rule legislation which was held up by the First World War which, in turn, precipitated the stormy events of 1916.

Ireland — A Nation traces the major social and political events from the 1798 Uprising to the 1914 Home Rule legislation. Particularly important scenes are those of the famine and of the emigration to North America, as well as the more conventional depiction of heroes/villains/martyrs such as Robert Emmet, Daniel O'Connell and Thomas Davis. The film was not shown in Ireland until 1917 (one print of the film sank with the *Lusitania* in May 1915, delaying the first Irish screening and Irish response for over eighteen months). Within a couple of days the British authorities banned it, even though they had already censored and passed it. Apparently Dublin audiences shouted "Up the Rebel!" and "Up the Kaiser!", and cheered at the intertitle, "England's difficulty is Ireland's opportunity".

An anonymous review of the production appeared in the second issue (February 1917) of *The Irish Limelight* — a publication billed as "THE ONLY IRISH JOURNAL DEVOTED TO CINEMA AND THEATRICAL TOPICS". The reviewer mercilessly highlighted the film's factual inaccuracies: "A messenger from Dublin was shown bringing the news of the passing of the Union in 1800 to Father Murphy (who was killed in 1798) as he was addressing his parishioners after Mass and straightaway the priest (then two years dead) converted his congregation into an insurrectionary band and placed himself at their head." To be fair, the reviewer did credit the film for its self-conscious propagandism and emphasis on story but did not welcome its disregard for chronology and historical accuracy in order to achieve its ends.

In his introduction to the Cinema Ireland exhibition in Dublin in 1976, Kevin Brownlow reveals that *Ireland — A Nation* caused riots in New York when it was screened. MacNamara further conveyed his nationalist sympathies by adding footage of a 1914 Home Rule meeting to the print sent to Ireland. A few years later, someone added to *another* print (which recently surfaced in the United States) footage from the 1919-20 period of De Valera's trip to New York and of the Black and Tans patrolling Dublin's streets.

Back in Ireland not all film exhibition was highly serious. In 1915, for example, it is believed that one travelling cinema at least encountered something truly 'Irish'. According to Liam O'Leary, an exhibitor at a village hall in the West of Ireland advertised the film "*Zigomar*, 3,000 ft in length". Somewhat to his surprise when he arrived for the screening, the hall was empty, although a large crowd was milling around outside. One local offered an explanation: "Sure, if it's 3,000 ft long we can see the most of it outside"!

Comical too, but this time intended, was F J McCormick's *Fun at Finglas Fair* (1915) which apparently centred on two criminals who escape from jail. McCormick was a famous Abbey Theatre actor who later appeared in *Odd Man Out. Fun at Finglas Fair* was previewed just before the Easter Rising at the Masterpiece Theatre in Talbot Street in Dublin; however, it seems to have been destroyed during the military action.

Film Company of Ireland and James Mark Sullivan

1916 is a date dear to many Irish people for obvious political reasons. The abortive Uprising precipitated the later War of Independence. On a personal level, Mr Bradlaw, the managing director of the Princess Cinema, Rathmines, had good reason to remember the takeover of the General Post Office. Unaware of the situation, Bradlaw tried to send a telegram only to be confronted by Major MacBride, who told him, "Go back or I'll shoot you." [For some reason MacBride was not at Jacob's biscuit factory where he was arrested and subsequently executed in prison by the British.] Thinking it a joke, Bradlaw replied, "Where do you bury your dead?" Luckily for Bradlaw, he then saw that MacBride meant what he said and soon retreated to tell his tale.

The Easter Rising, however, did more harm than good to the 'non-political' cinéphile and film historian. In the Dublin fires which resulted from the military action, many films were lost; in particular, the early films of the Film Company of Ireland disappeared. This company had

James Mark Sullivan

been set up early in 1916 by James Mark Sullivan, who had emigrated from Killarney to the United States when only a young boy. He later studied law at Yale University and had a successful legal practice.

Perhaps what encouraged him to return to Ireland and to embark upon film production were the successes of the Kalem Company and of the famous D W Griffith film, *Birth of a Nation*. It is not unlikely that Sullivan saw the potential of the story of Ireland as similar to Griffith's vision of America. In supporting Sullivan's aspirations *The Irish Limelight* reported to its readers in January 1917 that the company had a mission: "its work is not only to entertain with Irish humour, legend and story − the purpose of the Company is to make Ireland known to the rest of the world as she has never been known before; to let outside people realise that we have in Ireland other things than the dudeen, buffoon, knee breeches and brass buckles".

Sullivan set up his offices in Sackville Street and quickly tried to overcome the trauma of the burning of his nitrate films by immediately employing Abbey Theatre personalities as actors, directors and producers. One of the first employees was J M Kerrigan, billed as an actor-producer, who had been playing leading roles at the Abbey for more than seven years. He had the privilege − some would say the misfortune − to have acted in the first production of J M Synge's *The Playboy of the Western World* in 1907, which caused a riot because of the play's apparent calm acceptance of a less-than-chaste Irishman.

Before leaving for Hollywood in the 1920s, Kerrigan directed a number of films − *The Miser's Gift*, *O'Neill of the Glen*, *Puck Fair Romance*, *An Unfair Love Affair*, *Widow Malone* and *Woman's Wit* − but these have all vanished.

Meanwhile after the Rising the British authorities cracked down on cinemas: an entertainment tax was introduced and all cinemas had to close at 7.45 pm to be in line with the general curfew of 8.30 pm. A *Bioscope* report during May 1916 explained that the people were "not too keen on pictures at the moment. There is a spirit of restlessness and excitement abroad in the city"; the Grand Cinema in Sackville Street had been burned down during the insurrection.

However, production actually increased under such difficult conditions. The close relationship between the Irish Theatre Company (formed in 1914 by John MacDonagh, Joseph Plunkett and Edward Martyn) and the Film Company of Ireland proved to be fruitful. For once in the history of Irish film production the theatrical and filmic worlds coalesced neatly. An indication of this is the interview with Kathleen Murphy in *The Irish Limelight* for April 1917, following her well-received performance that year in the Film Company of Ireland's *A Girl of Glenbeigh*:

"I suppose I was always more than a little 'stage struck' and must count myself extremely fortunate in meeting with kindred spirits amongst whom were Mona Driscoll and Mr. Arthur Shields of the Abbey Theatre...one naturally misses the footlights and the audience and at the outset I found it just a little difficult to avoid looking at the camera, but everyone was very kind to me and in such a favourable environment one could hardly help but make rapid progress". Kathleen Murphy worked on some films for Fred O'Donovan, including his best film, *Knocknagow*.

Knocknagow

This major production of 1917 was adapted from Charles J Kickham's novel. Like Kerrigan, Fred O'Donovan had been acting at the Abbey for many years; by 1917 he had become their major director but joined the Film Company of Ireland. One of his first films was *Rafferty's Rise* (1917) in which he plays the ambitious constable, Rafferty, who (despite reading detective books) fails to be promoted and — more importantly — fails to impress his superior's (Brian Magowan) daughter, Kitty Hogan (Kathleen Murphy).

Knocknagow was shot during the summer and autumn of 1917 and released early in 1918. Taylor Downing in a 1979 article in *Sight and Sound* reminds us that the surviving print of this film, now in the National Film Archive in England, has many sections missing which makes the narrative exceedingly difficult to follow. In fact, even when the film was released in London in late 1919, reviewers complained

of its apparently wayward continuity. This is the film that Cyril Cusack remembers appearing in as a seven-year-old. The main role is played by Brian Magowan, a yeoman or middle class figure who is forced to emigrate due to lack of opportunity, while his peasant neighbours are evicted and their cottages burnt.

By relying on the book's attempted panoramic sweep, the film is structurally weak. However, the emphasis on poverty, wicked land-agents and ignorant absentee landlords gives an indirect judgment on the English presence in Ireland in 1917. This broad propagandism was picked up in British trade papers but by and large the film tries to capture the romanticised spirit of the original novel. Some critics believe that the film offers no consistent intellectual engagement with the real problems suggested in Kickham's novel and it is true that one senses an arrested

Knocknagow

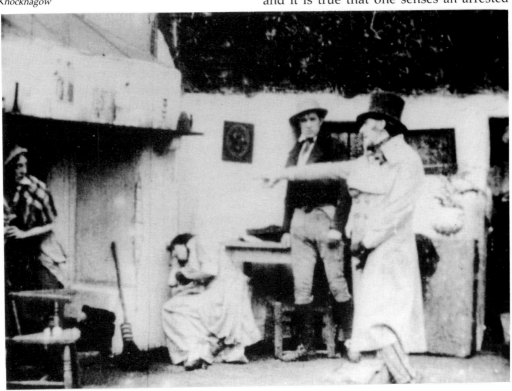

development in the way the absentee landlord exudes all that was good yet sickening about Victorian charity. Perhaps we should leave *Knocknagow* with a notion of how it was perceived in the press book that accompanied the early screenings:

"KNOCKNAGOW is essentially a pastoral play: you live among people who made Ireland — the Ireland of the '48 period./Their joys are keen; their sorrows heavy. It was the Ireland of the 'smile and the tear', and no audience can see KNOCKNAGOW, as presented by the Film Company of Ireland, without smiles and tears./ It appeals to the softer and sweeter emotions of the human heart./ There are no great thrills in the story, which is rather a sweet song of a summer evening in the 'long long ago' when our grandfathers were actively keeping alive an Irish spirit that has lent fire to the blaze of Irish inspiration that can be found the whole world round to-day". One wonders if this flowery language was in part an attempt to offset British censorship.

When Love Came to Gavin Burke

Less provocative that year was *When Love Came to Gavin Burke*, a film with quite a complex plot. A young farmer, Gavin (O'Donovan), is rejected by his love, Kate (Nora Clancy), in favour of a more financially stable partner, John (Stephen Gould). The decision proves to be a poor one and years later Kate's child, Grace, finds herself, like her mother, caught between two suitors, one with and one without money. These two bachelors, played by Brian Magowan and Valentine Roberts, fight it out on the banks of the Liffey before all is happily resolved. According to the June 1917 issue of *The Irish Limelight* there was quite a story to the duel:

"A week or so ago Brian Magowan and Valentine Roberts were booked for a life and death struggle upon a cliff edge with a genuine fall into the Liffey 240 inches below. The Homeric combat and the drop into the river came off all right, but Anna Liffey refused to stick to the scenario and put in a little bit of her own. The current swept the two actors towards the weir!/ With great presence of mind the camera man continued to turn the handle with one hand whilst with the other he called loudly for assistance./The two in the water struggled gamely but ineffectively./It was a thrilling moment!....Then the gallant lads went over the edge and coming to the quieter water below the weir swam quietly ashore!/ 'If you hadn't followed the instructions which I shouted at you,' said one of the heroes on the bank, 'you would have been lost.'/ 'Instructions?' said one of the dripping figures, as he glared at him. 'I couldn't hear you on account of the roaring.'"

A humorous eye-witness account of O'Donovan on set with Brian Magowan and Kathleen Murphy involved in a love-scene is also recorded in the same issue of the journal: "There was Miss Kathleen Murphy, dark haired, tragic-eyed, gazing fondly up into the honest open countenance of Brian Magowan and there was the gallant youth gazing lovingly down into the star-like orbs of la petite brunette...Raising a megaphone to his lips he [Fred O'Donovan] said: 'Place your hand upon her shoulder, Brian. Put your right hand on his shoulder, Miss Murphy. Now kiss — a good long one.'...They had to go through that touching scene three times before Fred O'Donovan was satisfied. I never saw a man with such particular notions about love-making."

John MacDonagh

More prominent than Fred O'Donovan

was John MacDonagh, who was born in Cloughjordan, Co. Tipperary. One of his brothers was Thomas MacDonagh, the poet and nationalist hero. John MacDonagh's first love was acting and while in New York finding bit parts in plays, he received an outline of a story from another brother, Joe, entitled *The Fugitive*. MacDonagh revised it and sent it to the Biograph Film Company who accepted the script and paid him US$100. MacDonagh was later to see his Irish-based script appear in an American Civil War setting in the film of the same name.

MacDonagh then met James Mark Sullivan who by that time had started on *Knocknagow*. Sullivan persuaded MacDonagh to make films for him, the most famous of which is *Willie Reilly and His Colleen Bawn* (1919 but released 1920).

Willie Reilly and His Colleen Bawn

This film is based on a traditional ballad and a William Carleton novel and is set in 1745 around the time of the penal laws. Willie Reilly, played by the indefatigable Brian Magowan, is a young Catholic who rescues a Protestant squire who, in thanks, introduces his saviour to his daughter Helen. The Catholic-Protestant love-story develops while debate goes on among liberal and reactionary Protestants as to the social role of the Catholic community. Reilly is implicated in a robbery but is wrongfully charged, yet because of the spirit of union between Catholic and Protestant he is able finally to win Helen, although he is exiled from Ireland for a number of years.

MacDonagh seems to have been a consummate craftsman who may have learned much from his New York experiences; he employed a wide range of shots, opting for cross-cutting and even surreal flashbacks. Billed as a film to help

harmonise the divided population, it must have been heart-breaking for the director to see the ensuing vicious War of Independence, Civil War and partition of the country, all of which rendered the film naïve. MacDonagh was undeniably an Old IRA sympathiser (there is an extant membership card) and probably his cast, too, many of whom were imprisoned — holding up the filming process for a number of months!

Willie Reilly was shot at St Edna's College at Rathfarnham, established by Patrick Pearse and Thomas MacDonagh in 1908 to further the Irish language and culture — a location not lost on a 1920 Irish audience.

During the filming of the final scenes of *Willie Reilly* MacDonagh made a film for the Republican Loan Campaign. It depicts, amongst others, Michael Collins and Arthur Griffith signing their names to a proposal for the public issue of the Loan. For the formal signing MacDonagh used the table which was supposedly linked to Robert Emmet when he was living in the Rathfarnham area. Somewhat confusingly, a reel kept originally at the National Library and now at RTE entitled *Sinn Féin Notabilities* is documented as showing Collins doling out subscriptions on the block on which Emmet was believed to have been executed. In any event, the Loan Campaign film naturally would not have been passed by the British Government, so it was given to "Volunteers" who would arrive at a cinema in a car, march up to the projection box and force the projectionist at gunpoint to screen it immediately before the authorities heard about it. Even so, MacDonagh was advised to flee and went to Scotland where for a time he continued to exhibit the film.

One further film that MacDonagh directed for the Film Company of Ireland was *Paying the Rent* (1920), photographed

16

Willie Reilly and His Colleen Bawn

by the ubiquitous Brian Magowan. The film's leading actor, Arthur Sinclair, plays the wayward Paddy Dunne who is diverted from paying his rent (on borrowed money) by a few friends who persuade him to go to the races at the Curragh. Fortunately, Paddy Dunne wins a long-shot bet and returns just in time to pay the land agent and the lender who has nearly married Dunne's daughter in lieu of the money. In his thesis on Irish cinema, Martin Dolan reports that the director employed a framing device in the shape of a shamrock and that he used continuously rhyming intertitles such as "Molly their daughter young and fair/had big blue eyes and golden hair". What these titles perhaps suggest is not so much a trivialisation of the Irish family (Dolan's assumption) but more a formal structure

through which the audience can latch onto the rhythm and punctuation of the silent film.

The Film Company of Ireland opened a studio in Dublin in 1919 but after the death of Sullivan's wife and child in a flu epidemic, the entrepreneur-lawyer became disenchanted. He returned to his legal practice in the United States and production came to a stop.

Norman Whitten and the General Film Supply Company

The documentary tradition in Ireland was systematically advanced by the activities of the General Film Supply Company, founded in 1917 by Norman Whitten. In

1915 and 1916 Whitten and his friends had previously recorded Dublin events; it is believed that one of Whitten's cameramen was jailed in 1915 simply for filming in the street. When the Rising took place shortly afterwards, Whitten took shots of Dublin burning, some 2000' of film. He gave the film to Pathé who rented a boat, picked up the material on the coast and quickly developed it to show in the United States.

Whitten's most experienced cameraman was Gordon Lewis who, it is believed, had filmed the funeral of Sinn Féin's O'Donovan Rossa in 1915. Whitten and Lewis went on to record the funeral of Thomas Ashe which took place on 30 September 1917. Other projects around this time include an animated film, *Ten Days' Leave*, from drawings by the Dublin cartoonist, Frank Leah.

Irish Events

The Irish Limelight periodical strongly supported Whitten's "gazette" of documentary projects, which he called *Irish Events*. One hundred of these films were made during the 1917-18 period. Whitten's aim was to create a niche for his company by finding what the Pathé and Gaumont Graphic gazettes did not cover on the local scene. One such street event was the return of the Sinn Féin prisoners in June 1917, filmed by Norman Whitten and reported in *The Irish Limelight*. Like any good journalist, Whitten was interested more in the topicality of the event than in the politics of the prisoners or of the British Government that released them:

"In almost less time than it takes to write it, he was out again in the street, the tripod was mounted in a chair, the eye of the Kinematograph was pointed directly at the oncoming procession and the first film of the ex-prisoners' homecoming was being taken./...When it became necessary to move out of the way of the oncoming crowds the camera man retreated to the sidewalk and from there took a few more feet of the procession as it passed. Then, chartering a side-car, he placed the precious box and tripod upon it and having ascertained that the men were being escorted to Fleming's Hotel in Gardiner Street, drove swiftly in that direction. He managed to get there with the procession and, at his request, two of the brakes containing the released prisoners were held back until he could get the men descending. Every facility was given to him and having made the most of his opportunities he rushed back to his offices."

By late afternoon three copies had been printed and were rushed by taxis to the picture-houses including the Rotunda. Whitten also despatched copies of his films to America. It is interesting that General Film Supply also serviced picture-houses with the Kalem Irish films such as *The Colleen Bawn* and *The Shaughraun*. But their main diet was topical events from the four provinces of Ireland — from Phoenix Park demonstrations in Dublin to the Twelfth of July celebrations in Belfast. *The Irish Limelight* was quick to compliment Whitten's enterprise since it promised to provide both employment and money for Irish people.

Gordon Lewis in an interview with the (anonymous) editor of *The Irish Limelight* in December 1917 documented one incident which happened during the filming of *Irish Events*. It reveals that Lewis and Whitten were not men driven essentially by politics but more by the search for exciting pictures, wherever they could be found:

"...the facilities given me by the [British] military authorities were highly appreciated. They threw gas bombs at the Tanks and these caused a fine sight and then infantry with shrapnel helmets dashed after the Tank across the ditches. It was like real warfare. I took a very nice piece from the inside of one of the Tanks. I sat on the driver's seat and held the camera on my knees with the lens protruding through the look-out hole and held on to the side of the hole like grim death. While we crawled along the driver of the Tank asked me would I care to go over one of the big banks and I said: 'Sure, it's the very thing I want!' We came to the bank, up and up we rose till I was almost lying on my back and then as it started to come down on the other side of the bank I drew in my breath in expectation of a switchback feeling. Suddenly I felt my lungs as if they would burst. I only then realised that we were among the gas bombs which were burning on the ground. Well, I did feel a bit queer, still I kept turning the handle...".

Irish Events became an incredibly diverse project but, given the times, it did have a strong political content. Whitten recognised this and tried to market the topical events as much as possible by compiling a long film, entitled *Sinn Féin Review 1 & 2* (1919), from a number of small reels. This film included the pilgrimage to Wolfe Tone's grave at Bodenstown, the Irish Women's Anti-Conscription procession in Dublin and Countess Markievicz's exhibiting a picture which she painted in Holloway Prison entitled "Easter Week".

The police had a private viewing of the film and in his report the detective in charge remarked:

"The film as it stands is a glorification of Sinn Féin and whenever exhibited would, no doubt, be good Sinn Féin propaganda and might in that way be objectionable to members of the audience holding different views" (12 April 1919). A few days later the films were confiscated by the authorities and things did not go at all smoothly, as indicated in the official report (17 April) of the seizure: "I went with all the available men of Westgate South Quay

Bks. to the Boyne Cinema House, Fair St., and asked for the Manager...a Sinn Féin suspect now living in Drogheda. He was absent and...[the] Caretaker of the Hall refused to give me the key when I told him my business. We had brought a heavy hatchet with us and on threatening to break in the door with it [he] consented to open it. I seized two films called the *Sinn Féin Review 1 & 2* and brought them to barracks". The films were later destroyed.

In the Days of St Patrick

One of Whitten's last but significant works was a feature film, *In the Days of St Patrick* (1920). This film is divided into a prologue, five parts and an epilogue. It allowed Whitten to introduce some Hollywood-style antics, such as chasing chariots and pirate boats out of which Irish raiders capture the young Patrick. Spectacular scenes in this film include the burning of Patrick's former pagan master's house and the confrontation between the Christians and the pagans on the hills of Slane and Tara. The film ends on a truly Catholic rather than Christian note with Cardinal Logue blessing "St Patrick's Children of Erin". And it is the Catholicism or appropriation of Saint Patrick by Catholicism that makes the film open to accusations of ideological one-sidedness. Since the film took about a year to make it must rank as one of Whitten's most sustained works.

William Power and the Celtic Cinema Company

Also active around 1917 was William Power who first set up a drama company to prepare actors for film performance before embarking on the light-hearted *Willie Scouts While Jessie Pouts* (1918) under the name of the Celtic Cinema Company. Matt and Bob Tobin were the cameramen; apparently the former was blind!

Power then made *Rosaleen Dhu* (1920), a story of a Fenian patriot who has to leave Ireland and join the French Foreign Legion. While abroad he marries an Algerian girl who, rather strangely, turns out to be the inheritor of an Irish estate. Power was praised by the local press for producing local pictures, a need the director deliberately attempted to meet. Power had a barber's shop in the back of which he and his team would process the film in wooden barrels. He also seemed to be in possession of a camera that could pan. Bob Tobin recalled that it cost £88.00, an enormous sum for the time.

Tragically, while on the production of *An Irish Vendetta* (apparently unreleased) at Leopardstown Race Track, Power was thrown from a horse and died. Soon after the Celtic Cinema Company folded.

Writings on the cinema

Writings on the cinema in this period could be found in the local and national newspapers, commenting on a particular film, controversial or not. As this chapter shows, *The Irish Limelight*, which survived for only a couple of years, popularised the cinema with well-written articles and features. The intellectual writers of the time were divided on the art of the cinema, although all agreed on the

need for more films depicting Irish history, legend and literature, particularly for children.

Professor Max Drennan, however, in the *Irish Monthly* in 1917 saw cinema as an attack on Irish values: "From the point of view of morals it might be profitable to draw a parallel between the use of cinema and the use of whiskey." In his suggested "remedies", he called for cinemas to be inspected, preferably by an "educated woman"!

A more balanced view was put forward by John Ryan in a 1918 issue of *Studies*, in which he admitted that the cinema was an important educational tool, "the most eloquent Instructor that has arisen since the days of Aristotle." He supported the idea of a national film industry, although he warned of the cinema's corrupting aspects, as is evident from his article's title, "The Cinema Peril".

Government and the cinema

By 1916 there were approximately 150 cinemas and halls showing films in Ireland, with around thirty each in Belfast and Dublin. The Grand Cinema in Sackville Street was burned down that year and many threats were made on other picture-houses. Dublin Castle became somewhat suspicious of the cinemas as they were possible meeting places for Sinn Féin suspects. In 1917 the Dublin Corporation employed two women to investigate the programmes of cinemas, theatres and music halls and the Dáil acknowledged the need for a national film censorship to improve upon the random decisions made by local authorities. In 1920 the major distributors had offices in Dublin and a branch of the Kinematograph Renters Society was in operation. There was a growing need for a government film policy to help business concerns plan ahead.

2: Insular states: 1922-1955

Odd Man Out

The War of Independence and the Civil War resulting from the partition of the country made the period 1919-1923 a particularly difficult one for cinema exhibition and feature film production. Cinemas were even attacked and bombed in Dublin in 1923. In March a land mine explosion, seemingly intended to cut the electric cable connected to the La Scala Theatre, blew the doors off the Pillar Picture House. Members of the orchestra were thrown from their seats but as the *Irish Times* reported, "the screen was undamaged, and a five-reel piece was continued during the height of the excitement caused by the explosion."

Interestingly, the Irish-related films most prominently shown in the capital celebrated the fight against the English - *Ireland — A Nation* and *The IRA in Training*. But as the Civil War began to take root, one production company,

inspired by Charles McConnell, Irish Photo Plays Ltd., embarked on the path of light comedy, utilising Norman Whitten as producer and John MacDonagh as director. As violence between Irish people increased, the general populace's hunger for entertainment prevailed over ideological arguments, just as it would do in Belfast and Derry in the 1970s. One exception to this theory was the opening of *Battle of the Four Courts* in Dublin soon after the rout of the anti-treaty forces in June 1922.

Irish Photo Plays publicised its activities on three films in the *Freeman's Journal* in May 1922. All three starred Jimmy O'Dea, the famous entertainer and actor, who later appeared in many other films, most notably in John Ford's *The Rising of the Moon* (1957). John MacDonagh wrote the scenarios for *Wicklow Gold* and *The Casey Millions* (both 1922).

The former comedy concerns the sneaky ploy of one Larry O'Toole, who secures marriage to his beloved by convincing his father that he will inherit land with gold sediments. *The Casey Millions* features two actors-cum-conmen who announce that they possess the skull of a deceased American millionaire. It does not take long for the would-be heirs to hand over the money in the hope that their heads are the same dimensions. O'Dea comes to the community's rescue by exposing the actors. The third film, *Cruiskeen Lawn* (possibly released 1924), revolves around one of Ireland's popular notions — a suddenly successful racehorse. The horse, whose name titles the film, accidentally drinks some "medicine" and becomes an overnight winner, solving the owner's financial (and marital) problems.

These productions were well-attended, raised little comment and were not the reason for the sudden interest in censorship at governmental level. It was rather the case that once Independence had been achieved, attitudes of insularity permeated both sides of the border. It was a time of grappling for a stable policy in many areas of cultural life. And in the South, the predominance of British and American films appeared to some as dangerous subversive forces getting in the way of building a national consciousness.

Censorship of Films Act (1923)

While the new state of Northern Ireland came under the jurisdiction of the British censor and of local authorities, the equally new state emerging in the South found that both Protestant and Catholic Church representatives wanted a national film censorship. What provoked this unanimity was the failure of the Dublin Corporation's Public Health Committee's plan to have twenty-two film censors, six each to be appointed by the Protestant and Catholic Archbishops of Dublin. Such a number proved far too cumbersome.

The Free State Government then introduced the Censorship of Films Act providing for one film censor, James Montgomery, and an Appeal Board comprising distinguished figures such as W B Yeats and Oliver St John Gogarty. Speaking in the Dáil, Professor Magennis, Chairman of the Appeal Board, made his opinions clear:

"There is not a boy or girl of 14 or 16 years of age who need not at the end of a year be a past-master in every detail of every form of vicious life in every quarter of the globe by merely going through this education of weekly *Seances* in one of our most respectable cinemas". Thus the censor's job was to protect the populace, as the act was worded, from "indecent, obscene or blasphemous material".

James Montgomery, censor

As an employee in a bakery, James Montgomery admitted to little knowledge of film. Yet in 1924 he had to pass some 10 000 miles of celluloid — 1307 films, of which he banned 104 completely and passed a further 166 subject to cuts. In support of Montgomery, Professor Magennis told English delegates in no uncertain terms that Ireland would prefer to have no films rather than forbidden ones. This stance only provoked a knee-jerk reaction from the industry in England who sent Montgomery a warning that, unless he became more lenient, they would not send films to the Irish Free State.

In 1925 the Censorship Act was extended to posters and displays outside cinemas. Meanwhile, Montgomery was rebuked for what some Catholics saw as a lack of rigour, which gave much validity to the film censor's belief that he was "between the Devil and the Holy See!". Some observers, however, believe that Montgomery's stiff attitude made other countries, particularly the United States, take notice of the type of films produced and exported; and the setting up of the Hays Office was perhaps partly due to objections to American films abroad.

Viewed over half a century later, the problems encountered by the censor when the 'talkies' arrived are nothing short of comical. Montgomery's preview theatre was not equipped to receive sound and so he could only attempt to evaluate the film from what he could see. Since he would still be held responsible for the dialogue, he passed films with a stamp "PLOT AND SOUND NOT CENSORED".

Naturally, this situation invited vehement public criticism and eventually the Amendment Act of 1930 covered this technological change by providing sound equipment for the preview theatre. The new act also stipulated that a dialogue script had to be submitted with each film. For seventeen years Montgomery dominated his post, overseeing a generally difficult period for Ireland and for the Irish cinema. Montgomery referred to his last years in office as a "sinecure". Whether or not he intended the pun we shall never know.

Cinema conditions

One of the dramatic events in Belfast during 1923 was the opening of the Classic Cinema in Castle Lane in December. The Public Record Office of Northern Ireland holds a souvenir programme from the opening in which one discovers that it was a most spectacular building, complete with café, dressing rooms, Ladies Rest Room, restaurants and a magnificent auditorium seating 1807 people. Fears of the films burning and causing panic were placated by a special section in the programme devoted to the projection room:

"This is an entirely fireproof compartment....The film projectors are built by the Ross Optical Co., London, upon the latest scientific optical basis, and are quite flickerless. It is impossible for ignition of any film to take place during the ordinary running of the programme. The mechanisms are so electrically connected that an entire programme can be run without stop, and no change from one machine to another noticeable". If this now sounds somewhat exaggerated, it was a major concern at the time, as illustrated a few years later when forty-nine people died in a fire at a cinema south of the border at Drumcollegher, Co. Limerick. Rather ironically, the audience was watching *The Ten Commandments*.

Most cinemas were not, of course, anywhere near the standards of the Classic Cinema. Many makeshift halls, built primarily of wood, were used in the 1920s and 1930s for exhibition purposes. These halls often relied on parked lorries with dynamos to generate light and power for the projectors. But it seems that however bad the working conditions, employees of the cinemas were sufficiently organised to join the Irish Transport and Workers' Union and to go on strike.

In 1923 management in Dublin wanted a paycut for some one thousand workers, arguing that wages were unnaturally high in Southern Ireland compared to Northern Ireland and Britain. Not surprisingly, as a 15% reduction was envisaged, the cinemas were closed for many weeks. While the exhibition side of the industry became embroiled with internal wranglings, production of Irish films continued.

Land of Her Fathers and Irish Destiny

During the year in which Montgomery took office, *Land of Her Fathers* (1924) was made. This was produced by John Hurley and stars Micheál MacLiammóir, Barry Fitzgerald and Maureen Delaney. According to George Morrison, the only copy was stolen in New York towards the end of the year.

In 1925 Dr Eppel, owner of the Palace Cinema in Dublin, produced *Irish Destiny*. This film traces a romance during the Black and Tans/War of Independence Days and was severely criticised by John Gerrard in *Sight and Sound* in 1948 for its poor technical quality. Brian Magowan stars and many who were involved in the actual war appear alongside him. Opening ironically with a scene of a pacifist playing chess with a priest, the production is notable for scenes depicting the burning of the Customs House and the escape of Volunteers from the Curragh prison camp.

The arrival of sound

The exhibition in Dublin of the Irish film of the Catholic Centenary celebrations in 1929 and the screening in Belfast and Dublin that year of Al Jolson's *The Singing Fool* established sound cinema in Ireland. There had already been several attempts in Belfast to match sound to pictures — in 1909 the St George's Hall showed the "Filmophone"; the Picture House showed Kinetophone films five years later and in 1926 Michael Curran brought in the "De Forest Phono Optical Sound-On-Film system" for one showing at the Lyceum. This system was also used a year later at the Central Cinema in Dublin.

The reverberations of sound cinema were felt throughout the world. For Ireland it meant that foreign films lost their popularity; subsequently the vast majority of films seen in local cinemas were British or American. Sound also brought the demise of musicians. From 1916 The Picture House in Belfast had a forty-member orchestra. This may have been the largest but even country cinemas had a trio and a piano. With the disappearance of live music from the cinema, the emphasis switched to pre-recorded pieces, although when a silent film did arrive in Ireland it was not uncommon for a piece to be specially composed by local musicians.

1929

The year of the Wall Street Crash and the ensuing worldwide depression saw two British films of Irish interest: a young Alfred Hitchcock made a very stilted *Juno and the Paycock* with Sara Allgood and Edward Chapman, and the first version of Liam O'Flaherty's *The Informer* was made as a silent by the German director, Arthur Robison, with Lars Hanson and Lya de Putti.

One of the key differences between this version and John Ford's 1935 film is that Robison stresses Gypo's motivation as a love entanglement as distinct from simple greed for money. Ford seems to be closer to the original text and, after an initial

Song o' My Heart

Irish Hearts

lukewarm reception, his film received popular acclaim. Four Oscars went to the picture, including those for direction and best actor. Victor McLaglen's extremely powerful portrayal of brute force with its primitive motivations helped Ford to focus on the allegorical elements of O'Flaherty's tale of betrayal. Ford's film has the dubious honour of being banned by the censor but it was awarded a certificate by the Appeal Board.

Foreign interest in Ireland continued when Frank Borzage, the American director, made *Song o' My Heart* (1930) in Ireland, with Maureen O'Sullivan and John McCormack. This film is interesting because it was the director's first sound film and probably the first to be made in Ireland.

The prize for the first *Irish* sound film may well belong to Ulsterman Colonel Victor Haddick (other sources say he was

from Limerick) for his *The Voice of Ireland* (probably 1932). This travelogue with commentary by the director and songs from the Northern Irish entertainer, Richard Hayward, is thought to have been made in 1932, although the standard reference works refer only to its first showing in London in 1936. Judging from reviews, the film's only merit seems to have been its sophisticated editing.

Irish Hearts/Norah O'Neale

The first Irish *fiction* film with sound, *Irish Hearts/Norah O'Neale* (1934), was made by Brian Desmond Hurst. Born in Castlereagh, County Down, Hurst was the seventh child of a blacksmith in the Belfast shipyard. He was educated in London and Paris, where he studied art, and moved to Hollywood in the mid-1920s. Once there, he worked as an assistant director and art director on some of John Ford's silent films. He returned to England in the mid-1930s, making first, independently, an adaptation of Edgar Allen Poe's *The Tell-Tale Heart*.

Irish Hearts was also an independent adaptation, this time of Dr James Johnston Abraham's novel, *The Night Nurse*, which focusses on a doctor's complicated love life while dealing with a typhus epidemic. Folk dances and rural scenery in Ireland seemed to be the mainstays of the film. Surprisingly, Hurst makes no mention of the film in his unpublished autobiography.

Riders to the Sea

Hurst was able to finance his next adaptation, Synge's *Riders to the Sea* (1935), by receiving £6000 from Gracie Fields, money which she never recouped. Many Irish Abbey Theatre actors star. The *Monthly Film Bulletin* reviewer criticised its naturalistic approach for such a poetic

play but highlighted the rendition of the women's keening and the startling close-up of a loaf of bread in the mother's worn hand.

Ourselves Alone

On the basis of these privately financed films, Hurst was contracted by British International Pictures to direct with Walter Summers *Ourselves Alone* (1936) from the novel and play by Noel Scott and Dudley Sturrock. For the script, Hurst made up to three hundred drawings. During the War of Independence a Royal Irish Constabulary Inspector takes responsibility for the killing of an IRA leader to allow the real killer, an English officer, to develop a relationship with the victim's sister.

Hurst's Northern Irish Protestant background raises some intriguing questions about the politics of the story. For example, in capsule reviews both officers are referred to as "British", but this does not adequately encompass Inspector

Riders to the Sea (1935)

Hannay, the RIC member, who would have been Irish and possibly Protestant. That a Unionist Irishman sacrifices his love interest for the sake of the potential love life between a Catholic nationalist and an English soldier has not a little irony to it. Most of *Ourselves Alone* was made at the Elstree Studios in England and was probably envisaged as a "quota quickie". It ran for five weeks in Dublin to packed houses.

Hurst continued to direct a wide assortment of films, returning only to Irish topics in *Hungry Hill* (1946) and *The Playboy of the Western World* (1962).

Cinematograph Films Act

In 1927 the Cinematograph Films Act was intended to raise the number of British films made, rented and exhibited in the United Kingdom in the face of stiff competition. This Act actually stipulated that films under this arrangement be made in Britain or in the "Empire" with a British scenarist. By 1938 (when a new Act effectively eradicated "quota quickies") the quota had risen to 20% and this increase matched the British production figures - from 131 films during 1928-29 to 228 films during 1937-38. Unfortunately, to fill the percentage many poor quality pictures were produced. A number of these were shot in Ireland.

One of the Irish beneficiaries of the Quota Act was the journalist and scenarist Donovan Pedelty. Like Hurst he had been working in Hollywood, gaining experience, and when he came to England in 1933 he wrote and directed a number of films. His productive period stretches only six years, although in that time he was associated with some sixteen pictures. Perhaps the two films of most Irish interest were *Luck of the Irish* (1935), from the play and book by Victor Haddick, and *Irish and Proud of It* (1936).

Both were distributed by Paramount and feature Richard Hayward in leading roles with some of his colleagues from the Belfast Repertory Company. Similar to *Cruiskeen Lawn, Luck of the Irish* hinges on a successful racehorse which although disqualified from a major meet is bought by a rich American whose transaction solves the financial problems of a country gentleman.

Richard Hayward

Irish and Proud of It concerns a garrulous Irish emigré living in England who is flown to Ireland by his fed-up friends as a practical joke. Lost in the Irish countryside, Hayward chances upon an illegal poteen industry; he is soon embroiled in its peculiar brand of politics but escapes back to England.

The making of the film proved to be quite a complex activity. Firstly, Pedelty was not allowed by the Irish police to acquire an actual whiskey still but they did provide him with plans so that he could make a replica at the Wembley Studios in London. Secondly, after shooting exteriors in County Antrim, the director took three weeks finding forty "Irishmen" in London to take part in a large fight sequence. The publicity release for the film documents that Pedelty could not stop a few of the men from carrying on the fray off the set after the final take. The stereotype of the pugnacious Irishman would appear to be not totally manufactured by the screen!

Pedelty's leading actor, Richard Hayward, struck out on his own, teaming up with Germain Burger to make the hour-long *Devil's Rock* (1938), distributed by Columbia Pictures. This romantic adventure stars Hayward and Geraldine Mitchel and local colour was prominent: the Lambeg Irish Folk Dance Society provided some dances and a local choir sang. The film was not appreciated by the *Monthly Film Bulletin* who dismissed it as amateurish.

Jimmy O'Dea

In the South, Jimmy O'Dea's O'D Productions employed Harry O'Donovan to direct *Blarney* (1938), a story of a jewelry robbery. In this instance the *Monthly Film Bulletin* reviewer thought that, despite O'Dea's good acting, the scenery, country dancing and border explanations would have been better left to a documentary film. 1938 was also the year of Maureen O'Hara's début in Alex Bryce's *My Irish Molly*, a sentimental musical comedy in which she was criticised in one review for some awkward moments and a lack of poise!

Key films of the 1930s

It is impossible, however, to discuss the mid-1930s in Ireland without fully considering three key films: Robert Flaherty's problematic *Man of Aran* (1934); *Guests of the Nation*, released in 1936 and directed by Denis Johnston; and Tom Cooper's *The Dawn* (1936). These films pose different questions as regards Irish film production and film representations of Ireland.

Robert Flaherty

Robert Joseph Flaherty came from Irish Protestant stock; his family migrated during the 1840s famine and settled in Quebec, Canada. His mother, however, was of German extraction and a Roman Catholic; Robert was the eldest of four children. Flaherty's father worked in the iron-ore exploration business north and south of the border between Canada and the United States. Film-maker Flaherty was born in Iron Mountain, Michigan on 16 February 1884. When he came to Ireland in the 1930s, he had an enviable reputation behind him, built mainly on *Nanook of the North* (1922) and *Moana* (1926). Just before he arrived in Ireland he made *Industrial Britain* in England in 1933,

Robert Flaherty

a hundred years previously. This anachronism tended to cast doubt on other, more faithful, depictions of Aran life. Robert Monks (see page 127) offers comments on Flaherty's cumbersome camera and John Goldman, the editor, believed that Flaherty tried to do too much with the equipment. However, the use of a long, 17" lens created some breathtaking shots of cliffs and the sea, taken from a distance of two miles.

Shot silent, *Man of Aran* presents Flaherty's skill at framing a shot but shows little evidence of his ability to capture rhythm and continuity. Some 37 hours of footage were reduced to a 76-minute film; the soundtrack was recorded and dubbed in London. The film cost £30 000 to make but within twelve months had grossed over £80 000.

Reviews of the film focus on the absence of certain topics − notably religion and sexuality − and convey the view that the film is a highly personal selection of events. Another criticism arose from the ethos of the 1930s: that Flaherty was not committed to the use of film for the improvement of society and, by implication, to the use of film to apportion

although the final editing and commentary were not under his supervision.

Flaherty's impetus to come to the West of Ireland was the notion of a life-and-death struggle with the sea. He sought something to resemble the intensity of Synge's play, *Riders to the Sea* (1904), and his book, *The Aran Islands* (1907), both of which Flaherty read before shooting. Pat Mullen's 1935 book, *Man of Aran*, provides an eye-witness account of the film's production. Mullen was Flaherty's main contact with the native population who occasionally had to be cajoled into appearing in the 'pictures'. As with many Indian tribes, some of the islanders believed that there was devilry involved in the practice of film-making.

What makes *Man of Aran* particularly problematic is Flaherty's decision to dwell on the shark hunting episode. According to Mullen, this activity had died out over

Man of Aran

blame for unnecessary poverty. During his stay on the islands Flaherty did not choose to live like the islanders. He rented a cottage, imported a cook and had men keep his peat fire burning! It was not until after World War Two that his film was evaluated fairly and its strengths and weaknesses balanced. Today one may view it as a docudrama or as a quasi-historical document in which the dangers and difficulties of living on the periphery of any land mass may be appreciated.

Guests of the Nation

Less ambitious in scope than *Man of Aran* was the challenge taken up by playwright Denis Johnston, who adapted Frank O'Connor's story, *Guests of the Nation*, for the screen in 1936. This titled silent took two years to make. Born in Dublin, Johnston was Director of the Gate Theatre from 1931-36 and drew on actors from the theatre for the film. Set during the War of Independence, it traces the slow awareness among some IRA Volunteers that two English soldiers in their custody will have to be executed.

One of the film's noticeable features is the experimentation with montage techniques. It is likely that the decision to choose a silent instead of a talkie was made as much from lack of money as from poor sound equipment. Johnston favours fast cuts after lingering close-ups and seems to have got carried away with some heavy symbolism: notably, the broken accordion falling to the floor and the blowing out of candles as the execution approaches. Nevertheless, the *Irish Independent* in January 1935 called it the best picture yet made in Ireland and Frank O'Connor himself thought that it told the story better than literature ever could.

The Dawn

Guests of the Nation is plagued by technical problems which are also all too visible in Tom Cooper's *The Dawn* (1936). Cooper, a garage owner in Killarney, borrowed equipment from the Kerry Electrical Company and set out to make a sound film depicting episodes from the "Black and Tans Wars". The production was a local, communal effort as may be gleaned from an account by Donal O'Cahill, one of Cooper's assistants:

"Voluntary workers all, and representative of every class in Killarney. There were boatmen, jarveys, hotel-keepers, merchants, mechanics, doctors, civic guards, shop assistants, bank clerks and engineers....For many months they were to be wholly at the disposal of the directors, devoting their Sundays and half-holidays to exterior work, and, on business days, snatching a hasty meal before rushing to the studio where, more often than not, they worked until three, four and often five am." Tom Cooper had been a Republican Flying Column leader and plays the IRA Company Commander, Dan Donovan.

The Dawn

The story centres around the Malone family, one of whose members is believed to have informed on the IRB (the forerunner of the IRA) back in 1886. But in 1919 family honour is re-established. The *Irish Times* in August 1936 situated the film's audience: "I warn you that if you are a Unionist or ex-Unionist, it will make you squirm. The Black and Tans are just too scoundrelly for words, in comparison with their IRA opponents." Having said that, the reviewer considered *The Dawn* the "most interesting and vital film ever produced in Ireland".

Guests of the Nation and *The Dawn* served to preserve notions of the near 'purity' of the War of Independence and, by implication, the 'impurity' of the Civil War which followed. Both films provoke set responses and perhaps one of the reasons for the half-hearted attitude to film production in Ireland at this time was due to the avoidance of 'open' films dealing with specific issues such as the fallout from the Civil War. As Liam O'Leary has said, these films actually did nothing to promote professional film production in Ireland. It seemed that Irish people were too content with American and British imports and too insecure to realise a native industry formed by native talent.

Tom Cooper made a second film, *Uncle Nick* (1938), while Donal O'Cahill directed *The Islandman* (1939); neither received good reviews.

Film literature in Ireland: 1920-30

This lack of focus or insecurity may be extracted from the film literature of the period. In 1928 Mona Price saw many current films as "the exploitation of the lowest sort of sensationalism and sentimentality in the masses". A year later in the *Studies* journal, the Reverend Cyril Martindale stated quite categorically that he felt films were degrading to the intellect and he even said they were pagan and immoral. Ironically, his criticism of "Americanisation via the films" would have many supporters now.

A testing ground for Irish film production and its critical reception occurred at the Peacock Theatre in August 1930 when Lennox Robinson introduced the first efforts of what later became the Irish Film Society. These films included a short, *Bank Holiday*, by Mary Manning; J N Davidson's *By Accident*, an hour-long drama which centres on a man who realizes he is a coward; and *Pathetic Gazette* (director unknown), described in reviews as a light-hearted look at the lore of Irish legend.

More interesting to a historian is the report of Robinson's welcoming the new enterprise, claiming that cinema had unfortunately got into the hands of the capitalists and that its potential as an art form was being undermined by the imperative to make massive amounts of money.

A flurry of publication marked the year 1936. A cinema manager was quoted in the March *Irish Monthly* as saying of his occupation: "It is not our business to stimulate thought. People come to us for relaxation." This pessimistic view to some was shared by John Desmond Sheridan who, two months later in the same journal, commented "the screen is a dead thing". In the same issue A P Bodkin argued, like many after him, that a search for uniquely Irish values would be the mainstay of an Irish film industry. Naturally, Liam O'Leary and the Irish Film Society added their voices to this call, in particular the need for Irish versions of Ireland and not American or British ones.

To this end, A P Bodkin promoted the notion of a Dublin Documentary Film Unit, not with the 'taint' of Grierson's apparent Marxism and materialism (which may have interested the Irish Film Society), but with that of Irish Christian history, and with the emphasis on the evolution of Catholicism. Although Bodkin saw the value of travelling film units, one can readily believe that he had in mind individuals such as Father Daniel Collier, "film priest", who made a number of short pieces depicting the life of Donegal peasants. Despite these concessions, the overriding mood in the 1930s and 1940s can be summed up in the title of an influential article by Gabriel Fallon in *The Capuchin Annual* for 1938 — "Celluloid Menace".

Nevertheless, in 1938 Fianna Fáil, the political party that ruled during the 1930s, began to promote the notion of Gaelic language films for school audiences, under pressure from certain lobby groups. At the same time Robert Flaherty was commissioned to make an Irish language film. The Dáil sanctioned £200 to be given to the project which turned out to be a disappointment. *Oidhche Sheanchais/A Night of Story-telling* (1935) was intended as a short to preface *Man of Aran*; it depicts an old man at a fireside telling stories. By all accounts the film failed to gain much attention, mostly because of the banal script provided by the Department of Education.

Unmade films of the 1930s

Much ballyhoo was made of the fact that the prominent President of the British Board of Film Censors in the silent era was an Irishman, T P O'Connor. Less well-known is that he was partly succeeded by Colonel J C Hanna who was Chief Censor from 1930-1946 and who had been stationed in Ireland between 1918-1922. James Robertson has studied the BBFC records from the 1930s and has revealed that a few scenarios of Irish interest were purposely stalled.

Perhaps the most important censures were of the scenarios entitled *Sir Roger Casement* (submitted 1934) and *Irish Story* (1939). The former was presented by Universal Pictures who wanted to portray Casement as an intellectual patriot who died heroically. Hanna's written comments on the scenario proved his military experience in Ireland went deep. The Chief Censor regarded Casement as an insignificant "traitor" who was justly punished. Warner Brothers proposed the latter scenario which dwelled on the Civil War. Hanna believed that the Irish Free State Government would not welcome such a divisive film nor the British Government since the IRA were presently active on the mainland. Neither scenario made it to production.

The Belfast Film Society

Between 1936 and 1946 the Belfast Film Society flourished independently from the Irish Film Society in Dublin, which started up in the same year. It is believed that the Belfast Film Society started with a showing of a Czechoslovakian film in the Old Grosvenor Hall, using a 16mm projector. Accompanying the Belfast Film Society was a monthly periodical, *The Belfast Film Review* which contained film and book reviews, news of visits of important people (such as the Director of the British Film Institute, Oliver Bell) and articles on cinematic topics. The November 1937 issue, for example, presented three quite different views of Fritz Lang's *M*. The Belfast Film Society's regular season consisted of five shows, chosen for their "*general appeal*" in addition to other "essential qualifications". Specialist films were screened to boost the regular programme.

The Belfast Film Society gradually merged with the Belfast branch of the British Film Institute and issued the

Review jointly. In the early days the editor was Ronald Marshall of Methodist College, Belfast. In a number of editorials he lamented the lack of good film criticism and encouraged members (numbering nearly four hundred by January 1938) to review films. The difference between the Film Institute branch and the Society was one of emphasis: whilst the Society generally only exhibited films — midnight screenings in cinemas such as the Apollo on the Ormeau Road — the Institute concentrated on lectures and discussions.

Liam O'Leary (right) with Donald Taylor Black

The Irish Film Society

Unaware, perhaps, of the Belfast Film Society, a number of film aficionados, including Liam O'Leary and Edward Toner, started up the Irish Film Society in Dublin. An abortive attempt to form a society had been made in 1930, when it was clear that the introduction of sound films blocked foreign films from Irish screens. In this respect, Ireland's interest in film societies imitated what was happening in England. Starting with just forty members paying five shillings a year, the Irish Film Society blossomed to over a thousand members. Branches were set up, albeit precariously, in places such as Cork, Drogheda, Limerick and Sligo. Little did they expect the furore over the showing of Eisenstein's *Battleship Potemkin*. Newspaper headlines such as "Spreading Deathly Poison" and "First Soviet

Propaganda Film in Ireland" greeted the Society's organisers one morning.

The Irish Film Society (IFS) was hampered not only by the mores of Southern Irish society but also by the simple fact that films often had to be rented from England from people who were reluctant to risk the delay in return that inevitably occurred.

As Edward Toner pointed out in an article in the 1943 *Irish Cinema Handbook*, the Irish Film Society had four main activities:

(1) exhibiting classical and foreign films;
(2) running the rather informal Film School which encouraged Irish people to make films and learn about cinema art (Colm O Laoghaire and Patrick Carey were students);
(3) overseeing the Children's Film Committee which worked particularly hard to construct adequate and suitable programmes for young people, including the introduction of films into schools;
(4) organising film lectures, discussions and literature, including *Scannán* magazine, under the general editorship of Richard Delaney.

The objectives of the IFS emerged slowly but surely into practice. In his book *An Invitation to the Film*, Liam O'Leary gives a detailed account of the Film School's aspirations, especially the way that it attempted to combine the teaching of film aesthetics with film production.

In 1940 their first film, *Foolsmate*, twenty minutes long and containing some two hundred separate scenes, was favourably reviewed in the local press. It traces an incident emerging from the Black and Tans period of the War of Independence. Other films followed: *Aiséirghe, Tibradden, Zones, They Live by the Sea, Dance School* and *This Farm is Ours*. O'Leary has said that the intention of these films was to promote a national consciousness in the minds of the people.

In 1942 the Children's Film Committee was established in tandem with frequent public debates on the issue of cinema and the child. A year later, the School of Film Technique was formed as a production unit of the IFS. This unit was designed to foster a film culture in Ireland among young people, with the expressed intention that a handful of students would 'graduate' to assistants on the current production. Their training included lectures on "The Basis of Creation", "Dance — The Poetry of Motion", "Music" and "Acting". The works of James Joyce, Liam O'Flaherty and the labour activist, James Connolly, were required reading.

Meanwhile, in 1945 the IFS established a travelling unit, "Comhairle na nog", which screened children's programmes in community halls around the country. In this year there were branches of the IFS in Waterford, Sligo and Portlaoise, from where *Scannán* was published and in which the editors called for an Irish film industry because, they claimed, there was enormous potential for scenery, stories and plots.

The Film School collapsed around 1948 because it proved too difficult to find adequately qualified teachers. Furthermore, the assumptions of the members of the IFS may have hindered development. These assumptions — that silent films were better than sound films, that American and British imports were generally pulp and that an excess of money encouraged bad cinema art — may, as Kieran Hickey has stated, have forced the stagnation of the production unit.

The Bell and Dr Hayes

The early 1940s saw three significant developments in promoting film culture and debate in Ireland: the emergence of the periodical, *The Bell* (1940-1954), edited initially by Seán Ó Faoláin; the appointment in 1941 of Dr Richard Hayes as successor to James Montgomery in the role of Irish film censor; and the forming of the National Film Institute in 1943.

The first two were neatly combined in a November 1941 issue of *The Bell* when the "Bellman" interviewed Dr Hayes. Hayes was a doctor, a soldier from the cause of Irish freedom and a historian of Franco-Irish relations. The interview needs to be republished in full in order to appreciate the interviewer's acerbic wit. The following extract reveals something of the delicate balance which Hayes, an Abbey Theatre board director, tried to maintain in his powerful position:

"You know the attitude of the people of this country to divorce....I myself have been criticised in several quarters for permitting pictures dealing with divorce — although they have been pictures in which the subject was treated seriously. My argument has been that such pictures illustrate a life that is so far removed from the life in this country that it's on an almost entirely different plane. I say...that each film in which divorce is a feature ought to be judged by one standard alone: Is it an incentive to Divorce or does it condone it — ennoble it in any way? If it does either of these things, then it is not a film for the Irish public. There was a case, fairly recently, when I got the distributors to change the title of a film from "I Want a Divorce" to "The Tragedy of Divorce." Hayes goes on to list his other "banned" subjects: abortion, birth control and illegitimacy.

Hayes explained that he normally saw two full-length films a day, in addition to trailers and re-runs of cut versions. The censor's rule of thumb was a moral code based on "the family" and "civilisation", a code which ensured that evil was not dressed in the cloak of good. Hayes particularly disliked American musicals and what he termed "lascivious dances". Although he rarely cut dialogue, Hayes insisted on having a script and a playback after the cuts were made. Amusingly enough, Hayes considered that if he did not understand American slang, then the "ordinary cinema goer" would hardly do so.

Hayes skirted the issue of the Emergency Powers Order which, since Ireland was neutral, banned newsreels of the war. This fact alone created two different cinema-going publics north and south of the border. Furthermore, 'partisan' sections from other films were cut. In particular, the censor objected to the propaganda and "vulgarity" of Chaplin's *The Great Dictator* (1940) and to the general use of Americanisms and Englishisms. On the subject of Irish films, Hayes believed the problem was one not of cost but of distribution in the face of the large American and British cinema organisations. Hayes justified his position by pointing out that unlike the adult audience at the Abbey Theatre, eighty per cent of the cinema audience was made up of children; therefore, films such as *Gone With the Wind* had to be banned!

Writing four years later in a 1945 issue of *The Bell*, Rex Mac Gall explained the sometimes torturous process for a cinema manager in Ireland to rent and exhibit a non-Irish film. Firstly, he would contact Head Office in London because, despite national boundaries, Ireland was considered part of the United Kingdom distribution network. The film would be shipped to Dublin, whereupon the renter applied to the censor's office for a certificate in order to exhibit the film. He would then pay certain fees, depending on whether it was a feature film or a short, purchasing 'fee stamps' (obtainable, strangely, from only one post office in the city!).

After the viewing the renter would receive either a rejection slip, a Memo of Exceptions (parts to be cut) or clearance. If rejected then there was always the Appeal Board, consisting of nine members but which could operate with a quorum of three. This board was noted for its idiosyncratic practices: for example, if the chairperson was absent, the third person who entered the room automatically took the chair. Technically, even if the Appeal Board reversed the censor's decision, the latter did not have to give certification; however, this power never seems to have been exercised.

Dr Hayes's exhibition theatre was about 20' square and the screen 6' by 5' high. At the back of the room there was a desk with two lights: one for his own notes and one for his dialogue script. Invariably the aspiring renter sat below Hayes, waiting for the result. Cuts had to be made at the renter's offices and even if the film was rejected outright, the renter could — and some did — edit, re-title and re-submit.

One surprising fact is that unlike Britain and Northern Ireland who allowed the *trade* to censor films while allowing local and district councils some autonomy, the Irish Censorship Act rigorously centralised control over what could be legally shown. Furthermore, there was censorship of films under the Emergency Powers Order (1939), for those "prejudical to the national interest". This order stipulated that no appeal could be made by the renter, except to the Minister of Justice. Mac Gall, an enlightened figure, could see that censorship was needed similar to the grading system adopted by the British Film Institute, so that more films would be shown to wider audiences and that the seriousness of film art could be more fully appreciated.

Many of the articles in *The Bell* give a marvellous panoramic view of Ireland in the 1940s and 1950s. For example, Michael Farrell wrote frequent pieces on country and small town theatres and in passing referred to the cultural impact of the cinema. When he visited Dundalk (*The Bell* January 1941) Farrell tells us that there were parks, a library, two weekly newspapers and the "much denounced lures of the cinema...offered in startling abundance". He explains that there was much competition in the town since one cinema was excused tax because it intended to put profits into parochial funds.

Meanwhile, the relationship between cinema owners and dramatic societies was strained because the town hall, the largest auditorium, was rented out as a cinema, thereby forcing theatricals into smaller venues. Farrell's detailed reporting reveals that the size of a town did not dictate the number of cinemas present as both Sligo (population 12 000) and Birr (population 3000) had two picture-houses.

The Irish Film Society took the opportunity to publicise its activities and screenings in *The Bell*: in the August 1942 issue, a piece appeared on the aspirations of the Children's Film Committee, including a call for suggestions from the reading public. Later, in 1945 and 1946 Lucy Glazebrook started a regular "Tour of Films" column about feature films showing in Irish cinemas. Although by necessity superficial, these reviews did spark interest in the more involved articles published soon after, written by Rex Mac Gall, Liam O'Leary, Hilton Edwards and Alberto Cavalcanti. Like the books written and edited by Liam O'Leary, Oliver Bell and Proinsias Ó Conluain, *The Bell* provided a forum to combat reactionary forces, such as the *Irish Catholic*, the Dublin paper which in 1944 set up a Film Information Bureau, aiming to encourage the "proper" use of the cinema.

The report by Melchior A A Sinkins for the *Kinematograph Weekly* of 13 January 1944, entitled "In the Land of the Gaels: Belfast, The Grim, Dublin, The Gay", provides a fascinating outsider's view of the Irish exhibition scene. In Belfast Sinkins found cinema managers going about their business armed with revolvers! Less sensationally, he found the Lord Mayor of Belfast, Sir Crawford McCullagh, very "film-minded" (he was a director of the salubrious Classic Cinema, then controlled by a British concern), the film-going public exceedingly well-behaved, the cinema staff well-trained and the cinemas closed on Sundays except for two theatres which catered exclusively for stationed troops.

One exhibitor, Protestant Billie Hogan, owned the Clonard Cinema on the Catholic Falls Road. Hogan obviously had a very understanding nature as, in April 1943 on the anniversary of the 1916 Rising, six armed men marched into the theatre and thrust a notice on the screen advertising an IRA meeting. Hogan's response was wistful: "It's no good kicking up a rumpus. At least they don't slash the seats." In tandem with the areas he would have to pass through, Hogan is reported as having first a Catholic then a Protestant escort on his way to deposit money at the bank.

In Dublin, which he preferred, Sinkins continued to find the Emergency Powers Order totally inexplicable. In line with the Republic's neutrality, any film depicting British or American troops (or German for that matter) could be withdrawn by a complaint from a Dáil member, even if the censor had approved the film. Often Southern Irish people would travel northwards to Newry and Enniskillen to see films banned in the South. As regards the trade, Louis Elliman dominated, owning thirteen of the forty-eight "decent" halls. Interestingly, Sinkins found training of projectionists in technical schools under the supervision of the Dublin Corporation; a similar scheme was planned by George Lodge of Belfast's Imperial Cinema for a four-year course at the Belfast College of Technology.

National Film Institute

The question facing the Roman Catholic Church in Ireland — and indeed in Rome — in the early 1940s was whether or not to take an active role in film culture. Following a papal encyclical, the National Film Institute became a reality in 1943. To some observers, it is little short of a crime that Ireland's rigorous censorship laws and general narrow-mindedness hampered the growth of the Institute. Its aims and objectives were admirably broad: "to direct and encourage the use of the motion picture in the national and cultural interests of the Irish people".

More specifically, the Institute had aspirations for the use of film in adult education, schools, the teaching of Irish and in the setting up of a National Film Library. A production unit was established and there were discussions and negotiations with a number of Irish amateur ciné clubs. The 1943 *Irish Cinema Handbook* lists many sub-standard 16mm and 8mm films made by Irish amateurs and organisations, including the Irish Ciné Group, founded in 1936 by John C Boyne, Gearóid Mac Eoin and Paul Marshall.

In 1944 the Government granted £2000 to the Institute, with a directive to acquire educational films for hire and to make films on behalf of the Government. The NFI was thus registered as a limited company. Initial films included the rise to power of certain contemporary figures and historical documentaries on Thomas Davis and the Young Ireland Movement. Naturally the Departments of Health, Local Government and Supplies as well as the Turf Development Board were actively involved in education by disseminating information on modern science, technology and safety measures. A Gaumont Cinema Co-operative, the Muintir na Tire film unit, purchased projectors and toured Ireland, showing educational and health shorts; another travelling film unit, the Glun na Braidhe, received a grant to promote Irish language and culture.

Many of those involved in the Irish Film Society, the Institute and these amateur groups overlapped, so much so that it would not be correct to say that they were in active competition. For example, the group of teachers, Comhairle na nog, who had made some films independently, joined the Institute in the late 1940s. Other films followed and by the 1948 Annual Report the Institute could boast a collection of 480 films in their library.

One of the partisan films made for the National Film Institute was *A Nation Once Again* (1945). Directed by John D Sheridan and Brendan Stafford, it was commissioned by the government of De Valera to help encourage support for its attempts to prove that Nationalism or Independence was a worthwhile gain, despite the post-war shortages of food and consumer goods.

The film is a celebration of the centenary of the death of Thomas Davis, the founder of the Young Irelanders. Davis stressed the unification of Ireland through language, history, literature and law and is seen as a link between Wolfe Tone and Patrick Pearse. De Valera's voice is heard in the film via a radio report praising Davis and the production ends with the national anthem, "A Nation Once Again".

The organ of the National Film Institute for a time was *Irish Cinema Quarterly* which contained news and articles about the film scene throughout Ireland. In a brief essay in the third issue, Liam O'Leary emphasized the need to tell a story effectively, citing his experience working on two road safety films at the National Film Institute for the Department of Local Government: *Mr Careless Goes To Town* and *Safe Cycling* (both 1949).

What is striking about O'Leary's

comments is that despite the practical nature of the films, his awareness of "visual form", "fluid narrative" and "atmosphere" mark him out as an extremely competent and capable director who did not seem to have the opportunity to branch out into feature films. Perhaps because of his Socialist leanings — if one judges from the agitprop *Our Country* (1948), a campaign film for the political party Clann na Poblachta — he did not sit comfortably with Irish politicking. Indeed, his *Portrait of Dublin* (1952), photographed by Brendan Stafford, started out as a leisurely view of the city but through committee pressure was turned into what Kieran Hickey calls "a time capsule of historical grievances and cultural boasts". It was subsequently shelved by the Minister for External Affairs, Mr Aiken, and Liam O'Leary's career as a film director ended. Needless to say, his report for the Cultural Relations Committee on the setting up of a viable film industry in Ireland was never implemented.

Perhaps inevitably, the National Film Institute toed the party-line in a number of ways but did make some valuable and successful films. Among these was George Fleischmann's *W B Yeats — A Tribute* (1950), which won a Certificate of Merit at Venice in 1950. However, there were instances of films shot but not finished or released, so conflicting was the creative environment.

Thus it was safer for the Institute to advance into the field of educational film hire at a time when television was not widely available. In this respect the National Film Institute followed the same pattern as the Scottish Film Council. The lack of money belittled any significant development in the areas now seen as crucial for the Irish Film Institute — archiving, education, exhibition and publishing. Sadly all these aspects were outlined at the time by John Grierson who gave an invited lecture at the Gresham Hotel in Dublin (later published in *Studies* entitled "A Film Policy for Ireland").

Return of Yeats's body in W B Yeats — A Tribute

Cinema trade in the 1940s

Despite the prudish censorship, the cinema was probably the most popular form of entertainment for working people. The Government cashed in on this by exacting a flat rate of import tax from each film. It was this tax that frustrated George Fleischmann who wanted to set up a lab in Dublin so that even the few Irish films that were produced did not have to be sent to London for processing. The Government received money from the processing traffic between Ireland and England and therefore were not particularly pressed to implement Fleischmann's idea.

Furthermore, the Government felt even less impelled to act since film theatres in the 1940s were blossoming. In 1944 the *Kinematograph Weekly* reported that 240 cinemas existed, 48 of which were considered of good quality. Four years later 350 existed, 150 of which the *Irish Monthly* believed to be of a professional standard.

Not surprisingly, take-overs by British and American interests held centre-stage in the mid-1940s. After the war Rank announced a large expansion in Ireland. To offset fears that British ownership would be politically charged, Rank invited Irish film critics to visit its British plants. When it took a major share interest in Allied Cinemas and Irish Cinema (owned by Maurice Elliman), Rank effectively controlled the distribution and exhibition market throughout the country.

Rank announced plans for building a studio in Ireland but nothing was realised. Meanwhile the lobby against the cinema seemed to grow. In 1943 the Clones Cinema in Co. Monaghan demanded that unmarried couples sit separately in the auditorium. The ban was lifted a few years later, reimposed and lifted again.

Foreign views of Ireland

While Ireland argued over the value of cinema and how to control it, films were made by foreigners using Ireland as their subject matter. 1947, for example, saw the release of *Captain Boycott* and *Odd Man Out*.

Captain Boycott

Frank Launder's *Captain Boycott* centres on a farmer rebellion against landowners in the 1880s. This covers Parnell's Irish Land League's resistance to Captain Boycott (Cecil Parker), a particularly vicious money-grabbing land agent. Stewart Granger leads the middle-of-the-road resistance movement, spurred on by Parnell's (Robert Donat) rhetoric. Noel Purcell, Kathleen Ryan and Alastair Sim also star.

Writing in *The Bell* in November 1947, Liam O'Leary summed up the limitations of the film to an Irish eye: "The background of *Captain Boycott* never means more than beautiful Irish scenery, a bunch of crude-looking louts obviously to be labelled peasants and a low-raftered community hall conveniently designed to congregate the protagonists at any given time. This Ireland is one of long winding roads leading inexorably to a pub."

Odd Man Out

In contrast Carol Reed's thriller, *Odd Man Out*, about a wounded IRA man, Johnny O'Queen (James Mason), trying to evade capture in Belfast, is a stirring cinematic achievement. If the division between the chase and the introspective sequences is too marked, what is undeniably assured is Reed's ability to capture a vividly realistic tension, such as that in the bungled getaway scene and in the accidental murder of the book-keeper. Cyril Cusack,

Kathleen Ryan, F J McCormick, Denis O'Dea, Dan O'Herlihy and Joseph Tomelty all feature in this film. One striking scene is where O'Queen sits hallucinating in the mad portrait painter's studio. The IRA man appears to see the paintings merge with actual people who circulate around him.

The 1950s

By 1952 film exhibition was well-established in Ireland and only 17 out of 2070 films submitted to the censor were banned initially. Of these, 10 were appealed and 5 won certificates. Seat prices in 1953 were de-regulated, advancing competition in the light of a study that found one in every three people in Ireland went to the cinema at least once a week, with some £3½ million spent on tickets. In urban centres this ratio was reduced to one in two. Not surprisingly,

the debate over the showing of the Queen's Coronation in 1953 set cinema and Nationalism against each other. Sinn Féin asked Irish unions not to allow the screening in Éire and under the threat of future damage, cinema owners decided to avoid the film. In Banbridge, Co. Down in Northern Ireland a bomb damaged a cinema that was showing a recording of the event.

Another important development in the early 1950s was the forming of an Irish Film Industry Committee by distinguished figures Lord Killanin, John Ford and Brian Desmond Hurst. Their report looked forward to an active native film industry but putting words into action proved to be another matter. An influential article, "An Irish Film Industry?" written by Hilton Edwards in *The Bell* in January 1953, argued also for the link between Nationalism and film production. In addition, Edwards raised practical matters:

he saw the need, as did Rex Mac Gall in *The Bell* in 1946 ("Towards An Irish Film Industry"), for a constant flow of financial backing.

Hilton Edwards

Hilton Edwards contracted the film "bug" while working with Orson Welles on his *Othello*. Edwards began with *Hamlet at Elsinore* (1951), a record of the open air production put on by Edwards and Micheál MacLiammóir in the Danish Castle. Forever adventurous, Edwards wanted to branch out into directing fiction films, although he did not want to be, as he said, "yet another little operator footling around with something that interested me and which I did not understand".

Return to Glennascaul

Edwards took the plunge with *Return to Glennascaul* (1951): "I got hold of a story that belonged to no-one, adapted it myself, so that I could ruin nobody's work but my own, procured the services of a fine cameraman [George Fleischmann] and a group of skilled and incidentally delightful people, whose very existence in Dublin gives me great hopes of a future for picture-making here. For actors, I had among others Orson himself, who generously agreed to play commentator".

Welles stars in this ghost story as a man who listens to a strange tale told to him by a fellow he has given a lift to on his way to Dublin. Fleischmann gives the film a marvellous atmospheric quality which more than makes up for the rather stiff acting. The sound was recorded in Peter Hunt's studios, for many years an Irish institution in itself, and was produced by Louis Elliman, a theatre owner, who provided initial backing — although George Fleischmann emphasizes (page 112) that the production was made on a shoestring.

As far as can be seen, the film was never released in the United States but for many years it was a support for *Marty* in the United Kingdom.

The Quiet Man

More famous and internationally acclaimed is John Ford's *The Quiet Man* (1952), for many the ultimate Irish-American nostalgia trip. As Hilton Edwards remarked in *The Bell* in 1953, "*The Quiet Man* is undoubtedly a highly professional and well-made picture with many merits, but I cannot for the life of me see that it has any relation to the Ireland I or anyone else can have seen or known." This realist-centered criticism is one that is often levelled at foreign screen versions of Ireland and its people and one which accompanies Ford's many Irish films.

If *The Informer* seventeen years earlier suggests a fixation with religious symbolism, then *The Quiet Man* reveals more clearly Ford's beliefs in the intertwining of religion, sexuality and community in rural Ireland. John Wayne and Maureen O'Hara star in this sometimes exaggerated and antiquated love-story. Nevertheless, the film is shot in beautiful Technicolour and is regularly shown on British and American television. Unquestionably, the Irish Tourist Board does not mind the stereotypes it presents but particularly outmoded today is the way Maureen O'Hara sets the male machismo in motion: Wayne must fight with O'Hara's brother before winning the right to marry the woman of his dreams.

No Resting Place

Nostalgia and humour hardly sum up Paul Rotha's *No Resting Place* (1951) which traces the fortunes of a group of tinkers, again in rural Ireland. The tinkers are hounded by the police because one of them, played by Michael Gough, kills a gamekeeper who has injured the tinker's son. Noel Purcell acts a suitably moral guard who chases the tinkers. Rotha's film is a docudrama that forces the viewer to see both tinker and guard in a spider's web, the creator of which, it is implied, is a conservative and puritanical Irish society.

North and South interact on television

Rex Cathcart's 1984 book on the BBC's role in Northern Ireland picks up two interesting incidents that relate to film screenings on television and their subsequent political ramifications. In March 1954, the BBC Panorama editor found himself at a loss for an Irish Saint Patrick's Day item. He eventually selected the Republican tourist film, *Ireland —*

Land of Welcome (date unknown). No reference is made in the film to Northern Ireland and by unfortunate implication, the Northern Protestant viewer inferred that the BBC considered Northern Ireland to have no claim to Saint Patrick.

If the feeling of *exclusion* raised Northern heckles in one film, it was, ironically, the possibility of *inclusion* in another film that caused a further argument. *The Promise of Barty O'Brien* (1951), screened soon after on the BBC, showed the magical effects of American aid in bringing electrical power to poor, rural Southern Ireland. The Prime Minister of Northern Ireland, Lord Brookeborough, referred in his letter of complaint to the BBC to the "unfortunate impression" that the film might have on British viewers "unaware that there are two distinct elements on the 'Irish Scene".

The Quiet Man

3: Internationalism and Ireland 1956-76

Mise Eire

Without a definite infrastructure for an Irish film industry, the role played by sponsoring institutions has proved crucial. In 1955 the Irish Tourist Board/Bord Fáilte was established under the Tourist Act. Financed by government grant, Bord Fáilte has sponsored many Irish documentary films to promote tourism in Ireland.

Dermot Breen and the Cork Film Festival

More significantly, Bord Fáilte supported the Cork Film Festival from its birth in 1956 until 1980, at which time the Arts Council assumed a major role. The festival heralded a new era for Irish film culture. Its first and most famous director was Dermot Breen, whose name became synonymous with the event until the 1980 festival.

When Breen was appointed film censor in 1972, he held for a while two of the most important positions in determining the course of Irish cinema culture. Breen's previous experience included organising the Irish tourist festival, An Tostal, and he had been a founder-organiser of the Cork International Choral Festival in 1953.

Breen's project was ambitious and long-cherished and on 21 May 1956 the first Cork Film Festival opened in the Savoy Cinema with a showing of *A Town Like Alice*. There were two Irish entries that year: Gerard Healy's film about the uses of electricity for industry and agriculture, *Power for Progress* and *Irish Symphony*, a documentary about the linen industry directed by David Villiers.

Although it started relatively small, the festival has over the years flowered into an international event of importance. Known for its seriousness and high estimation of the short film, Cork enables Irish people to discuss a wide range of cinematic topics with professionals from abroad. Louis Marcus in his interview (page 119) conveys a sense of the excitement the festival held for Irish people, worried that they were isolated from American and European movements.

The setting up of the Ardmore studios

Despite much exaggerated talk by Gabriel Pascal and George Bernard Shaw in the late 1940s about the setting up of an Irish film studio (to produce Shaw's then-unfilmed plays), it was another ten years before the idea became a reality. The state of Éire bears the responsibility for the setting up of the Ardmore studios, situated in Bray, twelve miles south of Dublin. The studios opened in May 1958 thanks to an investment of £250 000 provided by the Industrial Credit Company Ltd. and the Industrial Development Authority. As a working grant it was sufficient but no provision was made to train Irish film technicians to run the studio, nor were there auspicious circumstances in which to create an Irish film industry from Ardmore.

Louis Marcus's series of articles in the *Irish Times* in 1967 gives a detailed analysis of the limitations of the studios as they were constructed. Marcus emphasizes that the trouble with Ardmore was that it was designed not to develop an Irish film industry but to encourage foreign companies to make films in Ireland. For a while foreign directors arrived in abundance and in response in 1960 the Irish Film Finance Corporation (IFFC) was founded.

The IFFC was similar in concept to the British National Film Finance Corporation (BNFFC, established in 1950). However, whereas the BNFFC actively supported home-grown production, the IFFC was empowered to grant monies *only if* a distribution guarantee was already set up. Naturally, this ruling put the budding Irish film-maker at a distinct disadvantage.

It was not surprising, therefore, that conflict soon became associated with the name of Ardmore. One incident that illustrates this only too well is the rivalry between the Irish and British electrical trades unions between 1962 and 1964. The Irish felt that, since the Government had pumped money into the setting up of Ardmore, they should be employed there; the British argued that, since the finance enabling films to be made at Ardmore was primarily British, they should be hired. The issue died down only when Ardmore threatened to be strangled soon after birth if the dispute was not put to one side. As a mere facility Ardmore could not champion local employment; the most commonly hired Irish people seemed to be canteen workers and carpenters. The point is not that one should criticise Ardmore for what it was not, but that one would have at least expected various artistic, financial and governmental bodies to see it for what it was — "a piece of industrial equipment", as Louis Marcus called it, without a life of its own.

This mistaken optimism can be seen from the way Ardmore got off on the wrong foot from the very beginning. The first Irish managers to run the studios were Louis Elliman and Emmet Dalton. The former was an entrepreneur and the latter, who had been a soldier in the War of Independence and the Civil War, had experience as a film publicist and distributor. Both believed that Abbey Theatre players and productions could be used to create the backbone of the

Ardmore studios and, ultimately, a national film industry.

On the surface this seemed a sound proposition, although it is questionable whether or not they envisaged the general antipathy towards very stagey films. The filming in 1959 of the Abbey Theatre successes, *Home is the Hero*, directed by Fielder Cook and Muriel Box's *This Other Eden*, both foundered, perhaps because the distinction between theatrical film and filmed theatre was not clearly enough drawn.

Moreover, the vast majority of films made at Ardmore between 1958 and 1972 (some fifty-six) were produced, directed and serviced by foreigners. Of these, Michael Anderson's *Shake Hands with the Devil* (1959), Tay Garnett's *A Terrible Beauty* (1960), John Ford's *Young Cassidy* (1964), Joseph Strick's *Ulysses* (1967), John Quested's *Philadelphia Here I Come* (1970) and Robert Altman's *Images* (1972) seem the most interesting for an Irish audience. Other famous films, such as *The Blue Max*, *The Spy Who Came in from the Cold* (both 1966) and *The Lion in Winter* (1968), all have strong connections with the Ardmore studios.

Gael-Linn and the Radharc Film Unit

In opposition to the internationalism promised by both Ardmore and Cork, it is significant that two home-grown organisations should emerge to use the cinematic medium. It might be argued that while Ardmore and the Cork Film Festival imported American and continental culture to influence the direction of Irish cinema, Gael-Linn and the Radharc Film Unit offered to put film culture in a decidedly Irish context. To a Northern Protestant, it might be difficult to distinguish the net results of Gael-Linn and Radharc but the former, unlike the latter, had a wide enough brief to de-Catholicise the Irish language and thus pose a threat to the cultural space assumed by the Roman Catholic Church.

Gael-Linn was founded in 1953 to promote the Irish language and Irish culture in as many forms as possible, including through composers and musicians such as Gerard Victory and Sean O Riada. Gael-Linn's involvement in film production, however, did not begin until 1957, when Colm O Laoghaire, Vincent Corcoran and Jim Mulkerns started to direct and photograph Gaelic newsreels, each often only three minutes in length. This *Amharch Éireann* series lasted for five years and was distributed throughout Ireland by the Rank Organisation. Gael-Linn was made up not of altruistic amateurs but of people who felt that it was important for Irish people to see their way of life on-screen, if only to offset the imported lifestyles normally presented in their local cinemas. The arrival of Telefís Éireann and, more crucially, of television in 1961 brought the end of the newsreel, which ran to over 260 issues.

Whereas Gael-Linn appeared more concerned with a secularisation of the Irish identity, the Radharc Film Unit promoted a Roman Catholic perspective on Irish and international issues. Formed in 1959 by the Reverend Father Joseph Dunn, its aim was to produce religious programmes for Irish television. The unit opened a Communications Centre in Dublin in 1967 which contained full studio and editing facilities. Television had a direct effect on the National Film Institute which began to move away from non-theatrical hire and attracted new staff with a much wider interest in documentary film. Perhaps partly due to Radharc, very few of the Church-centered staff were left at the Institute by the early 1970s.

Concentrating on documentary work,

Radharc has won a number of awards for films such as *Turkana* (1966) and *Night Flight to Uli* (1969). The former centres on the trials and tribulations of the working nuns in the Turkana desert whilst the latter depicts the airlift relief to Biafra.

Radharc's Irish film production has been an ongoing activity - over 270 films between 1962 and 1988, divided fairly evenly between Irish and non-Irish topics. From Joseph Dunn's *The Restless Knives* (1968), which suggests that the Catholic Church has an important part to play in the Philippines, to his 1976 film, *The Black Irish*, and Desmond Forristal's *Nano Nagle* in the same year, Radharc has firmly inserted its Catholic ideology into Irish society. *The Black Irish* focusses on the emigration of Irish people from Kinsale to Monserrat in the Caribbean in 1632, escaping the violence of Cromwell. It also shows how their descendants have kept many Irish customs, including their religious practices. *Nano Nagle*, a dramatised documentary, is a portrait of the lady who initiated the first Catholic primary school in Ireland - Presentation College in County Cork.

Radharc has also made films on Irish saints, such as Desmond Forristal's *The Late Dr Plunkett* (1975), about the Archbishop of Armagh who was martyred at Tyburn. The documentary builds up an impressive portrait, using a number of Irish actors and actresses. The less-than-attractive role of Lord Chief Justice is played by Hilton Edwards.

In 1964 Radharc came to Derry to film places and people. Apparently, their film was never screened but Dermod McCarthy returned in 1975 to update the film. Commissioned by RTE, it contains footage from both years and was shown at the Foyle Film Festival in April 1987.

Cardinal Tomas O Fiaich filming in the Austrian Alps for the Radharc Film Unit

To critic Martin Dolan, Radharc's films are fraught with problems because they stress so much the importance of the Catholic Church over and above the possibilities of alternative solutions to social and political issues. Although this is undoubtedly true, Radharc has a specific brief with no hidden agenda and has expressed a certain attitude of mind prevalent in Ireland. In his book, *No Tigers in Africa*, Dunn succinctly sums up his own position:

"For me the idea of priests working in media is normal and natural, and should need no defence or justification....Sure I am biased. I am against the use of atomic energy in any form...I am for capitalism I think because my father was a shopkeeper and I haven't seen socialism work very well in the long term (it's too much like Christianity — expects everybody to be saints, and they aren't). I am a conscientious objector if such things exist anymore, and wouldn't ever shoot a bird or rabbit. I am anti-English and anti-Spanish because of what they did in their colonies. I generally support one political party which I am too cute to tell you about. And I am for Jesus Christ. Let the next man speak for himself."

Directors

Looking at particular directors in this period, four men emerge. That each made modest documentary films is a sign of the very lukewarm attitude government and private investors had (and still have) to the potential of cinema. Nevertheless, it may be said that without the pioneering efforts of George Morrison, Patrick Carey, Kieran Hickey and Louis Marcus and their record of international acclaim, the argument for a National Film Board would never have been won in the late 1970s. It is tragically ironic that Irish directors need to prove themselves abroad before gaining financial encouragement at home.

George Morrison

Born in Tramore, Co. Waterford in 1922, George Morrison is believed to have taken his first photographs aged only twelve. Eight years later, with a 16mm camera given to him by his father, he began his first film, *Dracula*. The cast included an architectural student, Dan O'Herlihy, who later starred in Irish-American films and took the Oscar-nominated lead in Buñuel's *Robinson Crusoe*. Morrison's *Dracula* was unfortunately never completed, due to a shortage of film stock.

In 1951 Hilton Edwards brought in Morrison as assistant director on *Hamlet at Elsinore* and he worked with Edwards and Micheál MacLiammóir on other films. By this time Morrison had already become interested in Irish actualities. Indeed, he will be most remembered for his two compilation films, *Mise Éire* (1959) and *Saoirse?* (1961).

Mise Éire and Saoirse?

In 1949 Morrison had written *Dead Sunlight*, a script for a proposed BBC feature on the last years of the Victorian era which, he says, envisaged all the techniques used ten years later in *Mise Éire*; the film was never made. Shortly

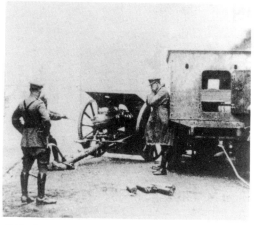

Saoirse?

after, in 1952, Morrison began cataloguing Irish-related film material; five years of research produced some 300 000' of material. Clearly, immediate action had to be taken or even scenes from 1916 would disappear.

Armed with his box of cards, Morrison obtained an interview with De Valera, the Taoiseach. Luckily, he was able to extract a small amount of money to embark on a few tri-acetate duplicates to be presented to the National Library of Ireland. But this was only scratching the surface and Morrison turned to Gael-Linn whom he persuaded to finance three compilation films.

Morrison envisaged a dialectic structure to the material: the build-up to the War of Independence, the movement to civil war and a critical look at post-Civil War Ireland. Only two films were made; the third was perhaps perceived as too controversial. The Irish revolution could not bear deep scrutiny in the 1950s and early 1960s for, as Morrison has written, even *Saoirse?* makes "no concessions to romantic nationalism". Both films were first shown at the Cork Film Festivals of 1959 and 1961. Morrison particularly enjoyed working with Sean O Riada on the musical accompaniment to the films, an affectionate account of which he gives in *The Achievement of Sean O Riada* (1981).

Mise Éire/I Am Ireland is a cinematic history of Irish events from 1896 to 1919. Particularly striking are the scenes of Royal Irish Constabulary men beating workers during the 1903 lock-out, the amnestied Sinn Féin prisoners (presumably from Norman Whitten's *Irish Events?*) and the funeral of Thomas Ashe. When the film opened in Dublin it was sold out for three weeks.

Saoirse?/Freedom covers the years between 1919 and 1922, from the first meeting of the Dáil and appointment of the cabinet, through Black and Tans raids in Dublin and the arrest of Kevin Barry, to the evacuation of the British forces and the outbreak of the Civil War. Morrison's necessarily selective process among the decaying nitrate film provides, by the simple order of the footage, a version of Irish history which may not appeal to our revisionist historians. However, the fact that it provoked *English* reviewers at a National Film Theatre showing to confront the debate of received notions of Anglo-Irish history can only be seen as beneficial.

By way of balance, it should be pointed out that such compilation films are not exclusive to the South of Ireland, as shown by the compilation of newsreels to construct *Ulster Covenant* (date unknown), which has a spoken commentary.

Morrison has continued to direct documentaries and short features, including *Saol Sona/Bright Future* (1967) and *These Stones Remain* (1972), as well as a documentary on Eamon De Valera for RTE in 1975. Among his published books are *An Irish Camera* and *The Life and Times of Eamon De Valera*.

Patrick Carey

Patrick Carey was born in London but grew up in Ireland from the age of seven. He worked in broadcasting for Radio Éireann, acted at the Gate Theatre, Dublin and became a stills photographer. When the Irish Film School began to falter, Carey joined a British documentary group and travelled around the world as a trainee camera operator.

He then worked on John Taylor's *World of Life* series of documentaries, photographing the award-winning *Journey into Spring* (1957). He also worked with the National Film Board of Canada, where he photographed the Oscar-nominated *The Living Stone* and *Sky* (1961). He accompanied Sir Edmund Hillary to Mount Everest in 1953 and went

Patrick Carey

to the Arctic as a camera operator on the Italian feature, *Top of the World* (1949).

When Carey returned to Ireland, he produced a series of highly acclaimed documentaries ("just moving pictures", as he calls them) on the natural beauty of the Irish landscape and on Irish tradition. The first and perhaps most famous film was *Yeats Country* (1965). The film was made for the Department of External Affairs with music by Brian Boydell and sound recorded by Peter Hunt. Winning a Golden Bear award at the Berlin Film Festival, an Oscar nomination and seven Certificates of Merit at festivals throughout the world, *Yeats Country* explores the Irish landscape that inspired the poetry of W B Yeats.

Carey was second-unit director for many films, including *A Man for All Seasons* (1966), *Ryan's Daughter* (1970) and *Barry Lyndon* (1975). He also co-directed the Oscar-winning film, *Wild Wings* (1967), with John Taylor. Back in Ireland, Carey made the short film, *Errigal* (1970), in both English and Gaelic versions. In this film Carey reduces commentary to a minimum in an attempt to exclude humanity in favour of the

elements and in particular the mountains of Donegal. As Carey has said, "the mountains are the characters in the story. The drama is in the battle of the elements. I have tried to convey this feeling of personality in a landscape by picture, supported only by music and natural sound."

Carey's natural vision is similarly evident in *Oisín* (1970), sponsored by the Irish Government for European Conservation Year. It has no soundtrack as such, merely the sounds of nature. In a programme note at the film's première, the director wrote that he tried to convey an Ireland that was proclaiming its own beauty and called upon people to listen to the natural sounds that surround them. Certainly the *Irish Times* and *Evening Press* reviews of Carey's films stress his wonder at Ireland's natural beauty and his grasp of Ireland's traditional roots. Carey now lives and works in Canada.

Yeats Country

Kieran Hickey

Born in Dublin in 1936, Kieran Hickey left Ireland for London in order to study and practise film-making. But he returned to start his own company, BAC Films, an operation he still runs today. Like other Irish directors of this period, his staple diet of documentary work was provided by commercial organisations and government agencies.

Faithful Departed

Kieran Hickey

One of Hickey's major achievements is a ten-minute documentary, *Faithful Departed*, which was broadcast on the BBC in 1967. Hickey uses the photographs of Robert French in the Lawrence Collection at the National Library of Ireland to illustrate the life and times of James Joyce's Dublin in 1904. Hickey's close attention to detail is shown by his choice of music, taken from songs mentioned in *Ulysses*. The famous Irish actor, Jack McGowran, narrates.

Hickey's other films include *Stage Irishman* (1968), an assessment of the 19th century playwright Dion Boucicault, and a half-hour documentary, *Jonathan Swift* (1967), from a script by David Thomson and using the voices of Cyril Cusack, Patrick Magee, Alan Badel and Siobhán McKenna. This revisionist look at Swift challenges the facile popularity of the man by revealing his underlying bitterness, pessimism and unstable mind. The documentary quotes from the wide variety of Swift's writings — *Gulliver's Travels*, letters, pamphlets and his *Journal to Stella*. Hickey experiments by including a cartoon sequence to emphasize the popular mythology surrounding the indignant Dean but ends the film with an image of Swift's brooding macabre death mask.

The Light of Other Days

Hickey embarked on a much more extensive usage of Robert French's photographs in the much acclaimed *The Light of Other Days* (1972), a broad sweep of Irish society between 1890 and 1914. Hickey's fifty-minute film is notable for its use of street pianos of the period for the musical background. This film was sponsored by the Esso Petroleum Company and interest in it prompted publication of French's photographs under the same title as the film. What Hickey's film highlights is the fact that Ireland was very much at peace between 1890 and 1914. The photographs of French and Lawrence stretch the length of Ireland, from County Antrim to County Kerry. Somewhat ironically, Lawrence's photographic studio and shop, located just over the road from the General Post Office (which was taken over by Patrick Pearse and company during the Easter Rising in 1916) was looted during the disturbances.

A scene from Faithful Departed

A scene from The Light of Other Days

Gael-Linn and Louis Marcus

Mention has already been made of Gael-Linn's newsreels and sponsored compilations of actuality footage directed by George Morrison. It should also be underlined that Louis Marcus owes his early documentary work to Gael-Linn.

Born in Cork in 1936, Marcus joined the IFS local branch while still at school; shortly afterwards, he started a film magazine, *Guth na Scannán*. His first film was a piece on the sculptor Seamus Murphy, *The Silent Art* (1959). This was followed by *Peil/Football* (1962) on Gaelic football skills, sponsored by Player and Wills (Ireland), who in 1963 supported a further film on the specific talent of Christy Ring. Eight further documentaries for Gael-Linn followed, of which the most acclaimed are *Rhapsody of a River* (1965), *Fleadh Ceoil/Folk Music Festival* (1967) and *Dubliners — Sean Agus Nua/ Dubliners — Then and Now* (1971).

Rhapsody of a River, commissioned by the Department of External Affairs but produced by Gael-Linn, is a loving look at Cork City and the valley of the River Lee. Louis Marcus and his cameraman, Robert Monks, were well served by the music specially composed and conducted by Sean O Riada. In addition, there is the traditional song, "On the banks of my old lovely Lee", as we take in dissolves from photographs to the present industrial growth along the river.

Fleadh Ceoil is an overview of the traditional Irish fleadh or fair, shot in Kilrush, Co. Clare. Included is an examination of Irish traditional music and how it affects the people who come to hear it. Following Kieran Hickey, Louis Marcus used the photographs in the Lawrence Collection to give a sense of turn of the century Dublin while contrasting that with the present in *Dubliners — Sean Agus Nua*. Besides Louis Marcus and Robert

Monks's *Conquest of Light* (1975), an affectionate look at the making of Waterford crystal glass, *An Tine Bheo/The Living Flame* (1966) and *Revival* (1980), on Patrick Pearse's concept of Ireland, may become Marcus's most historically important work.

Commissioned by Gael-Linn, *An Tine Bheo* combines the recollection of 1916 Volunteer veterans with shots of famous buildings and monuments associated with the Rising. In general, a traditional, heroic view of the Irish Citizen Army was presented. However, when Marcus was commissioned to commemorate the centenary of Pearse's birth in *Revival*, the Northern crisis had been going on for ten years. As the director wrote for the 1980 IFT Winter Festival Tribute to his work, "a bland pre-seventies approach to the subject was no longer possible".

Marcus's reading of Pearse's work, particularly that between 1903 and 1909 when he was editor of *An Claidheamh Soluis*, revealed a man who was not the mystic of popular belief but an intellectual who fully recognised the need to oppose Church control in education and to endorse anti-sectarianism throughout the island. In the film John Kavanagh plays Pearse and reads from the man's voluminous treatises. On pages 119-124 Marcus discusses some of his other films of this period.

Radio Telefís Éireann (RTE)

The setting up of a long-awaited television service in Southern Ireland meant the end of the Gael-Linn newsreels, but it promised much for the future. Created under the Broadcasting Authority Act of 1960, television transmissions began on 31 December 1961. A television service had been in operation in the North from the late 1950s both by the BBC and Ulster Television. RTE drama began to take a high profile in the 1960s and 1970s. In addition, documentary film work by independent directors, such as Éamon de Buitléar and David Shaw-Smith, was prominent.

Éamon de Buitléar

Éamon de Buitléar's films of the Irish countryside and landscape have been a permanent fixture on Irish and British television for over twenty years. Migrating birds, fallow deer, wild geese, otters and trout are only some of the wildlife that have come under the masterly scrutiny of de Buitlear's camera. His credits are too innumerable to do justice to in words. Most recently his series of films for RTE has borne his own name - *Éamon de Buitléar's Ireland* — illustrating his dominance of the field.

David Shaw-Smith

De Buitléar shared a series with Dutchman Gerrit van Gelderen who took on David Shaw-Smith, then a floor-manager at RTE, as an assistant. After working for a couple of years with Gelderen, Shaw-Smith branched out on his own and made the internationally acclaimed *Connemara and Its Ponies* (1971). The Irish independent director then solidified his reputation with the RTE series, *A World of Houses* (1975), and perhaps his most important work, the *Patterns* (1979-83) and *Hands* (1977-88) films. On pages 147-153 Shaw-Smith gives a full account of his film-making philosophy and practice.

Colm O Laoghaire

A Gael-Linn associate, Colm O Laoghaire made two notable films in the 1960s which convey a sense of the balance struck by film directors in their use of film in Irish culture and society. *Our Neighbour's Children* (1960) was produced to highlight the problems of the children at Baldoyle

Hospital. When the film was run in theatres, some £5000 were quickly raised. O Laoghaire's focus is on the charity of priests and nuns in the hospital and the toys bought by the donations. Robert Monks, the cameraman on the film, gives a full account of the film's production on pages 125-126.

This communal sense was evident, too, in *This Most Gallant Gentleman* (1966), a short film on the movement of Roger Casement's body from England to Ireland. O Laoghaire's film, sponsored by the Department of External Affairs, stresses the importance of Casement to the nationalist cause and the reburying as an active political event.

1967 — John Huston, Louis Marcus and the Film Industry Committee

The series of articles in the *Irish Times* written by Louis Marcus in 1967 had a number of spin-offs, including two PhD dissertations and the staging of an Irish film season at the Toronto Film Society in June 1970. More important, however, was the setting up of a Film Industry Committee. This committee was headed by John Huston who, as Louis Marcus relates (pages 122-123), did not seem to fully understand the infrastructure required for the setting up of an Irish film industry. The report was drawn up and written, therefore, by Louis Marcus and others interested in the Irish documentary film. Twenty-three members were on the committee, serving both artistic and technical aspirations.

The report was published in July 1968. It recommended a National Film Board empowered to give grants and loans to Irish film-makers and to market the films made. The report also accepted that foreign personnel would inevitably be involved in the short term, but the major emphasis was towards Irish talent. An Irish Film Archive was also envisaged. A Film Bill was drawn up in 1970, but then came the cataclysmic events of that year, especially the arms crisis involving the present Taoiseach, Charles Haughey, who then had just been sacked as Minister for Finance, pending a court case on the importation of guns and ammunition. The projected Irish Film Board would have to wait for another decade before getting off the ground.

Peter Lennon's Rocky Road to Dublin

In the heady days of 1968, this film achieved a certain degree of notoriety. Its programme note detailed its major theme in a parodic manner: "An attempt to reconstruct in images the plight of an island community which survived nearly 700 years of English occupation and then nearly sank under the weight of its own heroes — and clergy. Or: what do you do with your Revolution once you've got it?" Peter Lennon, a Paris-based journalist, was noted for his critical articles on Irish society published in *The Guardian*. His film allows distinguished Irish figures such as Seán Ó Faoláin, Conor Cruise O'Brien and Douglas Gageby to exclaim on matters Irish and in particular what could have been after the expulsion of the British.

The editing of the film was carried out in Paris and Lennon announced a world première in Dublin. Respectable members of the establishment attended, wrongly assuming that the film had passed through all the "correct" channels. *Rocky Road to Dublin* expresses an unashamed disenchantment with the lot of the children of the Irish revolution. It is Lennon's implicit scoffing at the "well-behaved obedience", expected by elders of their children, and his depiction of the youthful escape routes via alcohol and disco-dancing that provoked a furore. Lennon was just able to smuggle the film out of Ireland before it was seized.

Meanwhile, in Paris in June 1968 Lennon's film was receiving rave notices. His film was also chosen for the Critics' Week at Cannes, a screening which took place before the revolutionaries broke up the festival. Then the universities of the Sorbonne and Nice got hold of the film and while *The Grapes of Wrath* played to the wives of striking post-office workers, *Rocky Road to Dublin*, along with Eisenstein's *Battleship Potemkin*, was shown to Renault car workers as a sobering comment on what awful events could follow a revolution.

Similarly devastating in its analysis of urban Dublin, Brian MacLochlainn's *A Week in the Life of Martin Cluxton* (1971) for a while became RTE's most requested feature-length drama for rental by foreign exhibitors. It traces the heart-rending story of a young borstal boy who comes to reject his working class family, and other social and religious "nets". His seeking a life of crime conveys more about the weaknesses of Irish social structures than about his personal problems. The film won prestigious television prizes in Italy and Czechoslovakia as well as in Ireland.

Joyce and the screen

The theory that acclaimed literary works inhibit excellent cinematic adaptations is borne out by the various films made from the novels of James Joyce: Joseph Strick's *Ulysses* (1967) and *A Portrait of the Artist as a Young Man* (1977), and Mary Ellen Bute's *Passages from James Joyce's Finnegans Wake* (1965). Many have argued both directors have inevitably misrepresented Joyce and, in doing so, emerged without any satisfactory results. Perhaps it is simply that Joyce's way of showing the interior workings of his characters' minds — his stream of consciousness technique — is uncinematic.

Certainly Strick's rather stilted version of *A Portrait*, filmed mostly from an objective point of view, fails to bring the story of Stephen's development to life. Even the "Circe" episode in *Ulysses*, the most dramatic in the novel, is underplayed despite Milo O'Shea's sympathic characterisation of Bloom. The famous Molly monologue seems to be rendered without any feeling for the complexities of the woman's emotions and situation. Bute's film is a brave attempt but seems destined to fail because of the huge structural and linguistic difficulties of Joyce's novel.

Queen's Film Theatre opens

The economic climate for film exhibition in the late 1960s was not a healthy one. With the increasing popularity of television, 'B' movies, newsreels and matinees began to disappear. Parallel with developments in the United Kingdom, an art cinema — the Queen's Film Theatre (QFT) — was established, attached to the Queen's University of Belfast. Michael Open and the QFT are almost synonymous terms and interviewed on pages 131-134 he describes his involvement and opinions. In his book on the history of Belfast cinemas, Open points out that screens in the city diminished from forty-two in 1957 to twenty in 1969, and then to five in 1978.

The QFT was very much a trendy venue in the 1970s in a not-so-trendy city. The QFT was thrust into the limelight ironically enough at a time when bombs in the city reduced most of the Belfast cinemas to a heap of rubble. Previously in 1972, the Arts Council stepped in with financial support to keep the art-house going after its many years of losses. The Arts Council still supports the QFT, support without which the cinema would close. In recent years the QFT has succeeded in presenting a balanced but challenging programme for its patrons. A recent programme, for example, included Ridley Scott's *Bladerunner*, Akira Kurosawa's *Ran* and Michel Deville's *Death in a French Garden*.

Film and "the troubles"
A Sense of Loss

It would be quite naïve to suggest that "the troubles" in Northern Ireland have not made their mark in the cinema. In the period pre-1977, some of the most interesting documentary work was achieved by foreign directors. One significant film within this group is *A Sense of Loss* (1972), directed by Marcel Ophuls. When Ophuls arrived in Belfast, he had to undergo hospital treatment which set him thinking about the doctors' somewhat macabre and varied lifestyle, at a time when bombs were wreaking devastating physical injuries on civilians.

Ophuls and his team chased after ambulances to be near the scene of death. Then, through an Irish intermediary, Ophuls would visit the bereaved family after a few weeks and ask them to fill in the story surrounding the death. To his credit, Ophuls tried to give balance to the film by tracing four deaths but one, that of a British soldier, is missing because the Ministry of Defence refused access. Ophuls did not interview members of the Provisional IRA — "I didn't want to sit down and have civilised talks with people when I knew that, in two or three days, I would be talking to their victims," he said. Even so, when shown in America, the Provisional IRA supporters identified with the film and came to hand out leaflets before the screening.

In the film a Protestant bookshop owner relates how his mother was killed when his premises were burned down;

Bernadette Devlin claims that "it is better to die in the middle than to suffer a constant death at the dark end", and Ian Paisley's rhetoric is seen from a sinister low angle position. In general, Ophuls's sympathies lie with the non-partisan — the innocents who die for other people's causes.

Not as well known as Ophuls's documentary is the Berwick Street Collective's *Ireland: Behind the Wire* (1974), depicting the poor social conditions of what the film terms "the nationalist population". Although very partisan, the film is significant in that it was one of the first to reveal that violations of Human Rights were being committed by the security forces in Northern Ireland. Furthermore, there is some shocking footage of Bloody Sunday, the occasion when British Paratroopers shot dead many civilians in Derry.

A Sense of Loss

RTE dramas

Contrary to popular opinion in the North, films made by RTE about the crisis in Northern Ireland did not take a partisan line. Gerry Murray and Ted Dolan's *Down There* (1973) followed the visit of Belfast working-class Unionists to the South to see the site of the Battle of the Boyne, meet a Bishop and see Maynooth Seminary.

John Kelleher and Joe Mulholland's *Three Funerals* (1975) takes up the structure of *A Sense of Loss* and concentrates on three deaths: those of a young soldier, a young girl and an IRA hunger striker. The producers include interviews with the respective families. Pat O'Connor's *Shankill Road* (1976) focusses on the staunch Protestant community in Belfast. These films attempt to argue with a fair degree of success that the nationalist claims of the IRA and Southern Ireland's genesis need to be more closely examined for flaws.

Victims trilogy

By contrast, the flaws that Deirdre Friel's famous *Victims* trilogy (1976) exposes are extracted from a wide variety of situations. Writer Eugene McCabe sets up a number of argumentative dramatisations which begin in *Cancer* with two men on their way to visit a brother dying of the deadly disease. As they travel they argue about the problems of the North while around them we are shown police checks and soldiers.

The main focus of *Heritage* is on Protestant Eric, a young UDR member, who is driven to distraction and (apparently) suicide by the sectarianism around him in rural Fermanagh. In *Siege* an IRA unit is despatched to keep hostage a colonel who lives in a large house. The plot enables McCabe and Friel to explore many issues, the most important of which being the place of women in Irish society and politics, and the relationship between stunted sexuality and violence.

Ryan's Daughter

Much less provocative is David Lean's *Ryan's Daughter* (1970), for which a fictional village was built on the Dingle peninsula in County Kerry. The location ensured some breath-taking scenery for this drama set in 1916.

Ryan's Daughter

An unhappily married young girl, Rosy Ryan (Sarah Miles), becomes the lover of an equally unhappily married British Major (Chris Jones) who commands the army garrison near the village. The unemployed villagers resent Rosy, partly for reasons of class and partly for her liaison with the Major. Called the "whore of a British soldier", she becomes a likely suspect in the betrayal of an IRA unit who have come to the village on a stormy evening to collect a German shipment of arms. The villagers converge en masse on Rosy's home to serve punishment for this alleged crime against the community (in fact it is her father who has informed the British). She is stripped and shorn, somewhat similar in fashion to the tarring and feathering of women that was happening in the North of Ireland while the film was being shot. Rosy and her husband eventually leave the village for Dublin and the Major kills himself.

Trevor Howard as the mediating priest and John Mills as the village idiot give powerful performances but the film does not cohere. The love affair and the problems of a passionless marriage sit uneasily with the 'troubles' which Lean draws upon. One feels the lack of characterisation in many places, undoubtedly caused by having to reduce 11½ hours of film to 3½ hours of screen time. Particularly risible in the film is the way the petty-minded villagers seem to operate only as a mob. Nevertheless, Lean's production was very popular at the box-office in Ireland.

Barry Lyndon

Lean's panoramic sweep is also favoured by Stanley Kubrick in his approach to 18th century Ireland in *Barry Lyndon* (1975). Similar criticisms were made with regard to weak characterisation but, as with many of Kubrick's films, the emphasis seems to lie on a kind of *visual* truth.

Barry Lyndon (Ryan O'Neal) is a gullible hero, who is ensnared in the highly developed and ritualistic rules of the aristocracy. Much of the enjoyment of the film comes from the knowledge that we are watching a late 20th century version of a 19th century novelist's view of 18th century Ireland.

Like Lean's version, *Barry Lyndon* is a long film (187 minutes) which in itself brought the director much censure, given that his story is not a particularly stimulating one. However, this type of criticism fails to take account of the many formal devices used by Kubrick to contextualise Barry Lyndon's apparently foolhardy attempt to rise above his station. The most significant instances are when the obtrusive narrator tells the audience what is about to happen before we are allowed to see it. This technique is in a sense consistent with very rigid social strata where the exceptional or original is excluded and where the individual is dwarfed by society.

Hennessy

A film released in the same year as *Barry Lyndon* also focusses on one man's attempts to outwit the accepted norms. Don Sharp's *Hennessy* examines the isolated actions of Niall Hennessy (Rod Steiger) who seeks revenge after witnessing the accidental killing of his wife and child by an English soldier (who in turn is killed by an IRA gunman). But instead of joining the IRA, with whom he has a past association, Hennessy sets out on his own to blow up the British House of Commons on the opening of Parliament.

To Hennessy family is more important than Ireland's 'freedom' and his revenge is a personal act. While wrapping a jacket full of gelignite around his body, he tells the MP he is impersonating, "It's got nothing to do with politics at all."

Interestingly, the IRA, as well as the British police, seek to stop Hennessy, because they believe the killing of the Queen would set back Irish unification fifty years.

National Film Studios of Ireland (NFSI)

Between 1971 and 1973 the Ardmore studios were virtually idle; the last film made had been Robert Altman's *Images* (1972). On behalf of the government, RTE bought the studios for £975 000 but the former insisted that the latter would not operate the facility. Then John Boorman, the English director, arrived and started work on *Zardoz* (1973) and post-production work on *Deliverance* (1972). Boorman's arrival may have been a beacon for the government because the National Film Studios were set up in June 1975 by Justin Keating, Minister for Industry and Commerce.

The first board comprised Boorman (as chairman); Vincent Corcoran, producer of short films; William Harpur, Head of Film at RTE; Ruaidhir Roberts, General Secretary of Irish Congress of Trades Unions; Martin Marren, a lawyer and Sheamus Smith, as managing director of

Vincent Corcoran

the studios. The official opening was in November 1975; in a press release from the studios Boorman announced, "We intend to create a place of excellence. We are going to make pictures for the international market". At Cannes in 1976 this hype extended to the studio brochure which included a miniature bottle of whiskey.

Between 1976 and 1977 the studios were busy: 176 television and cinema commercials; Calvin Floyd's *Victor Frankenstein, The Last Remake of Beau Geste* and, perhaps most importantly, Joseph Strick's *A Portrait of the Artist as a Young Man*, with an all-Irish cast and crew. Government paved some of the way for the studios with the 1976 Corporation Tax Acts, which allowed producer profits from international sales of pictures made in Ireland to be exempt from taxation. A system of proportionate tax relief was also set up for pictures made partly in Ireland.

Internally, the establishment of the studios encouraged the Arts Council to offer a Film Script Award to help Irish screenwriters. The award in 1976 was intended to give the winner provision of facilities at the studios. And at the 1976 Cork Film Festival, Tom Cooper (*The Dawn* 1936) was awarded the first National Film Studios of Ireland Award for "outstanding contributions to the Irish Film Industry".

Restrictive practices

1976 was, however, a troubled year for the exhibition side of the industry in Ireland. In February, Irish Cinemas Ltd., one of the two Rank subsidiaries in Éire, reported losses of up to £100 000. In addition, there were the first rumblings of discontent from suburban and independent cinema owners at the tendency of downtown Dublin theatres to monopolise first-run feature films, often not releasing them to other areas until eighteen months had passed. The issue was referred to the Fair Trade Commission and top executives from the London-based Kinematograph Renters' Society became involved in the discussions. The latter offered to cut release time from the city centre to the suburban cinemas from fourteen to three months; however, the offer was dropped when the Examiner of Restrictive Practices, Austin Kennan, said an investigation would be carried out. There then followed protracted public hearings, a published report and finally an informal agreement to quicken the release time to non-city centre cinemas.

Censorship

In 1980 a special issue of *Film Directions* dealt very thoroughly with film censorship in Ireland. One of the fascinating aspects highlighted in an article by Ciaran Carty is that three out of the six Éire censors up to 1980 were medical doctors, as if somehow the state regarded film excisions in a literally surgical sense! Dermot Breen, who was appointed in 1972, was regarded by renters as the most level-headed of all. Yet *Variety* reported in May 1976 that he considered 315 films in 1975, passed 131, cut 154 and banned 30. Of these 30, 10 went to the Censorship Appeal Board where only 3 won limited or no restriction certification.

In the North, where control was placed, as with the rest of the United Kingdom, in the hands of the local authorities and their elected or nominated committees, relatively few films passed in England were rejected. Michael Open mentions some of the most important, some would say ridiculous, occasions when the Belfast Committee revealed its prejudices.

In the 1940s, a film showing the birth of a baby caused much hostility, although it was eventually passed as an "adults only" screening; in the 1950s, a complete misreading of the purposes of a film about the effects of marijuana, entitled *The Devil's Weed*, again called for "adults only" viewing; and even in 1968, Joseph Strick's *Ulysses*, with its occasional four-lettered words, ran into trouble (although it was able to be screened at the QFT under club rules). The same was the case for *The Last Tango in Paris* (1972), although by that time this and other controversial films found a haven in the Tonic Cinema, Bangor, outside the Belfast Committee's jurisdiction. Open quite rightly bemoans the loss of Kubrick's *A Clockwork Orange* (1971), which somehow in all the arguments was never shown in Belfast.

Film writings

Critical writings in this period included the National Film Institute's journals, *Irish Film Quarterly* (1957-59) and *Vision* (1965-68). These contained articles on the early Cork Film Festival, the educational usage of film and the film scene around the world in such countries as Canada and Poland. Significantly, the issue of children and the cinema was often raised. Séamus O'Connor called for a National Film Archive in an essay in *Studies* (1965), and this argument was well served in 1976 with Liam O'Leary's 'Cinema Ireland 1895-1976' exhibition as part of the Dublin Arts Festival. The brochure for the latter gave a broad and fascinating sweep of Irish involvement in film-making and film culture throughout the history of the cinema.

There were also more traditional reports on the cinema scene in Dublin and Ireland in general by Michael Paul Gallagher in *Studies* and by Anthony Slide and Pat Billings in the *International Film Guide*. There were also numerous features in magazines such as *American Cinematographer* on American and other 'foreign' documentaries on "the troubles" in Northern Ireland.

4: The new wave: 1977-88

Eat the Peach

The Irish Film Theatre

Although no specific division of years can be discerned in the 1970s, the setting up of the Irish Film Theatre (IFT) in Dublin in 1977 with a £5000 loan from the Arts Council/An Chomhairle Ealaíon and the formation of the Federation of Irish Film Societies may be perceived as major commitments to promoting film culture in Ireland.

The IFT, like the Queen's Film Theatre in Belfast, was run under club regulations, enabling uncensored films to be screened. The IFT was able to show 250-300 films each year until its closure in 1984 due to various economic crises. In 1981 the IFT had around 10 000 members and 90 000 admissions. It has to be said that the theatre programming was too ambitious, a lesson the QFT learned in the early 1970s and subsequently modified its position,

even though it relied — and still does — on the Northern Ireland Arts Council's subsidy to continue operating.

While it survived, however, the IFT and its club membership removed the need for an Irish Film Society. The Winter Festival in 1980, for example, featured forty films, many of them Irish, over a period of just two weeks. In addition, the festival celebrated the short films of Louis Marcus, which in itself reveals the fervent belief in an indigenous film culture. For a time a regional IFT flourished in Limerick and before the axe came plans were made for Cork, Galway and another screen in Dublin.

Film Directions magazine

One of the less publicised acts of the IFT and the QFT in combination with both Arts Councils in Ireland was the establishment of *Film Directions*, "a film magazine for Ireland", as the cover proudly stated. The editorship was shared between Michael Open in the North and David Collins (and later David Kavanagh) in the South.

The magazine had been in existence in the mid-1970s as a newsletter published from the QFT by the Arts Council of Northern Ireland, but with the support of the South it became a more substantial product. A debate about the current film situation in Ireland in the first joint issue of *Film Directions* in 1977 conveyed to the disinterested reader that there were similar problems both north and south of the border — namely, a lack of visual education, of art cinema distribution and exhibition, and of money for Irish film directors. For example, the Northern Ireland Arts Council budget for film in 1977 was between £7000 and £9000!

This inadequacy was forcefully taken up in a 1984 issue of *Film Directions*, in which an article rightly bemoaned the fact that Northern Ireland does not have money specifically geared to film, unlike England, Scotland and Wales. Between 1973 and 1983 the Northern Ireland Arts Council's Film Committee handed out a total of £195 000 to a wide variety of film-related projects. After 1983 the Visual Arts Committee was established which provided money only for the QFT and for the production of films relating to the arts and to individual artists in Northern Ireland (such as documentaries on Basil Blackshaw and John Hewitt).

For some reason the Arts Council of Northern Ireland has not been able to persuade Government to provide separate money for film for the province, under the principle of equality of film funding throughout the United Kingdom. More optimistically, in 1988 the Northern Ireland Film, Video and Photography Association wrote a report, entitled "Fast Forward", which recommends a Media Council to help develop film and video production in the province. The British Film Institute, Channel 4 and the Arts Council of Northern Ireland are interested parties in this suggestion.

Film Directions for a while became a mixture of theoretical articles written by Kevin Rockett and Richard Kearney and more practical pieces of biography about certain films and directors by various authors. In its letters' page, Rockett's writing was attacked for being "opaque" and "would-be scholarly" and the policy of the magazine was questioned. This in turn led to a written showdown in a February 1979 issue when Rockett and Open appeared to take positions — one posing the need for a "rigorous theoretical language, verbal and filmic" and the other advocating a very gradual introduction of film theory terminology.

After the IFT Board decided to withdraw distribution of *Film Directions*, the Dublin Arts Council withdrew from the joint publication status of the magazine. The specific reasons for these actions remain unclear to this day but certainly it strikes one as little short of bizarre that the cultural importance of a *joint* magazine did not have precedence over arguments about film theory to which, after all, *Film Directions* was actually open. In any event, *Film Directions* continues today and is cleverly joined up with the QFT programme. Perhaps as a potential rival, the IFT published its own *News* between 1978 and 1982, providing a forum for Irish critics and film-makers to air their views.

The role of the Arts Councils

The two Arts Councils in Ireland have in recent years been a source of guidance and financial assistance regarding film activities. In the North, the Arts Council has been involved in quite a number of ventures, including for a while 'film tours' throughout the province. A constant grant is made to the QFT and *Film Directions* but other than these institutions money has been made available to film societies. More recently, grants have been awarded to the Northern Ireland Film and Video Association and the Belfast Film Workshop. In addition, the giving of awards to film-makers and small production companies has been a consistent policy to the extent that the project must relate to the arts in Northern Ireland. For instance, Flamingo Pictures received a sum of £10 000 towards their documentary on the Ulster painter, William Scott — *Every Picture Tells A Story* (1984).

The Arts Council in the South seems over recent years to have been more ambitious as regards grants to specific productions. One commendable aspect of the Council's Film and Video Project Awards (formerly Film Script Awards and Film Project Awards) is that applications from the North are also considered. For example, the 1986 awards included £6500 to Double-Band Films (Michael Hewitt, Dermot Lavery, and John Hughes) and in 1985 £4000 were given to Belfast-born Alastair Herron for his 16mm project, *Aisling*. Other awards in 1986 included £10 000 to Joe Comerford's *Fallout*, a short 35mm film, and £8000 to Pat Murphy for a screenplay based on Josephine Poole's novel, *Moon Eyes*.

Sadly, in 1988 the Film and Video Awards fund was inexplicably reduced to £30 000. Of the sixty-six applications, only six awards could be handed out, among which Cathal Black received £20 000 for his new film, *Hano*, Fergus Tighe £2500 for *Johnny Culchie* and Thaddeus O'Sullivan £2500 for his *Artaud in Ireland*.

More generally, the Arts Council in the South supported the Cork Film Festival in

its difficult times as well as the IFT, which needed help in 1983 as attendances started to drop off quite drastically. The early 1980s recession affected the number of film societies affiliated to the Federation of Irish Film Societies — from forty-seven in 1981 to thirty-seven in 1982. The National Film Institute, which became the Irish Film Institute in the early 1980s, received money for the setting up of the Irish Film Centre. In the 1986-87 period this meant capital grants to the tune of £95 000, which was in addition to the regular grant for education and development of media studies. That the capital grant came from the National Lottery funds reveals the rather ad hoc attitude the Éire Government continues to have towards a national film culture.

The Film Bill and the Irish Film Board

As pointed out by other writers on Northern Irish film culture, a separate financial body to promote film is regarded by most European countries as a necessity to build up an industry. In the South of Ireland this became a reality after exhaustive campaigning. The Government's Film Industry Bill passed and Bord Scannán na hÉireann/Irish Film Board was established in 1981, with a brief to "assist and encourage by any means it considers appropriate the making of films in the state and the development of an industry in the state for the making of films".

This sounds wordy and perhaps it is not surprising that a public hearing was held on 4 April 1982 to help direct the board's policies. Incredibly, the hearing took place on the day after the Government's announcement to close the National Film Studios. Yet again the impression was given that what one hand gives the other takes away. Published by the Film Board, the Proceedings are fascinating because of the diversity of opinion and of occupation of the delegates. Director Tommy McArdle argued for the production of Irish films and for their systematic distribution "in the thirty-two counties of Ireland". In apparent opposition, Morgan O'Sullivan, now head of MTM Ardmore, argued for international investment, reminding all that financial considerations were paramount in creating a "cost-efficient industry".

Meanwhile, Liam O'Leary gave an impassioned speech for the need for a National Film Archive to give recognition of Irish film culture and production throughout the 20th century. As the Chairman of the Irish Film Board, Muiris Mac Conghail, replied, "Mr O'Leary has just blackmailed us into establishing a National Film Archive."

Once this airing of views from all sides of the industry was over and digested, the Film Board, with its meagre grant of £500 000, quietly and competently got on with the business of helping Irish film production, including the negotiation of tax incentives. In the 1982-87 active life of the Film Board, nearly fifty films were supported, the most famous of which are Neil Jordan's *Angel* (1982), Pat Murphy's *Anne Devlin* (1984) and Cathal Black's *Pigs* (1984).

As well as marketing films where requested, the Film Board helped Irish students attend the National Film and Television School in the United Kingdom, arranged a producers' training course and commissioned a feasibility study concerning an Irish Film Archive. To this latter point, the Film Board promised money to the Irish Film Centre's development in Eustace Street, Dublin.

The Irish Film Centre

Under the assured directorship of David Kavanagh, the Irish Film Institute has lobbyed successfully for establishment of an Irish Film Centre (IFC). The Friend's Meeting Hall just off Dame Street, Dublin has been purchased and two cinemas planned, one with 250 seats geared to popular contemporary films and one with 100 seats for national film weeks, archival material, festivals, retrospectives, lectures and seminars. In this way, it is hoped that the previous IFT one-screen programming problem will be avoided and every effort will be made to make the surroundings comfortable and varied. Apart from the invitation to include schools in the activities of the Centre, the building's space will allow for a bookshop, exhibition space and a café. In brief, the IFC will resemble the National Film Theatre in London.

As at July 1987, the ambitions for the Centre's Archive is to allow for ninety square metres of storage space for access prints, to provide restoration facilities and to open an area for the general public and researchers to view material. No copying of nitrate films will be carried out on the premises but it is hoped that a connection can be established with a foreign laboratory which has already completed most of its own copying. Perhaps in the future material lodged at the National Library and RTE may be transferred to the Archive. It should be pointed out that permanent storage space of master material will not be part of the Centre's brief; most likely, a building outside the city will serve this purpose, just as the British National Film Archive keeps its major collection outside London.

While the Institute has been preoccupied in recent years with the establishment of the Centre, it has still worked hard through its education section to promote media studies in school curricula at the secondary level. The Institute provides in-service courses for teachers, liaises with the City of Dublin's VEC Curriculum Unit on teachers and students' materials and helps out on units in other teachers' courses. In the public eye most strongly is the annual summer school in connection with RTE which has a bold educational and theoretical slant.

Following on from the Project Arts Centre's Irish programme (the centre had a 16mm sixty-seat cinema in operation from September 1976 to October 1978), one of the major activities of the Institute in the 1980s was the Green on the Screen Festival at the Metropole Cinema in Dublin in 1984. This festival of Irish and Irish-related films, nearly 160 in all, drew public attention to the absolute need for both an archive and a film centre.

Cork Film Festival

Although the Cork Film Festival fluctuated in popularity between 1977 and 1988, it still made an important contribution to the cultural scene. Specialised programmes planned for the 1978 event, for example, included "Focus on the emerging cinema" and "Women in the cinema". Australia was chosen for a six-day programme of contemporary features and Dermot Breen arranged a film techniques course for fifty teenagers, inviting high profile BBC and educational personnel to impart their knowledge. Breen concentrated his efforts at the festival regarding prizes on the short film. Awards bestowed came under the following titles: scientific and industry-sponsored film, short fiction film, film on art, animation or cartoon film, general interest or documentary film, the Federation of Irish Film Societies Award and the European Community Commission Award.

When Breen died in 1979, Robin O'Sullivan took over and feature films were re-introduced for the 1980 event, along with a film selector, Donald Taylor Black. Technical awards were emphasized and it is pleasant to note that Kieran Hickey's *Criminal Conversation* (1980) won a special mention for its camerawork, even though the film's ironic look at Irish marital relations received a cautious welcome from the Cork audience. The Waterford Award for the best Irish entry went to Declan Lowney's *Wavelength* (1980), a pertinent sketch of a Dublin commercial radio station.

At this festival a number of interesting activities were laid on. In the opening speeches, Maureen O'Hara gracefully received the City of Cork Award for distinguished contribution to the cinema; the Prime Minister (Taoiseach) Charles Haughey promised a film industry policy for the umpteenth time; and a programme of films on cinema and Ireland attempted to balance Irish views of Ireland with non-Irish views. This latter led to a lively final debate about the Film Board Bill.

One controversial film, *Curious Journey* (1979), written by Kenneth Griffiths and apparently suppressed by British television, made use of interviews with members of the Old IRA. Irish journalists lambasted the film for implying that the present IRA were similar "heroes".

According to David Simmons in a *Film Directions* report, the fringe critical debates continued with a fervour in the following year when Tiernan MacBride, Chairman of the Association of Independent Producers (AIP), pointed out that the three appointees to the Film Board — John Boorman (National Film Studios), Louis Heelan (formerly of the National Film and Finance Corporation) and Robin O'Sullivan (Cork Film Festival) all at the time headed money-losing institutions! More seriously, MacBride complained of the Government's tardiness in nominating

Irish film-makers to the board, something which did eventually happen and which coincided with the resignations of Boorman and Heelan before April 1982.

In the festival, Thaddeus O'Sullivan's 1980 film, *Jack B Yeats: Assembled Memories 1871-1957*, won a Certificate of Merit and more significantly, the opening night presentation was an Irish film, Joe Comerford's *Traveller* (1982). The award for the best Irish film, however, went to Pat Murphy for *Maeve* (1981), financed by the British Film Institute. Also at this festival, Neil Jordan's documentary on John Boorman, *The Making of Excalibur*, was praised for its polished production values but criticised for its lack of critical distance.

After 1981 the festival seemed to lose its high profile, not emerging successfully again until 1986 under the joint directorship of Theo Dorgan and Michael Hannigan, officers at the newly built Triskel Arts Centre in Cork. The latter has a screen and this was used mainly for the less 'popular' films. The Cork Opera House, with its one thousand seats, proved a splendid venue for the major films, including Colin Gregg's *Lamb* (1985) and Canadian Denys Arcand's *Le Déclin de l'Empire Américain* (1986).

Budawanny

The former film received three standing ovations. On the historical side, Liam O'Leary's involvement in the Irish Film Society was focussed upon. While Cork's future seemed uncertain in the 1980s, the Dublin Film Festival emerged and, recently, the Foyle Film Festival in Derry. The competition between Cork and Dublin was highlighted in 1987. Bob Quinn withdrew his new film, *Budawanny* (1987), from the Dublin Festival because the latter had brought their event forward, giving the impression to some that they were downgrading Cork.

Ardmore

As the formulation of the Film Bill and Film Board slowly ran its course, a great deal of attention was focussed on the National Film Studios. In an interview with Michael Open in *Film Directions* (1981), Sheamus Smith said that help had already been given to independent Irish film-makers and that he assumed that this would continue. And although Smith had critics among the independents, he was more preoccupied with the less attractive side of Ardmore: in May 1979 *Variety* reported that materials and labour were more expensive than in Britain, that the studio could only handle one big picture at a time and that the nearest processing labs were in England. This over-reliance on one picture was pinpointed in the NFSI's participation in the 1977 European co-production, *The Purple Taxi/Un taxi mauve*.

With hindsight, the NFSI's seven per cent stake (bought for £260 000) in the English language areas outside North America was a mistake. While Ardmore tried to attract foreign investment, the Association of Independent Producers argued for five films to be made at the studios every year, three of which were to be Irish-originated.

This argument became academic when the Government, after threatening to "pull the plug" if the studios did not pay their way, proceeded to do exactly that in early April 1982. The studios had been losing about £500 000 each year, despite the appearance of an upturn coinciding with Boorman's work on *Excalibur* (1981). It was not until 1986, after two other sales fell through, that Morgan O'Sullivan's Tara Productions and MTM Enterprises bought the studios to bring film and television work to the country. On pages 135-138 Morgan O'Sullivan describes his vision of the new Ardmore.

The demise of the Irish Film Board

The activities of the Irish Film Board were cut abruptly short by the Prime Minister, Charles Haughey, in June 1987. His Government argued that the return did not justify the outlay of £500 000 and that, in any case, new tax incentives would better facilitate film production. In vehement opposition, an "Action Committee", comprising a wide variety of people involved in the Irish film scene, met at the Irish Film Centre in July to lobby for a "single state agency for film". The group's arguments for the reinstatement of a central film body cannot be overstressed, for who else can oversee script assessment and development, marketing, promotion, training and international co-productions? Now that there may soon be a Media Council in Northern Ireland, Mr Haughey's decision to abandon the Irish Film Board looks penny-pinching and short-sighted.

Directors

Neil Jordan

When asked today about Ireland and the cinema, the name of Neil Jordan will most likely first spring to mind. The release in 1982 of *Angel* (*Danny Boy* in the United States), with the support of the new Irish Film Board (twenty per cent) and Channel 4 (eighty per cent), launched Jordan onto an international stage. His meteoric rise was hitherto unknown for an Irish feature film-maker.

Sligo-born Jordan made his name first through *Night in Tunisia*, a collection of short stories, many of which seem influenced by the cinema. Jordan had aspirations to attend the National Film School in London but did not have the money, and he ended up working on a number of jobs, including bath attendant.

Angel

However, after proving he could write good dialogue, Jordan was commissioned to write television scripts. He was not given a free rein until he worked under John Boorman at Ardmore, producing a documentary on the making of *Excalibur*. Even so, the common response to *Angel* is one of amazement that a first feature film could be so strongly cast and directed. This and subsequently *The Company of Wolves* (1984) and *Mona Lisa* (1986) are fundamentally about love and the perversion of violence.

Angel

In *Angel* Danny (Stephen Rea) sets out on his murder mission because of his love for the deaf mute girl, shot because she happens to be in the wrong place at the wrong time. There is, of course, personal guilt involved, as Danny had cavorted with the girl outside the ballroom and so bears some responsibility for her death. Love, too, prevents Danny from sharing his obsessive, murderous thoughts with his singer girlfriend, Dee (Honor Heffernan). At one point after they have made love, she tells him with a strong note of accusation, "You've moved me." She realises that Danny is keeping something from her and this mystery is only serving to deepen a half-aware, tragic attraction. Auntie May's love for Danny prevents her from informing him about his ominous ace of spades in their game of cards, while the absence of love is patently obvious in the abandonment of the canteen girl by one of the murderers. Danny sleeps with this girl and inquires whether or not he resembles her former lover, thereby tying together a murderous love-bond. Consistent with this connection, Danny catches his prey while the latter is physically intimate with another woman.

The specific details of who is killing whom for what reason are left, it seems, intentionally vague. Poetically, it does not seem to matter. Probing into the psychology of the obsessive, Jordan inserts a number of dances and songs which seem to communicate a slow but sure movement towards death. Perhaps the most disturbing section in the film is Danny's meeting with Mary, a widowed farmer. She cuts his hair, trys to kill him, tells him of her loss and her lack of love, and when given the opportunity to take control with Danny's gun, she kills herself instead. It seems she would rather die by violence than live without love.

The Company of Wolves

The Company of Wolves

Another unusual kind of love is evident in *The Company of Wolves*, an extended dream sequence set off by a young girl's fertile imagination. The film can be read as a revision of the Little Red Riding Hood story, where the attraction of the girl for the wolf seems to outweigh the traditional fear. The sets of the sometimes grotesque medieval village and surroundings are simply stunning and the use of wolves quite brilliant (apparently on the set at the Shepperton Studios, the wolves were not averse to killing and eating one of their pack!).

Strangely, the film ran into distribution problems: the British Board of Film Censors gave it an 18 certificate which meant that few children (its intended audience) could go and see it on their own and even London Transport banned its poster for being offensive! This is all the more strange since the joint script between Jordan and Angela Carter is very subtle in its layered narrative and framing devices. The wolves come smashing through a picture frame in the final sequence of the film, marking the end of this rich fantasy.

Mona Lisa

If the emotional journey is presented surrealistically in *The Company of Wolves*, then it is a testimony to Jordan's supreme versatility that it is presented extremely realistically in *Mona Lisa*. The ex-con George (Bob Hoskins) is posted by his ex-boss (Michael Caine) to chauffeur Simone (Cathy Tyson), a high-class prostitute. In the process the two are interlocked: George in his wish to help and please her; Simone in her need of George to help find her secret female lover.

Jordan's love-story is bolstered by the co-writing of the script with David Leland. Jordan wrote the final draft with Bob Hoskins in mind, an actor who excels in the part and for which he shared the Best Actor Award at Cannes.

The menace of *Brighton Rock* pervades *Mona Lisa*, for one is never too sure how far the Soho underworld will go to achieve its dubious ends. This uncertainty is what makes the final shoot-out all the more shocking. In the end George realizes that to Simone "he was just her driver for a while, that's all. Whatever else might have happened — whatever about the hotels and the look in her eyes and the whole damned thing, he was just her driver — just for a while…and that's the story." The tragedy of the film is that George becomes obsessed with a woman who appears to have everything he has not — grace, style and control over emotions. The film concludes on an upbeat note, for this self-knowledge enables George to strengthen his previously uneasy relationship with his daughter.

Bob Quinn

If Neil Jordan may be regarded as an *international* Irish director then Bob Quinn is a *national* Irish director. Born in Dublin in 1935, Quinn has had an extremely diverse working life — journalist, teacher, fisherman, radio announcer, bottle washer, telephone operator, assistant chef, farm labourer and, most lately and prominently, writer and film-maker. Never satisfied with institutions, Quinn walked out of RTE one day and decided not to go back.

He then started his own production company, Cinegael, in Carraroe, Galway where he now lives. Appropriately enough, the Galway Film Society, as part of its contribution to the city's arts festival, put on a retrospective of sixteen works by Quinn in August 1987. The director discourses at length about his attitude to the film scene in Ireland on pages 142-146. His major achievements are *Caoineadh Airt Uí Laoire/Lament for Art O'Leary* (1975), *Poitín/Poteen* (1978), *Atlantean* (1984) and *Budawanny* (1987).

Caoineadh Airt Uí Laoire

Caoineadh Airt Uí Laoire/Lament for Art O'Leary sets up a relationship between 18th century colonial oppression and the present day. By using the structure of a rehearsal of a play that deals with the killing of one of the few returned Wild Geese, Quinn is able to bring into sharp relief the problems in interpreting received

Caoineadh Airt Uí Laoire/Lament for Art O'Leary

notions of history. Criticised by Kevin Rockett as a confusing interpretation, it nevertheless deals with very complex issues in an original way, especially when historical sections are inserted, breaking up the rehearsal of the play.

Lament was sponsored at some point in its production by Official Sinn Féin, now called The Workers' Party, who ceased hostilities in the North in the early 1970s because of the sectarian nature of the violence. John Arden, the English playwright, portrays the character in opposition to O'Leary. The latter's final six years of life is Quinn's focus.

This is an Irish language film; the self-consciousness of the actors wearing 18th century costume calls into question the dividing lines between the present and the past. The uncovering of the film's construction allows for little escapism; indeed, Art O'Leary often addresses the camera, saying that he is play-acting. Quinn's aim here seems to be to utilise 'confusing' formal devices to break down stereotypes of what it means to be Irish or screen-Irish.

Poitín

What is most striking on the surface about *Poitín* is simply that the dialogue is spoken

in Gaelic, possibly the first *feature* film in Irish with a native Gaelic-speaking cast. (*Lament for Art O'Leary* is hard to categorise as a feature film in the accepted sense of the word.) Cyril Cusack plays the old poteen maker who employs two agents (Niall Toibín and Donal McCann) to sell his illegal drink.

Amusingly, the poteen still Cusack operated was an authentic one. The agents, however, run foul of the police and lose their produce. Undaunted, the two break into the police barracks, steal the poteen, sell it at a fair and decide to keep the money from the transaction. Inevitably, it seems, the two drink away the proceeds and then look for more satisfaction, in the search for which they frighten the poteen maker's daughter (Máireéad Ní Conghaile), before the old procurer metes out a suitable revenge on his wayward employees.

Winner of an Arts Council Script Award, *Poitín* has successfully done the rounds of art-houses and festivals in Britain, Ireland and the United States. However, it should be emphasized that, in keeping with Bob Quinn's nationalist thinking, the world première was in Carraroe, presenting to his audience a much more down-to-earth picture of Connemara than that in John Ford's The Quiet Man.

This alternate version of "Western" life provoked some angry telephone responses to RTE when it was shown on Saint Patrick's Day in 1979: "Disgraceful and disgusting", "It's a national disgrace" and "Burn that film and don't let it out of the country". One can almost hear Bob Quinn chuckling to himself. Further mischeviousness ensued at the end of one screening of the film in Galway: a labelless bottle was passed around the audience who indulged in the colourless liquid only to taste some lukewarm water!

Niall Toibín in Poitín

Atlantean

Forever interested in exploding Irish myths, whether imported or self-manufactured, Quinn made *Atlantean*, a series of three films for RTE, and produced a book resulting from the series. In the films he examines the plausible case that Irish people are not descended from the Celts but from the inhabitants of North Africa who moved from Egypt and surrounding areas to the Atlantic seaways and only then to western areas of Europe and, subsequently, inland. One of his most provocative statements is the assertion that early Irish Christianity was fundamentally Gnostic.

The *Atlantean* films were shown on RTE 2 in March 1984 and unprecedently reshown in May on RTE 1. They were also sold to a number of television stations abroad. It is clear that however successful the films were and are, other series, such as Frank Delaney's *The Celts* for the BBC, have continued to be more influential. Perhaps now that Quinn's research is in book form, some scholars will take up more thoroughly his observations on the similarities, among others, of sean nos singing, language and the sheela na gig figures in Ireland with their counterparts in North Africa and the Middle East.

Budawanny

Quinn returned to fiction film-making with *Budawanny*, premièred also in Galway to an audience that was meant not to include film reviewers (although it seems a few nipped past the entrance door). Quinn's private viewing invitation went instead to art critics, since he believes that film is art and therefore in need of art *criticism* and not film *review*. As Quinn wrote in a piece for the première's audience: "I would ask you to imagine yourselves at an art exhibition and adopt the same attitude as you would when viewing a painting, a sculpture or a piece of music. If you enjoy it, well and good. If you don't, at least you will have been given the choice."

Quinn's tale revolves around a priest (Donal McCann) who makes his housekeeper (Maggie Fegan) pregnant and around the various changes in his mind and in his community that this action forces. What is striking about the eighty-minute film is that it is almost totally in black and white, which conveys not just a kind of simplicity but a purity of treatment. At Quinn's own admission, he was striving to avoid pyrotechnics (a radical shift from the 1970s and *Lament for Art O'Leary*) to capture the innocent consistency found in the old silent films.

There are echoes in the film of Bergman's *Winter Light*, in which it also seems that religion is perceived as a hollow form or duty that must be performed to give order to the world and to help weak individuals. *Budawanny* is a loose adaptation of *Súil le Breith*, the book by priest Pádraic Standúin, who achieved notoriety in the 1970s by picketing the dole office in Galway to make the point that the Government should pay his livelihood and not the small community of Inisheer, his parish. Standúin was eventually transferred to the Aran islands, which strikes Quinn as somewhat suspicious, even though Standúin claimed that it was by choice. Clare Island is the setting of Quinn's film and when completed he sent a videotape to Clare so that the island community could have the first public viewing of the film.

Pat Murphy

Surprisingly, the West of Ireland, with its powerful, though traditional, mythology, remains an unexamined area for the country's leading female director.

Dubliner Pat Murphy moved to Belfast when she was a teenager and grew up as "the troubles" began to take root. She attended art college in Belfast but later left for colleges in London where she actively began to be involved in performance art and video. As a painter, the media of tape-slide and video came naturally to her and she soon began to think in filmic terms.

This progression in her thinking coalesced with her scholarship to the Whitney Museum in New York where she met a group of women film-makers, including Lizzie Borden, who stimulated Murphy's aspirations to examine Irish themes on film. She returned to the Royal College of Art School of Film and Television in London, graduating in 1979.

In the meantime, she had been busy: receiving an old family photograph album from her mother, Murphy photocopied the stills and used them as a platform for a film entitled *Rituals of Memory* (1977). To add to the theme of elusive history and memory, the film included letters and isolated conversations.

Maeve

While at the Royal College of Art Murphy took a course on oppositional cinema and Northern Ireland. Viewing the endless amount of television documentary work on the province by non-Irish directors suggested to her that there was something missing in their accounts. Returning to Belfast, where later she helped form the Northern Ireland Film and Video Association, she set out to make video recordings of people simply telling their own stories. The material she accumulated became the basis of *Maeve* (1981) and, much to her surprise, the British Film Institute gave her £73 000 and RTE £10 000.

Teaming up with John Davies, another student from the RCA, and a British crew, the production was shot mainly in Belfast,

On a Paving Stone Mounted

with some scenes in London. *Maeve* traces the emotions and feelings of a young Catholic woman who returns from London to her home in Belfast to face the onslaught of family duties and political (in this case Republican) allegiances.

The sense of displacement anchors the film in a context similar to that explored by Thaddeus O'Sullivan in *On a Paving Stone Mounted*. Maeve (Mary Jackson) discusses with her boyfriend Liam (John Keegan) the inactive role of women in the Republican Movement. She is disenchanted with the would-be Socialist Republican Movement simply because it can only accommodate male ideology.

Prominent in *Maeve* are the choices of form and of point of view, not only in the switch from realistic drama to very stylised dialogue, but also in the oscillation between seeing woman as outsider and as the missing piece in the Republican jigsaw. In legend, Mebh or Maeve of Connaught invaded Ulster: in a sense Murphy and Davies's film is an invasion into the male ideology of both the British soldiers who attempt to humiliate Maeve and the chauvinist attitudes of her father and boyfriend.

The choice of landscape is also potent: a discussion between Liam and Maeve takes place on Cave Hill, a locale associated with the United Irishmen, an organisation that joined Protestant and Catholic together against English oppression in the 1790s. And the film's final scene, depicting the Giant's Causeway upon which the three women walk, seems to suggest an assertion of female authority in a place which reverberates with male mythology.

Why this film provoked extended comment in journals such as *Screen* and *The Crane Bag* is not only because Murphy is a female film-maker who is actively making a feminist film, but also because her film avoids simple answers or solutions and actually encourages contradictions. In an interview, Murphy situated her production neither in the liberal camp (such as Derek Mahon's 1980 adaptation of Jennifer Johnston's novel *Shadows On Our Skin*) nor in the agit-prop camp (such as Arthur Mac Caig's *The Patriot Game* in 1978). She does not provide conclusive reasoning, except that the political issue in Ireland is perceived partly as a personal issue concerning the oppression of women.

However, the problems with the film's politics immediately spring to the fore. If the film is an insular critique of the Republican Movement then it achieves its aim. But if it attempts to do more — and this has been the impression of many critics — then the absence (except for one brief scene with an old Protestant woman) of any discussion of the Protestant Irish is so glaring that Murphy's film is close to Mac Caig's in emphasis. Why is it, the Irish Protestant asks, that there is no examination and recognition of the fact that the majority of the security forces in Northern Ireland, the RUC and the UDR, are populated by *Irish* people?

Anne Devlin

Less controversial but perhaps a more important film is Murphy's two-hour epic, *Anne Devlin* (1984), in which the director reclaims a woman into Irish history. Catholic Anne Devlin had an association with Protestant Robert Emmet and his supporters, who rebelled against the union of the British and Irish parliaments in 1801. The subsequent rebellion in 1803 was a disaster and while other 'friends' of the cause lied their way out of imprisonment, Anne Devlin refused to do so and later became a Republican martyr.

Murphy received money from an Arts Council Script Award, the Irish Film Board and a private investor to finance the project. Although it took four years to research, write and organise, the film took only six weeks to shoot, mainly in and around a large house in the Roscommon town of Strokestown. Further filming at Dublin Castle and Kilmainham jail rounded off the production.

Murphy was fascinated by the journals of Anne Devlin and wrote the script with actress Brid Brennan in mind, who is excellent as this unsentimental and strong character. In sympathy with this characterisation, Murphy deliberately avoided close-ups in fear of romanticising Devlin; we are encouraged to see her from afar, in the context of history and community. Perhaps the most powerful statement in *Anne Devlin* is the way the audience understands that, whereas Robert Emmet dies for his beliefs, Anne Devlin is one of the few who actually wishes to *live* for them.

The place of women in the Republican Movement is yet again advanced as a problematic area and it is significant that the film speaks through the journals, Murphy's source, rather than through action, from which women have traditionally been denied. The interrogation of Devlin is immensely powerful due to the woman's stoicism; her strength lies in her ability not to have her memory of events perverted by her captors. Murphy's account of the 1803 period is undoubtedly a success, beautifully photographed by Thaddeus O'Sullivan and scored by Robert Boyle.

Pat O'Connor

Like Murphy, Pat O'Connor had to leave his homeland for visual education. Born in 1943 in Ardmore, Co. Waterford and brought up in Lismore, O'Connor left Ireland in 1965 to seek work in London. At that time, all he could readily find was employment as a navvy. O'Connor then moved to Los Angeles and UCLA, where he took some film courses. But it was not until his move to Toronto and systematic film training with a 16mm camera and use of a television studio that he began seriously to think of a career. On graduating in 1969, he returned to Ireland and joined RTE as a trainee producer/ director, working on documentaries and the drama series, *The Riordans*.

The Ballroom of Romance

O'Connor was able later to concentrate on single dramas, including Neil Jordan's *Night in Tunisia* (1982). But it was the adaptation of William Trevor's *The Ballroom of Romance* (1982), produced jointly by RTE and the BBC, that shot O'Connor into the limelight. A reasonable budget of £200 000 was set for twenty days filming in County Mayo. Costs were cut by using an actual ballroom and the local people.

The film centres on a spinster who returns to the ballroom where in her youth she had danced full of romantic aspirations. Sadly, she finds the only comfort in the company of a drunk man.

The sensitive direction and photography won a BAFTA Award for the best single drama and encouraged RTE and the BBC to work again on another William Trevor adaptation, *One of Ourselves* (1983).

Cal

More importantly, when David Puttnam saw *The Ballroom of Romance*, he was certain that O'Connor could delicately develop character in the adaptation of Bernard Mac Laverty's novel, *Cal*. Mac Laverty wrote the screenplay but worked closely with O'Connor for some five months in revising it. For eight weeks on a budget of £3½ million they filmed in Drogheda and County Kildare in the Republic of Ireland (the North was considered too unstable and risky).

Cal (1984) is a tragic love-story of immense power. The main character, Cal (John Lynch), drives a car for the IRA so that a gunman can kill a policeman. Guilt draws Cal to the widow Marcella (Helen Mirren) like a moth to the flame. Their relationship dominates the narrative, in spite of the creeping note of sectarianism. It has been suggested that the film presents no specific political perspective

Cal

and that it dwells too much on the human tendency for guilt and the subsequent need for redemption.

Equally, however, one can point to the implicit bias against the Protestant community in both novel and film, an observation most critics have avoided. Cal's house is fire-bombed by Protestants, he is beaten by the RUC and by a gang of Protestant youths, and the Protestant foreman Dunlop is considered a "bastard". More telling, perhaps, is the choice in book and film of depicting Catholic Marcella as an *unhappy* wife to her Protestant policeman husband and how unhappy again she is with her subsequent life with Robert's Protestant family. What this close reading of the film's events suggests is a Catholic narrative voice in search of a Catholic reader. In itself, this emphasis is not a bad thing, but when combined with the political thriller genre and a Northern Irish setting, a film director can unintentionally strike very uneven and damaging chords in the viewer.

O'Connor has recently made the critically acclaimed, but non-Irish-related, *A Month in the Country* (1987) and has since been working in the United States and Canada on two films, *Stars and Bars* and *The January Man*.

Joe Comerford

Resembling O'Connor in one respect, Joe Comerford's reputation has slowly but surely built up through short films such as *Withdrawal* (1974) and *Emtigon* (1977), to two larger ventures: *Down the Corner* (1978) and *Traveller* (1982).

Withdrawal focusses on the suffering of a drug addict. We see a perturbed woman listening to the television set from which we hear a disturbing monologue; then, after close-ups of her wringing hands, we cut to a man in the corner who is in the act of shooting up. This half-hour fiction film was re-edited with the co-operation of RTE 2. The new version presents more clearly the lives of four people in a mental institution and their ploys to avoid suffering.

The film is based on a book by David Chapman, to whom the production is dedicated and who died just as the original film was completed.

Emtigon is an abstract, expressionist exploration of powerful images, accompanied by the electronic music of Roger Doyle. What we gather from this fourteen-minute film is a sense of an old man who abuses a young woman.

Down the Corner

It was *Down the Corner* that enabled Comerford to bully his way into the public eye. This film investigates life in Ballyfermot, a working-class area of Dublin. Originally conceived as a Community Arts Project, the film was supported by the Arts Council, Dublin City Corporation, RTE and the British Film Institute. Strangely, the NFSI's involvement was not substantial.

Down the Corner

Comerford examines and observes the lives of a group of children who live in a deprived environment. The main event of the narrative, as such, is the robbing of an orchard.

The static nature of the piece suggested to Michael Kelly of the *Irish Socialist* that Comerford, whether aware of it or not, gave a message that working class life was "squalid and meaningless". Kelly's criticism emerged from his observation that the film favoured a slice of life technique over an attempt to situate events in an economic and historical context.

This lambasting caused Kevin Rockett in *Film Directions* to enter the discussion to point out that the term "realism" as used by Kelly was problematic. Rockett went on to examine the film closely, arguing from a highly theoretical position that *Down the Corner* fails to impress simply because it does not question its formative principles. He claimed that it does not specify the setting for the story, that it does not prepare the viewer for the cinematic codes it employs (for example, the use of black and white photography for an incident in the past), and that it does not avoid the stereotype of the oppressed, such as the depiction of the despairing, drunk and redundant worker.

Rockett's point that just because a film is made independently it does not follow that it will be "independent" or refreshing in the techniques it employs is well taken but, equally, Rockett's criticisms are partly misdirected because he makes no allowance for whom the film was primarily made. The central aim of *Down the Corner* was that it would be shown to the people of Ballyfermot and as Joe Comerford has said in *Film Directions*:

"I worked on the basis that if I concentrated on the actors and I was working with a group of technicians who were doing the same, then the end product would be a document of how a group of people lived in a particular environment, rather than an exploration of the aesthetics of film....It had more social criteria than artistic criteria in its production." By all accounts, Comerford did not have as full a control over the production as he would have liked and it was reported that there was some friction with the local people.

Traveller

A more intellectually challenging film is *Traveller* which has also attracted extended critical comment. It was funded mainly by the British Film Institute (though RTE contributed to the Arts Council Script Award which Neil Jordan's screenplay won in 1978).

The film traces the mostly illegal adventures of two travellers or gipsies, Michael and Angela (Davy Spillane and Judy Donovan), who have been paired in marriage by their respective fathers. Angela's father, Devine (Johnny Choil Mhaidhc), sends them to the North to collect some stolen goods and on the way they meet Clicky, a Republican sympathiser (Alan Devlin). On their way back, their van crashes. In trying to seek help, Michael, spontaneously it seems, robs a post-office and they end up moving south and west before returning to Devine whom Michael kills. The three leave for England and, subsequently, for America and Australia.

Comerford's film is a complex furthering of the itinerant issue in Irish society that was explored in Paul Rotha's *No Resting Place*. *Traveller* has little dialogue, many static shots and uses a voice-over technique, all of which prevent the viewer from empathising with any of the characters. As Kevin Rockett has indicated, some interesting oppositions are constructed: Michael's father deals in horses and traditional crafts, while Angela's father smuggles electrical goods; Michael and Angela's marriage is set against their inability to communicate with each other; and the family unit structure confirmed by the agreed marriage competes with the taboo of incest which is hinted at between Angela and her father.

Comerford's sense of reality as a series of conflicting impulses, extremes with no middle ground (though the characters may be seen to "progress" by exiling themselves from Ireland), is patently clear. However, more problematic is the character of Clicky whom Kevin Rockett sees as a pivot in his argument that the film, though not dealing specifically with the Northern crisis, has interwoven into its texture links between and among the Catholic Church's beliefs, "the troubles" stretching into the South and Irish Nationalism. But as Kevin Barry has argued, convincingly, in a *Crane Bag* article, the production has little material to sustain a wider political interpretation; rather, it is a piece that deals specifically with a group of people who mostly elude the "traps" of Irish history, politics and social structures.

Reefer and the Model

Recently Comerford has completed the feature, *Reefer and the Model* (1988), which won the Europa Prize at the Barcelona Film Festival in competition with some fifteen other features. Producer Lelia Doolan visited over one hundred production companies to raise the £1 million budget. The film was shot totally in Galway and on the West coast of Ireland where Comerford once worked on a fishing trawler, an experience which seems to be at the heart of the project.

Kieran Hickey

Although Kieran Hickey returned to the documentary format in 1986 with *Short Story: Irish Cinema 1945-1958*, an account

Exposure

of the pioneering film work of Hilton Edwards, Gerard Healy and others, his work in the late 1970s and early 1980s has been in the area of fiction: *A Child's Voice* (1978), *Exposure* (1978), *Criminal Conversation* (1980), *Attracta* (1983) and, more recently for the BBC, *The Rockingham Shoot* (1987).

T P McKenna plays a mischevious broadcaster of ghost stories in *A Child's Voice*, set at the time when the "wireless" was the mainstay of entertainment and news at home. The twist in this story, however, involves the inability of the broadcaster, who writes his own stories, to make one of his characters obey his directions. The "disturbing gentleman of the wireless", as he is known, eventually receives his rebuke.

McKenna also figures strongly in Hickey's provocative film *Exposure*, a Film Script Award-winner which revolves around the reactions of three male surveyors towards a young French woman photographer while ensconced in a hotel in the West of Ireland. Niall O'Brien and Bosco Hogan join McKenna to make up the rather emotionally inarticulate trio, who seem better able to drink to excess and intrude childishly on the photographer's (Catherine Schell) belongings than to accept that there are women who have a solid sense of their sexuality and career path. On the surface, it appears that the men oppress the woman with their crudeness but as Barbara O'Connor has pointed out, when the photographer develops a picture of the three men in the last scene, her control over their images suggests a subversion of traditional patriarchy.

Another critique of the traditional male-female relationship in Ireland is present in the hour-long *Criminal Conversation*, a term for adultery often used in legal language. Two couples share Christmas Eve together, get drunk and reveal their secrets. One of the men admits to an affair with the other's wife and the comic joviality turns sour.

This change in tone apparently forced a similar reaction from the Cork Festival audience. The mixed reaction has to be understood in the context of Éire, where divorce is still illegal (indeed, a move for legality was overwhelmingly defeated in a recent referendum) and where a 'wronged' husband may sue the adulterer for compensation. Hickey's film, nonetheless, was the first Irish-made production to be billed as a major evening event at the Cork Film Festival.

The oppression and victimisation of women are suggested in Hickey's *Attracta*, adapted by William Trevor from his own story. Set in a provincial town, it charts a kind of 'descent into madness' of a Protestant school-teacher, Attracta (Wendy Hiller), whose parents were killed by the Old IRA. It is another woman's story, however, of how her soldier husband was killed by the current IRA, that pushes the teacher over the edge. Communal guilt seems to pervade the thoughts of Attracta who considers her educated life a failure, as she berates herself, exclaiming, "I told them how in this town the two people who killed my parents became my friends. It was a story I should have repeated over and over again in my schoolroom."

A second schoolteacher, this time of a different persuasion, is portrayed in *The Rockingham Shoot*, a television play written for BBC Northern Ireland by John McGahern. Bosco Hogan indulges masterfully as the nationalist pedagogue who tortures his students with rigorous Gaelic spelling tests! The latter is used in retaliation for his truant students, who have been temporarily employed by the 'English' aristocracy at Rockingham Castle to help on the pheasant shoot.

As in Cathal Black's *Our Boys*, some

savage beating is portrayed. Yet McGahern's script and Hickey's direction point to the romanticism and magic of Rockingham's hold on the children and to how the schoolmaster represses his own imagination by his unremitting Republican ideology.

Cathal Black

A John McGahern story is also the basis of Cathal Black's *Wheels* (1976), in which a man returns from the city to his country birthplace, with all the attendant memories and frustrations. Like the story, the film succeeds in its concentration on the inability of people to communicate. Neil Jordan in *Film Directions* has written perceptively on *Wheels*: he isolates its meticulous faithfulness to the written text and yet also its life as an independent tracing of the original, such as the way the first person narrative of the story is translated in the film to a voice-over.

Much more controversial is Black's *Our Boys* (1980), which, given the problem of insufficient funding, took three years to make. The Northern Ireland Arts Council offered £3500, RTE donated some old black and white film stock, the NFSI gave free use of sound and lighting equipment and the editing was undertaken for free by Windmill Lane Studios.

This forty-five-minute film centres on the Christian Brothers education system in Ireland and how its narrowness unbalances children. Black includes interviews with former pupils who talk about the often barbaric punishments meted out by the Christian Brothers in the name of education. In addition, he traces the closedown in the early 1960s of one such school. Black mounted the production in an old Methodist establishment because, according to the director, "it's not the sort of picture you'ld dare shoot in a Catholic School". Honestly

presented as a personal view of elements on the Irish education scene, the film provoked a reviewer in the *Tipperary Star* to classify Black's film as a vilification of an esteemed profession and merely a "presentation of a few individual hang-ups".

Equally challenging is Black's next film, *Pigs* (1984), made for only £130 000. Here we are thrust into the world of a Dublin squat. This derelict Regency mansion, however, has a charm of its own and Thaddeus O'Sullivan's photography marvellously captures the incongruity of such decay and of the assorted down-and-outs who populate the shelter.

These characters comprise George, the con-man; Orwell, a pimp; Mary, a prostitute; Ronnie, a drug-dealer; and Tom, who is mentally-ill. Black concentrates on homosexual Jimmy (played by Jimmy Brennan who also wrote the screenplay and narrates) and his search for peace and a means of living. Gradually his mansion community breaks up and he is left to the police who are able to force him to sign a statement that he has collected dole money fraudulently. There is an undeniable theatrical air about the production which stresses the script's interest in character over narrative.

Thaddeus O'Sullivan

Although known mostly for his lighting camerawork for Cathal Black and other directors, Thaddeus O'Sullivan has directed four notable films — *A Pint of Plain* (1972), *On a Paving Stone Mounted* (1978), *Jack B Yeats: Assembled Memories 1871-1957* (1980) and, most recently, *The Woman Who Married Clark Gable* (1985).

On a Paving Stone Mounted, a film dealing with the permanent Irish problem of emigration, is the most intellectually challenging. It has no key character with whom the audience can associate and this

78

The Woman Who Married Clark Gable

immigrant experiences, even in his or her own memory of the homeland. The English section develops for O'Sullivan as a story about how to be Irish in London, how to articulate Irishness and how to form images of Ireland from elsewhere.

The Woman Who Married Clark Gable

More light-hearted and straightforward in technique is O'Sullivan's half-hour film, *The Woman Who Married Clark Gable*. Bob Hoskins plays George, a Protestant Londoner who has married Mary, a Catholic Irishwoman (Brenda Fricker) in 1930s Dublin. An uneventful married life suddenly takes a bizarre turn when the husband grows a pencil moustache and with his wife goes to a Clark Gable movie.

The slight (very slight!) resemblance between Gable and George fascinates and disturbs Mary to such an extent that for her the illusion becomes real and their marriage often becomes strained. George, puzzled by his wife's behaviour, shaves off his moustache and normality is restored. A particularly striking feature of the film is the crisp black-and-white period photography by Jack Conroy.

Strongbow Films and Eat the Peach

While travelling into Ireland's peaty interior looking for an item for an RTE magazine programme, Englishman Peter Ormrod chanced upon a 60' high barrel tower. The director discovered that it had been built by Connie Kiernan, an Irishman who had been so inspired by the 1964 Elvis Presley movie, *Roustabout*, with its Wall of Death scene, that he decided to construct his own. The unusual nature of this Irish craftsman set Ormrod thinking about the basis of a screenplay which,

is partly underscored by the subjective camera movement.

The film seems preoccupied with memory which, for a new immigrant from Ireland, often fluctuates between lamentation and bitterness. For a while, O'Sullivan departs from the subjective camera treatment to more conventional shots of English representation in Ireland through such banalities as newspapers and English 'B' movie films on the Irish cinema circuit. These images serve to highlight the disparity between media images and actual experience.

The film is also composed of 'Irish' and 'English' sections, divided by a scene where a boat moves away from the dock, suggesting a no-man's-land of neither British nor Irish culture. The Irish section of the film includes images from two very native events — the pilgrimage up Croagh Patrick mountain and Puck Fair. The former is a Christian ritual while the latter's celebration of the goat suggests a pagan rite. These two elements on the Irish psychological landscape, Slane and Tara, relate to the doubleness that every however, took almost ten years to be realised as the film *Eat the Peach* (1986).

Ormrod, whose credits include the well-received RTE series, *Caught in a Free State* (1983), and work for the BBC *Play for Today* series, found support for his project through his old boss at RTE, John Kelleher. Kelleher had made his name as executive producer on the mini-series, *Strumpet City* (1980), which RTE sold to more than fifty markets. Kelleher left RTE in 1983 and first took over the *Sunday Tribune* newspaper before starting his own independent production company, Kelcom.

It was not until Kelleher joined up with David Collins to form Strongbow in 1985 that Ormrod's germ of an idea came to fruition. Kelleher's travel record — some three hundred Dublin to London flights in three years — was necessary to seek the required extra finance for *Eat the Peach*.

The film itself touches upon many aspects of Irish society. We see the withdrawal of foreign investment with the closure of a Japanese factory, the subsequent unemployment and the uneasy attitude in the South toward "the troubles" in the North. But the main thrust of the production is the realisation of a dream, no matter what complications Vinnie (Stephen Brennnan) and Arthur (Eamon Morrissey) have to encounter.

Niall Toibín masterfully plays Boots, the boastful would-be promoter, complete with fake American accent and cowboy hat and boots. Despite their success in building the wall and in arranging a television camera crew to film its opening, no sponsors come forward to further the project. In frustration, Vinnie sets fire to the wall but seems to have already begun on a new project when he later shows Boots a homemade helicopter. The film nicely captures the power of an individual's dream despite the heavy odds against him.

The End of the World Man

Aisling Films

It should not be thought that Dublin is the only city in Ireland that harbours production companies. In 1983 in Belfast Aisling Films was founded by Belfast-born Bill Miskelly and Derry-born Marie Jackson. Miskelly entered the BBC in 1967 as a film editor, moving on to direct around forty documentaries and television features for the company, including work by Brian Friel and Bernard Mac Laverty. Marie Jackson met Miskelly while working at the BBC. She had been progressing from researching stories to directing short documentaries, one of which won a BAFTA Award.

Their first venture together was a one-hour television film, *The Schooner* (1983), adapted by Jackson from a Micheál McLaverty short story. A young Belfast boy, Terry (Johnny Marley), is on holiday at his elderly great aunt's farm on a remote

Irish island. Aunt Annie (Lucie Jamieson) cannot rid her mind of memories of her husband, a ship carpenter, who went off to sea and never returned. She oddly believes he will magically reappear, though her loss has made her embittered. The aunt's strictness seems to relax when Terry is allowed to play with the husband's model ship, a schooner. The boy is a reminder to the old woman of the vitality of life and this feeling is compounded after he returns safely from an evening playing by the rocks. The loss of the model ship in the waves symbolises to the aunt that her husband is truly dead.

The End of the World Man

The Schooner was well received and allowed Jackson and Miskelly to see if they could successfully market their own product without the buttressing of the BBC. In the event, RTE, Channel 4 as well as television companies in Holland, New Zealand and Scandinavia bought the film. With this success, Marie Jackson continued writing with two main motivations: to create a picture with two girls as the leading characters and to show Belfast in a new light. The result was *The End of the World Man* (1985), which has proved to be the most successful film given funding by the Irish Film Board. Its many awards include first prizes at Berlin, Chicago, Los Angeles and Vienna.

In the film Paula (Leanne O'Malley) aged ten, and Clare (Claire Weir) aged eleven, rebel against plans to make their favourite glen into a car park in downtown Belfast. Their anger is directed against "The End of the World Man", a nasty Department of Environment civil servant (John Hewitt), who also spends his weekends as a vocal evangelist. As Bill Miskelly has been quoted as saying, the film deals with universal issues of CND and conservation but: "We're not trying to

make any big statement by having one kid a Catholic and the other a Protestant, either. We are simply saying that where Catholic and Protestant do grow up together — not that they do much in Belfast anymore — they have to be told they are different before it means anything to them".

Another children's film written by Miskelly and Jackson is in the pipeline, provisionally entitled *Michael and Billy J.*

Other Irish directors and films

Tommy McArdle's two feature-length films, *The Kinkisha* (1977) and *It's Handy When People Don't Die* (1980), concentrate on the desiccating effects of the use of myth in our lives. In the former film, the action centres on superstition. A mother believes that, because her child is born on Whit Sunday, it will either kill or be killed unless she, in turn, kills a robin. By doing so, the woman is able to enter back into her community, thereby repressing her individuality.

That individuality is taken up more forcefully in the latter film, which is set in a Wexford village at the time of the 1798 rebellion. Both the village wiseman and the priest encourage the men to go off and fight but one apparently mad character, Art (Garret Keogh), refuses to do so, preferring the instinctive or animal side of life. Art's working out of the specific myths which he is prepared to believe in presents much of the interest of the film.

McArdle seems to suggest the film's focus on this individual is not merely a pacificist or self-preservation attitude to nationalism and war but an alternative understanding of a community's shared myths. This provocative film was re-edited to reduce its running time by twenty minutes, although criticism in *Variety* and *Film Directions* agreed that a number of scenes still needed a sharper focus to help the audience.

Drawing attention to media-constructed myths about Northern Ireland is the major focus of *Acceptable Levels* (1983), a Frontroom/Belfast Film Workshop joint production, directed by John Davies, co-director with Pat Murphy of *Maeve*. The script traces the common foreign television feature story of how kids in a ghetto area of Belfast are growing up.

During the filming and interviewing, a riot develops outside and a young girl is killed from, it seems, the use of a plastic bullet by the security forces. The crew films the whole incident yet excise most of it in the editing room back in London, given the various pressures a controversial film on the province has to withstand when shown in Britain.

A kind of ghettoisation is also present in Joe Mahon's *The Best Man* (1985), shot in and around Derry. Billed as a social comedy, the film won awards for best actor (Seamus Ball) and best film at the 1985 Celtic Film Festival in Newcastle, Co. Down. Produced by a Catholic priest, Dennis Bradley, the production focusses on middle-class life in the city and particularly on the way one inveterate drinker does his best to lure his friend away from the clergy to the pub.

Social issues are prevalent as well in Neville Presho's *Desecration* (1981), a Film Script Award-winner. This film examines the conflict between an ancient monument restorer and an impetuous businessman keen to mine the deposits on the monument's site. Even the sympathies of a third man, a city geologist, cannot save beauty from big business.

The Courier

More recently, the new Dublin production company, Cityvision, has made *The Courier* (1987), a thriller set in Dublin in the underworld of drug-dealing. Joe Lee and Frank Deasy direct, supported by Neil Jordan as executive producer and by Irish actor Gabriel Byrne in a leading role. A young courier, Mark (Padraig O'Loingsigh), angered at the murder of his girlfriend's brother by drug boss, Val (Byrne), determines to plant damaging evidence that will bring the latter's operation to a halt. In a shootout Val is killed by the police.

The malaise of modern-day Dublin pervades the film, an oppressive presence for the young Irish people who are exploited by crooks and police alike. It is significant that Mark and his girlfriend leave the city at the end of the film. As they walk along the shoreline, we are reminded of the ending of Ingmar Bergman's *The Seventh Seal*, when Joseph and Mary escape the plague. It is perhaps as a mixed genre production that *The Courier* is best approached.

Padraig O'Loingsigh in the title role of The Courier

Clash of the Ash and Boom Babies

Another feature-length début is Fergus Tighe's *Clash of the Ash* (1987), which

David O'Meara and Joe Savino in Sometime City

David O'Meara and Joe Savino in Sometime City

centres on the trials and tribulations of a leaving certificate student (Liam Heffernan) who, although good on the hurley field, has much more to combat in depressed 1980s Ireland, not least the restrictions of parents and teachers. Tighe deserves the highest praise, working as he did on his project while on the dole before the Irish Film Board came up with finance to help develop a script and pilot film. On the basis of the latter, the Arts Council further supported the film, while Tighe borrowed equipment and went into debt.

A similar story of the thinnest of shoestring budgets is to be told about the making of Siobhán Twomey's excellent début feature, *Boom Babies* (1986). Made for a meagre £18 000, the 24-year-old Dubliner's script revolves around the conflicting lives and dreams of two grown-up children of the 1960s baby boom in Ireland. Twomey herself got just £400 for her nine months' work — eight and half months raising the money and eleven days for the shooting of the film.

Niall Toibín's daughter, Aisling, stars as an unemployed, middle-class Southside Dubliner who has her car stolen by an unemployed, working-class Northsider

(Andrew Connolly). These popular, though illegal Irish pastimes — stealing cars and joy-riding — serve to bring the two together and their relationship is nicely drawn with a tightly written script.

Riders to the Sea

J M Synge's classic Abbey Theatre play was taken as the subject of young Irish director Ronan O'Leary's début film. The forty-seven minute long film numbers three Oscar winners among its international cast and crew and yet was completed on a budget of only £95 000. The film stars Amanda Plummer and Geraldine Page in her final screen performance before her death. It also features an interesting début from Barry McGovern, best known for his stage interpretation of Samuel Beckett.

Written in 1904, Synge's short play tells of the primal struggle between an old woman and the sea, the sea that has robbed her of the lives of her husband and her six sons. O'Leary's powerful version was castigated by Irish critics when premièred at the Cork Film Festival but has proved successful on television and video release in the United States.

Boom Babies

Sam Thompson: Voice of Many Men

Documentarists

Undeniably, the period 1977-88 has been one of impressive feature débuts by Irish directors. However, the documentary tradition established by Fleischmann, Marcus, Hickey and others continued parallel to RTE's scheduling. Louis Marcus's major project in 1978, *The Heritage of Ireland*, unfortunately coincided with Robert Kee's *Ireland — A History* for the BBC and so has not been as widely shown as it should be.

In the 1980s Donald Taylor Black has been making a name for himself by concentrating on Irish artistic and literary figures - *At the Cinema Palace — Liam O'Leary* (1983), *Remembering Jimmy O'Dea* (1985) and *Sam Thompson: Voice of Many Men* (1986). The latter film stars the ubiquitous Stephen Rea, who performs pieces from Thompson's autobiographical

writings in a Belfast setting. Taylor Black has recently produced *Oliver St John Gogarty: Silence Would Never Do* (1987).

One must also mention the scrupulous dedication of Seán Ó Mórdha's literary documentaries for RTE: *Is There One Who Understands Me?/The World of James Joyce, Samuel Beckett: Silence to Silence* and *Oscar Wilde: Spendthrift of Genius*, written by the late Richard Ellmann before his recent biography of the Irish playwright. Also for RTE, David Hammond and his Belfast Flying Fox Films made *Steel Chest, Nail in the Boot and the Barking Dog* (1986). The names refer to three nicknames of former Harland and Wolff shipyard men. Hammond's company had only two weeks to shoot the film; nevertheless, the production won the Golden Harp Film Award which Hammond had won previously in 1972 for

Steelchest, Nail in the Boot and the Barking Dog

his BBC film, *Dusty Bluebells*, about street games in Belfast.

Non-Irish directed films on Ireland

Of the many films on "the troubles" between 1977 and 1988, four of note are the Dutch film, *The Outsider* (1979), and the British-financed *Ascendancy* (1982), *Boy Soldier* (1986) and *A Prayer for the Dying* (1987).

The Outsider

Reviewed by *Variety* as a "thoughtful terrorism drama, starring the IRA", *The Outsider*, written and directed by Tony Luraschi, is one of the few non-Irish films to examine seriously the crisis in Northern Ireland. Craig Wasson stars as an Irish-American who is influenced by his nostalgic and patriotic grandfather to join the IRA. However, he soon becomes disenchanted with the Ulster scene, narrowly escaping murder by both the IRA and the British Army at the end of the film. An impressive Irish cast, including Niall Toibín, ably supports this studiously realistic approach to "the troubles".

Young Michael is haunted by his grandfather's stories and songs — "Some fell by the wayside/Some died with a stranger" — and this message is only reinforced when he hears a singer in an Irish pub repeat the song. Ironically, unbeknown to Michael until his return to Detroit, his grandfather was an informer. In Ireland, Michael's first important job for the IRA is the kidnapping of a magistrate from Brookeborough, Co. Fermanagh. He is tried in a kangaroo court and executed. Michael is unable, however, to pull the trigger and a friend has to do it for him. Curiously, this magistrate is portrayed as and by an Englishman and not as an Irish Protestant which would have been more accurate. The impression is left, therefore, that the IRA have not killed a fellow Irishman. To Luraschi's credit, he inserts a short scene where Michael and his driver meet the mainly Protestant Ulster Defence Regiment. He hears their accent and asks his companion if they are British. The answer he receives, "Yes and no", is perhaps the most perceptive statement in the film.

The making of *The Outsider* in gloomy Dublin backstreets (serving as a Catholic Belfast ghetto) did not go totally smoothly. The Dublin inhabitants approved the project but also prompted a donation to their residents' association. Rumour has it that the American crew received an unsigned letter supposedly from the IRA, who suggested that they would not interfere during the filming.

Nonetheless, the army paraphernalia from Britain, including a tank, needed constant security. Every blank shell fired after each action scene had to be accounted for. Strangely, *The Outsider* was filmed in the spring of 1978 but not released until December 1979 and even then it was often rejected. Perhaps the scene of the police (led by Ray McAnally) torturing a blind Republican sympathiser (Bosco Hogan) had not a little to do with it.

Ascendancy

On a much smaller budget from the British Film Institute, Edward Bennett made *Ascendancy*. His film charts the psychological descent of a well-to-do Belfast Protestant woman around the end of the First World War. Connie, played by Julie Covington, suffers from paralysis of the arm, a physical impediment which symbolises her numbed mental state. Connie's father appears to be a major partner in the Belfast shipyard and it is clear that his daughter would prefer to live in a less prosaic and more imaginative world. However, she is trapped in a different kind of past than the tiresome sectarianism she sees around her. She mourns for her brother, killed during the war while fighting for the British army in Flanders.

Bennett seems to suggest that this personal loss is so debilitating that Connie cannot contextualise any further violence, which she experiences in abundance when wandering the streets of inner city Belfast. Richard Kearney views the film's aesthetics as part of a general trend in the depiction of Irish women on the screen. He pinpoints the idea of the suffering woman in Irish culture, a figure who can only accuse men of bloodthirsty violence. Connie seeks sanctuary with other women in a nearby Catholic church, but rather than see this as a facile image of 'peace women', one feels that the cause of the violence lies just as much at the door of Irish women as it does of Irish men. Winner of the Golden Bear at the 1983 Berlin Film Festival, *Ascendancy* has since been shown on television.

Boy Soldier

Also about Northern Ireland is Karl Francis's *Boy Soldier*, a film unashamedly Welsh in perspective. Funded by Channel 4 (Wales), *Boy Soldier* traces the fortunes of one Welsh soldier, Wil Thomas (Richard Lynch), who kills a civilian in panic when his friend is murdered in a street disturbance. The ramifications of this sudden act bring to the fore not just "the troubles" but the role of working-class Welsh men in the British army. It seems that the English disregard of the Irish is close, if not exactly the same, to their disregard of the Welsh. This attitude explains the harsh treatment the soldier undergoes for refusing to admit his guilt in the killing of the youth, since as Wil sees it, he did only what he had been trained to do.

Perhaps most striking in the film is the director's quick montage of Wil's memories of Ireland and Wales, a technique that serves to blend the small Gaelic-speaking nations together. The essential contradiction in Wil's fate is that because he is a good soldier, following orders, he must be sacrificed. Just as tragic is the punishment of Deirdre (Emer Gillespie), an Irish Catholic, for an innocent love-affair with Wil.

A Prayer for the Dying

More recently, Mike Hodges's melodrama, *A Prayer for the Dying*, starring Mickey Rourke as a drifting IRA gunman, Martin Fallon, has attempted to convey a soulless individual's torment. The turning-point for Fallon is the accidental blowing up of a school bus filled with young girls. Fleeing to England, Fallon cannot fully escape without first doing some dirty work for Jack Meehan (Alan Bates), a sinister mobster-cum-undertaker. Reluctantly, Fallon murders his given target but is seen by a priest (Bob Hoskins). The relationship between Fallon and the priest's blind daughter serves to highlight the gunman's spiritual waste. At the end of the film, we see Fallon slowly slipping down the figure of Christ to his death. As a mixed genre film, Hodges's vision of a man in an extreme situation works well, although the cross symbolism could have been toned down a little.

Period pieces

The Dead

It is interesting that two classic ambiguous fictions about Irish society were screened and released in 1987: John Huston's *The Dead* from a story by James Joyce and *The Lonely Passion of Judith Hearne* from Brian Moore's novel. Huston's film was not long completed before he died and is undeniably a brilliant and moving swansong.

Unlike previous adaptors of Joyce, Huston, who had lived in Ireland for many years, seems to capture the underlying nostalgia and gentleness of the short story with effortless efficiency. Donal McCann's expressive face as Gabriel, Anjelica Huston's saddened air as Gretta, Maria McDermottroe's energy as the playful Molly Ivors and Helena Carroll's warmth as Aunt Kate all stay in the mind long after viewing. Sean McClory's (Mr Grace) recitation of a Lady Gregory love poem is simply overwhelming, an apt addition to the script. As Gabriel ponders his wife's passion for another man, now dead, his voice calms us with beautiful acceptance that we are all shades, all in receipt of the snow which falls "Upon all the living and the dead".

The Lonely Passion of Judith Hearne

Whether Gretta or Gabriel's epiphany enables their barren marriage to be reactivated is left, like the story, unconfirmed. Equally uncertain in book and film is the fate of the heroine in *The Lonely Passion of Judith Hearne*. Jack Clayton has taken more liberties with Moore's work than Huston did with Joyce's story. 1950s Belfast becomes 1950s Dublin and the ending is a major departure, with Judith having the opportunity to reject the man she strove to marry.

In flashbacks we learn that Judith (Maggie Smith) is an orphan who has been brought up by her sober and religious aunt (Wendy Hiller). When the aunt becomes senile, Judith feels obliged to care for her, despite offers from the doctor to have her committed. When the aunt dies Judith is middle-aged and with little money to her name; she is also an alcoholic. Once drunk, her rowdy behaviour seems to be the reason why she moves boarding house fairly frequently. Marriage seems out of the question for this lonely lady until she meets fellow boarder, Mr Madden (Bob Hoskins).

What they both have in common is loneliness, exacerbated by poverty. Foolishly, Judith raises her hopes but, once disappointed, she resorts to the bottle for comfort. Eventually, her actions lead her to a rest home. At the convalescent hospital, in both the novel and the film, she sees that religion and marriage are not the wherewithal of life. This knowledge is a cold comfort. The desperation in Maggie Smith's performance is impressive and Marie Kean as the stingy landlady rivals in presence her masterly portrayal of Freddy Malin's mother in *The Dead*.

Other Irish and Irish-related films

The Outcasts

Englishman Robert Wynne-Simmons won an Arts Council Script Award for his project *The Outcasts* (1982), a film funded

Sheila

The Outcasts

by Channel 4 and the Irish Film Board. The setting is rural Ireland in the 1840s, just before the famine. A travelling fiddler appears to bewitch people by his powerful, evocative playing. A young girl, Maura, spends an evening with the fiddler but on her return to the village she is blamed for an unfortunate happening, to the point that on one occasion the villagers attempt to drown her. However, the fiddler intervenes and saves her. She is then given access to the magic of the power within her, released by the fiddler. This power bewilders her as she returns to her cottage. Starring Mary Ryan, Mick Lally and Cyril Cusack, the production won the Best Film Award at the 1983 Brussels Fantasy Festival and the Best First Feature Award at the San Remo Festival in 1984.

Lamb

Bernard Mac Laverty has written only two novels, both of which have made it to the screen. *Lamb* is his earlier fiction and is taken up with immense sensitivity by director Colin Gregg. In the 1985 film Liam Neeson plays the priest who takes a borstal-boy, Hugh O'Conor, to London. The boy suffers from periodic epileptic attacks and their relationship is the force of the film, a brooding, melancholic traffic of emotions which ends in the priest's mercy-killing of the boy, since he is unable to save him from further pain.

Failure, too, is the major theme in Kevin Billington's *Reflections* (1984), an adaptation of scriptwriter John Banville's novel, *The Newton Letter*. William Masters (Gabriel Byrne) is writing a book on Newton, a noted celibate. Newton's would-be biographer, however, seems to lose faith in both celibacy and monogyny as shown by his relationships with the local people who own the lodge in County Cork where he has gone to write his volume. Because he cannot understand the life around him to any satisfactory extent, it is logical that he abandons the book.

Writings on the screen

Just as Irish feature film-making has come of age in this period, so too have critical writings on the cinema. In addition to articles in *Film Directions* and *IFT News*, Kevin Rockett, Luke Gibbons and Stephanie McBride have published informative pieces in *Screen*, *Framework* and *The Crane Bag*. Just recently, *Film Directions* has announced a second auditorium for the QFT (late 1988) and an Irish section for the new Guild of Regional Film Writers. It is not too premature to argue that Irish film culture is now firmly on the map.

The future of Irish cinema

Despite the closure of the Irish Film Board (which may still be resurrected in some form), the future of Irish film-making can now be seen in a cautiously optimistic light. The number of independent production companies has grown; perhaps more importantly, television stations in England and Ireland, faced with the prospect of cable and satellite competition, seem eager to contract out programmes and series. For example, in July 1987 RTE allocated Irish £1.8 million for freelance film production.

In contrast, the much-debated $20 million international movie on the life of Michael Collins, to be directed by Michael Cimino, seems to be permanently suspended with scripting problems. It is overwhelming to think how many Irish films could be made for the same amount of money.

To some extent, it does not matter if cinemas and distribution networks are owned by multi-national or American and British companies as long as films about Ireland are being made by Irish directors and by Irish production companies. The market place is its own arbiter; if the film is good enough it will survive and do well; if not, it will die a natural death.

What is really the issue here is *funding* from diverse sources for Irish directors and production companies: the more films are produced, the more pressure will come to bear on worldwide distribution networks to give access to Irish films. It is undeniably true that Ireland needs more producers and marketing executives to negotiate deals and draw money into the country. The new Irish production companies have taken a first bite at the offered fruit; it should not be long before we Irish can pick the tree ourselves.

Interview with Grace Carley

Grace Carley was born in Waterford City in 1961. On leaving University College, Cork in 1982, she was appointed Executive Assistant to the newly formed Bord Scannán na hÉireann/Irish Film Board. She subsequently became the Board's Marketing Executive, responsible for international promotion of the Board and its product. She resigned in September 1987, shortly after the Government's announcement that the Board was to be wound up. She is now Director of Television Distribution with Liberty Film Sales, a London-based film marketing agency, where she also has special responsibility for feature film production. We conducted our interview with her in June 1987.

How did you become involved with the Irish Film Board?

I came out of university and was looking for a job and got into the Film Board. The Board was established in 1981 but didn't appoint a staff until August/September 1982. At that time they appointed a chief executive and myself to start up the whole procedure of administering a film board, the funding, the legal side and so on.

For the first two or three years it was basically just the two of us; subsequently as more productions got made and there was obviously a need to try and sell these productions, I took over the marketing as well. So the staff here is myself and Michael Algar, with Muiris Mac Conghail as chairman — that is not an executive position, it is just a part-time, official, government-appointed position. Basically what the Board does is decide on the projects it will support and decide on general policy, and then we carry out whatever that is.

What have you learned about the marketing side in the last five years?

I suppose that I have really only begun to learn in the last two to three years about marketing and it is very much a case of making it up as you go along: there is very little to tell you how to market a film. The reason for that is that no two films are alike. So you're not in the position of marketing, say, shoes which have a particular target market and there is a particular way of selling shoes, I presume.

With films, each one is the prototype. Obviously there are certain ground rules but generally each film has to be handled separately. Because of our financial position and our general resources and manpower we don't go to every single possible market or festival; we go to the main ones — Berlin, Cannes, usually an autumn television market or London.

Was the attendance at Berlin and Cannes a policy from the start?

No, it wasn't in fact. It wasn't until 1984 that we began to go to festivals for a couple of days to find out what they were all about and how best we might have a presence at them. In 1984 Michael Algar went over to Cannes for five days and subsequently in 1985 and in following years we took an office in a fairly good location in Cannes. So it means that we are in an identifiable location now, people will know where to find us, and it seems to work very well for us.

How is your time taken up at Cannes?

Generally you do your best to get as much publicity as possible for the films you are trying to sell; you try and get in contact with the most appropriate people that you hope will buy the films; you try and talk to the press; set up screenings and pull along people to see those.

And Berlin?

Berlin is more easily managed in that it is very compact, it's all in one place, the press are there, the buyers, the sellers, etc. Market screenings are set up and the press can go to them, you can get good reviews - people like *Variety* and *Screen* are there and it is much more useful from that point of view. But Cannes you just have to be there. It is the best place for making contacts, everyone is there. The whole business is built so much on personal relationships; you've got to get to know the buyers, build up good, even social, relationships, nurture them in a way — it's quite difficult, I think.

Who have you had success with recently?

It has varied depending on the film. This year, for example, we only had Bob Quinn's new feature film, *Budawanny*, which was sold to Switzerland, as a result of a contact we made in Berlin. There was also interest in it from Australia, again as a result of Berlin, and further interest will come up in the months after Cannes. I know some people talk about making huge deals in Cannes but generally I think you make an initial contact there and then in the succeeding months you actually close the deal or maybe continue the contact.

And when you sell to, say, Switzerland, what sort of financial package are you talking about?

You're not talking about an awful lot of money in relation to the film because the guy who is buying it only sees it going into about three or four different cinemas around Switzerland before being sold onwards to television. So he will give a minimum guarantee which is basically an advance against royalties and it won't be much more than about $10 000.

How important is it for the Board to have their films shown at the London Film Festival?

The London Film Festival has been a good outlet for Irish films and certainly in the earlier years gave us great support in bringing our films to a wider audience. Our first participation was in 1983 when we had five films at the festival and since then we've always had two or three. So it is good from the point of view that there is a lot of foreign press there, certain foreign distributors, foreign film festival directors and so on. But you would reach a much wider audience in Cannes, for example.

Ireland has a number of new, small independent production companies such as Strongbow, Cityvision and Windmill Lane. Has this rise been coincidental with the Irish Film Board or because of it?

I would argue that it is absolutely because of it. If you look at Cityvision, for example, in 1982 they had just made a very small, low-budget video about unemployment to which the Board contributed. Since then we have been supporting them every single year, mainly through grant-aiding for various projects they have been doing, whether they are non-broadcast video or drama — recently they made *Sometime City* for which we put up fifty per cent of the finance.

I would strongly argue that without the Board Cityvision would not have survived and they would not have come to the position they are in today of making their major feature film, *The Courier*. Even the script for *The Courier* was written with money from the Board — they got £8000 to develop that script and the first commitment to finance the film was from the Board, which is putting in £100 000. I think it is important to stress that because unfortunately people in government will tend to look at the industry and say, "Oh yes, the industry is doing fine, let's close down the Film Board."

And Strongbow?

In the case of Strongbow I think that the industry had developed to a certain stage by the time Strongbow was set up so there was an infrastructure here that enabled companies as big as Strongbow to carry on film production in the way they're doing. Regarding *Eat the Peach*, the Board put money into it years ago for script development and again was also the first to commit production finance to it.

Even though our commitment to production finance is in general about £100 000, which doesn't make a hugely significant impact on the budget, it is still very important for people in the international industry to see that a project from Ireland has the stamp of approval from the Film Board. Because the question that will be asked of an Irish producer looking for money is: "Has the Film Board put up any money for this?"

Is it the Board's responsibility to vet screenplays very rigorously?

Yes. Again because we've so little money and there is so little to go around, we have to be sure that what we're supporting is the best available. So we get between fifty and one hundred applications each year; a lot of them might be very short synopses or treatments and are fairly easily assessed. More of them would be full-length scripts.

The process is that the scripts go to independent readers, then go to a project assessment sub-committee of the Board which looks at the entire package, not just the script, to see whether it is a viable type of package, whether it is going to raise finance elsewhere, whether it is significant to the development of the film industry here. They then make a recommendation to the full Board who also read everything and then they come to a decision. So the Board does go very thoroughly through anything that is put in front of it and it will stand over to the end anything it supports. That whole process takes about four to six weeks.

Has the Board's grant of £500 000 increased at all?

No.

What about next year?

I would say there's very little chance. In fact this year in the budget the Board's grant was cut to £250 000. Then, following some rumblings, the Government did a great U-turn and decided that it would actually bring it up to £500 000 by replacing the other £250 000 from national lottery funds.

So the change of government recently has in fact adversely affected the situation?

Well, it almost did.

Are you fairly optimistic about next year?

No. Not at all. I'm not optimistic about next month. I'm serious.

From a pessimistic point of view, what do you think the Government has in hand?

What we need to get the film industry really moving, and not just depending on luck and companies like Channel 4, is a fiscal measure that will encourage investors to put money into the Irish film industry, and encourage private investors, corporations and private individuals in Ireland. At the moment there is no particular tax incentive that is sufficiently attractive to enable people such as banks, pension funds, insurance companies to put money into the industry. The BDS scheme has restrictions on the amount you can invest and it is only for private individuals, not corporations. Even Strongbow would admit that it is not really a suitable scheme for the film industry because it presumes there will be an ongoing process of manufacture: with a film it usually takes a year to set up, a year to finish and then a year or more to see any of your money coming back. So it is not the kind of structure that will enable the funds coming in from the sale of one set of goods to finance the manufacture of the

next — it really doesn't work very well that way.

What we have suggested to the Government, and they've had a proposal now from us for eight months, is an extension of the BDS to allow corporate investors to invest up to £250 000 in a film project and that can be limited to one film project or can be extended to cover a package. So it takes out the elements that are totally unsuitable to the film industry.

The last Government had come to a certain stage with this proposal and was reasonably in favour of it — it had gone to the highest level of civil servant and with various modifications on the way seemed to be fairly acceptable at that level. Now that proposal is still under consideration by the new Government. Anything that will bring money into the industry and keep it going is acceptable as far as we're concerned.

Can I ask you now about some of the Irish seasons you have had in other countries? You had one at the Cinémathèque in Paris recently, I believe. How easy is it to put these events on and what is the financial cost involved?

The main difficulty in having these events is having the manpower required to put it all together. In the case of the Paris event (and previous to that we had one in Germany) the Irish Film Institute looked after most of the organisation; they had one person who spent all of his time putting it together. We also had some people in Paris who were looking after that end of it.

So whereas it is quite easy to get sufficient interest from organisations such as the Pompidou Centre or the American Film Institute, it is the actual physical getting it together that is the difficulty. We would like to do more seaons but we just don't have the manpower here. I would say the cost of the French one in total was probably about £7-8000, which is a lot of money for what is basically going to be a cultural event and which really won't have that much significance financially.

I am interested in the situation when you sell a film to another country. Since the Irish Film Board puts money into a lot of these productions, what stake does it take with regard to the handling of the film distribution? Do you take on full responsibility to distribute them?

We would rather not be sales agents for the films that we're involved with. But there are particular films which don't have a sales agent lined up and there are certain producers who would prefer if we did handle it, so we're happy to do so. The nature of our representation is that we would be at these festivals anyway and that for no extra cost to the producer we can promote their films and attempt to get sales for them.

We're quite happy for people such as Film Four International and Palace Productions to take on the sales of a film because they have much more resources and experience than us, and they're likely to be more successful. But in all cases where we have production investment in a film, we do have the right to a share of the profits, so for every pound we put in we get the appropriate percentage back. So we would get our investment back and then go in for a share of the profits after that.

So in the case of Bob Quinn he actually asks you to promote Budawanny?

Yes. In the case of *Budawanny*, we were actually the majority financiers in that, so we did ask for the rights. The only other financiers in that were the Arts Council

and there was a pre-sale to Channel 4 — but they weren't interested in selling it. So it was obvious that we should take sales rights on that and he was happy that we did so.

You mentioned the Arts Council — in previous years before the Film Board was set up it played a fairly major role in promoting film. What about its role now?

It is fairly insignificant in a way because their total budget for film is £50 000 a year and they give that out in the form of script awards. What they try to do is complement rather than duplicate what we're doing; they will look at films more from an 'art for art's sake' viewpoint rather than the commerical overview that we would have. So it is quite useful in that it might bring films to our attention that we otherwise haven't been aware of or it might provide the necessary £15 000 to actually finish a film.

Michael Algar I believe is leaving the Board in August. Will a new chief executive be appointed? Or will you be promoted?

This is a burning question! Up to now there haven't been any interviews or appointments made, even though an advertisement appeared in March and applications are in. My major fear would be that because the Board itself is outgoing in October, they might be prevented from appointing anyone.

So it remains to be seen whether we will have a new chief executive, I don't know that we will. I wouldn't be surprised if Michael has his contract extended; I'm not sure he wants to but he may be asked to stay on.

So it's a real state of flux here at the moment?

Slight bit of flux here at the moment, yes, I would say so.

How do you see the new Irish Film Centre in Dublin?

The Board actually put £50 000 into the purchase of the Centre and has committed another £50 000 from next year's budget towards the further development of it. One of our major concerns is the archive area of the Centre and the Irish Film Institute has undertaken to develop that area on our behalf to a great extent in return for our funding. We're very concerned about the lack of an archive here: we are the only European country apart from Albania not to have an archive.

The second element is training: we're statutorily charged with trying to provide training for film personnel and to have a venue available such as the Irish Film Centre would be very useful for that purpose. For example, in 1984 we ran a producers training course which made use of the Institute's premises at the time.

So am I right in saying that a copy of each film that the Irish Film Board has put money into is kept by the Board?

To a greater or lesser extent, yes.

For eventual transference to the archive in the Film Centre?

Yes...I don't think that's an absolute necessity. Each contract that we have in relation to an investment stipulates that we get a print of the film. But this can also be used for festival purposes or any other purpose that we see fit. I would hope that when the archive is set up that it would be sufficiently funded to actually be able to buy brand new prints of everything, because the prints that we have here may be scratched or messed around a bit,

having done all the circuits. Since we set up and since *Angel* there is no trouble actually identifying exactly where all the material is.

A criticism could be levelled against the Board that the brief is a little too loose and that you are trying to do too much. In Canada, for instance, they have a tighter brief and the majority of its productions are documentaries. How do you feel about this?

I can see the argument. But I don't think that just by making documentaries you will develop a wide range of skills. A documentary film can be made with three people and a director; but that doesn't exactly provide employment or develop skills that will be significant enough for future films.

I would be inclined to agree that with the existing manpower and resources we do try to do too much. We do everything from support film festivals, to marketing, promotion, training, production, development, everything.

It might well be that in the future the Board will have to decide what it's going to concentrate on and that may be concentrating just on the development of feature film scripts, with a certain amount of money towards the production of them.

I was also thinking of the relationship between the film and theatre worlds in Ireland. Do you think there could be more connections between the two as there is, say, in Sweden?

Yes I think there could be markets, particularly, say, American television markets for filmed stage plays or for stage plays brought into the realm of film. But we are not in the business of commissioning; we react to what is presented to us and it is not an area we have looked into. If you look at the Swedish film industry it is heavily, heavily subsidised, they have the resources, an enormous film institute and so on.

Do you think then that Ireland needs an Ingmar Bergman for there to be a significant turn around?

I don't think any one individual director would have such an effect; maybe an individual politician. If you look at New Zealand, they have managed to make a significant impact on the worldwide film industry and one of the major reasons is that their Prime Minister, David Lange, is totally committed to the film industry. They also have the tax incentives to attract private investment.

I would like to ask you about the Board's attitude to Ardmore. It generated some bad feeling in the past with its policy of attracting foreign directors and crews and of not using home-grown talent. How do you see the new Ardmore?

Yes it has created bad feelings, but also among politicians because of the consistent money-losing venture that it turned out to be after and even before it became the National Film Studios. It seemed to give politicians the impression that film-making was a loss-making venture and not something they should be involved with. Which is why we have quite a hard time convincing Government that we can do an economical job and it is worth developing the independent sector here.

I think the studio did have a benefit though in that a lot of the productions did use Irish technicians and developed quite a good body of technicians here: we probably have better technicians than we deserve to have for a young industry. The down-side is that it didn't develop the kind of people here who would actually initiate projects, so that once the foreign productions had gone away, there was nothing left to fill that void.

The attitude towards the new Ardmore studios is quite positive. It is good to have a major American interest such as MTM Enterprises but it is also good to have someone like Morgan O'Sullivan to maintain the Irish aspect and the Irish interest in the studios. The way he has set up the studios seems to be possibly the best way, that is the four-wall idea of just having crews in when there is something happening, rather than having forty people fully employed even if there was no work going on, which is how they ended up in 1982. This is why they lost money, really.

MTM and Tara Productions will provide employment here, the studios are available to anyone who wants to come and use them, and there will also be a gap filled regarding the hire of equipment. So I think it will have benefits for the industry here.

What about proposals that come from Northern Ireland?

The Board has always looked at projects from Northern Ireland in the same light as those from the Republic. We've put significant money into one particular company in Belfast, Aisling Films, for *The Schooner* and then much more into *The End of the World Man*, which is probably the most successful film the Board has been involved with. We have also committed development funding to their next project.

The situation in the North is very difficult because they don't come under the arm of the British Film Institute and there doesn't seem to be any significant funding for film coming from their own Arts Council. If there are good projects coming from the North, we're happy to be involved with them.

How do you go about the selling process and what films are you currently selling?

We send video tapes, brochures and lots of reviews. We have a policy of promoting everything we're involved with or have been involved with. The ones I am directly selling are *The Outcasts, Anne Devlin, Budawanny,* a couple of documentaries from Donald Taylor Black and also *Eh Joe, Sometime City* and *Boom Babies.*

    The difficulty with the short films is that they are all between 34 and 38 minutes, whereas a television half-hour is between 25 and 27 minutes; it's very hard to slot them in. So the best you can hope for is to sell them as a package, although that is also a bit difficult because they are unrelated in content and format. It's a very slow process.

What about Anne Devlin?

I think it is a wonderful film but it is exceptionally hard to sell partly because of the historical context, which is not a very well-known event and also because the film doesn't dwell on the more popular aspects of 'bloody revolution'. It has sold well to Australia; I had interest at one point from other areas. It has been through every American distributor imaginable and we're not having much success there. It is a very specialised film and the American market is very difficult.

Is there anything else you would like to say that we haven't covered?

I think it's fairly well covered: I hope I don't make it sound too negative. It does get quite frustrating when there is so little money and so little prospect of any money coming up. A third of my time is spent answering for every penny we spend and we have to provide reports and so on, so one can get bogged down in the usual bureaucracy and administration. The main message is we need more staff!

Interview with David Collins

Having spent eight years in arts administration, **David Collins** founded his own film company, Samson Films, in 1983. He has produced three films since then, including the critically acclaimed short, *The Woman Who Married Clark Gable* (1985), starring Bob Hoskins. He is Managing Director of Strongbow, the Dublin-based independent production company which he set up with John Kelleher in 1984 under the terms of the Business Expansion Scheme. Their productions include the feature, *Eat the Peach*, and the television series, *When Reason Sleeps*. David Collins is a board member of the Irish Film Institute and a member of the Association of Independent Producers.

Can I start by asking how you raised the finance for Eat the Peach?

John Kelleher had a project called *Eat the Peach*. At that stage he had an independent production company, Kelcom, and he approached me to help him raise the money. We developed a structure — Strongbow — able to qualify for Business Development Scheme relief. This is an investment incentive provided by the Government here whereby people can subscribe for shares in approved companies and claim tax relief on their subscription: that is the basic attraction. We raised £1 million from the public in March/April 1985. The cost of *Eat the Peach* was £1.7 million; we raised just over £600 000 of that from Channel 4 and about £100 000 from the Irish Film Board. Obviously within the budget we put in our cost of financing and a certain contribution towards company overheads in the first year.

Did you approach private corporations?

The BDS scheme is only available to individuals — the maximum anyone can subscribe is £25 000. Effectively now in Strongbow we have about 330 shareholders. We have since raised further funds and now the total amount raised is about £1.4 million — the average investment being around £4000. Quite frankly it takes an awful lot of £4000s to contribute a significant sum towards the financing of any feature film or television drama series. So it has been our plan to encourage corporate investors but this requires some form of taxation incentive. We've put a number of proposals to the Government on that. *[In the 1987 Finance Act a measure was introduced based on proposals developed by Strongbow.]*

How many countries have you sold the film to?

At present, ten.

You describe yourself as a film and television company. What balance do you maintain between the two?

We work in a very small market — Ireland represents less than half a per cent of the world market. It is impossible to recover the production costs on any drama we might do from Ireland alone. In the United States, for example, it is possible to raise all the finance plus profit from this one market and so the rest of the world can be a potential source of pure profit. Within Ireland it is absolutely the other way around. Because of that we have to export our ideas and product and we need to be involved in as many aspects of the business as possible. We could not afford to specialise in feature films alone. *[In September 1987 Strongbow acquired a majority interest in another leading television company — Green Apple Productions.]*
The division between features and television for Strongbow at the moment is about equal. Feature films are more sexy to do; however, we have learned a certain amount as producers which we can bring to television drama. Firstly, with television drama you're dealing with international broadcasters and it is less risky. Secondly, there is much more cross-fertilisation between the television, video and feature film businesses than ever before. So in the search for production finance one always has to take television into account. That undoubtedly has certain aesthetic implications; the product offered must have a wide appeal.
However, it is extremely important for an Irish producer to have the opportunity to raise some of the finance from his own

market. We feel by and large that Radio Telefís Éireann could do more in this area. We feel that there should be more generous, or anyway more imaginative, tax incentives available for the corporate sector; and we also feel that the Irish Film Board should be properly funded. If thirty per cent of the money needed for a project was available from Ireland, it would transform the situation. However, we are also very concerned at the cost of making films here — it is not much different to the United Kingdom.

But low-budget films are being made, for example, in the United States — by people such as Spike Lee and Jim Jarmusch.

Yes they are and I feel there is a certain hangover here in terms of old and outmodish customs and practices. It is a question of being competitive. Either you find your thirty per cent is being supplied because your costs of production are that much lower or alternatively you have to find the mechanism of raising that money because the resulting production economically benefits the state. These remain key issues.

John Kelleher said in an interview that as a company you now needed to 'internationalise' as the next stage of your flotation. Has it become a problem to say which projects, how many projects and which subject matter? How much would, for example, John Banville's Birchwood *cost to get off the ground?*

Maybe £700 000. *Birchwood* is a very beautiful subject which could break out of an art-house release. However, its subject matter is not immediately amenable to television broadcasters, so the financing is not easy. And it is also heavy on production design, camerawork, casting — so it can't be made without reasonable production values.

We have quite a number of projects that are amenable to an international approach. There is nothing to stop us making films in America or in England and yet make a substantial contribution to the Irish economy. Since we started we have sold product worth over £2 million sterling. That has gone into the Irish economy so I think the tax-break has already justified itself in terms of the multiplying effects which are used to calculate the economic sense or nonsense of granting incentives to invest.

How many people do you employ here? Yourself and John Kelleher...

And three others full-time. John is more on the marketing side, whereas I'm more on the financing side. Plus a legion of consultants! Legal, accounting and so on. It is a complex business to actually maintain and run a public limited company.

I read that one of your consultants is Chris Sievernich who was involved with Paris, Texas. *What is your reasoning behind that: is it because of a specific project or is it because that person will be able to give you access to a larger market?*

Both of those. I think particularly when you're establishing yourself you want to build up as much support as possible, even of a moral kind. He has just finished producing *The Dead* with John Huston and we may have an interest in that project. It would obviously have been an extremely nice film to make here but unfortunately the local finance was not available.

The capital involved in film production is very, very mobile: there are an awful lot of films being made in Yugoslavia, South America, Mexico — sometimes it is due to tax reasons, sometimes to the perceived

production costs and so on. In Spain you can make a full-length feature film for about US$600 000 — you would be pushed to do that in Ireland or England. And what perhaps protects us to a certain extent is that an English language production reaches the largest market. However, I think that independent producers will soon be commissioned by European consortia on the basis of productions which have 'Pan-European' values. The budgets will be fixed and maybe the only place to make it is Portugal. So let's go to Portugal and make it there. This mobility is growing; it may not have reached the stage yet where it has transfigured individual production set-ups in individual countries, which are still bound by language and by a shared attitude towards all kinds of production practices.

Can I ask you about Ardmore? There are two issues: the use of Ardmore as an Irish centre, though owned by MTM, and the question of your international policy. What do you think the effect of that will be on Irish film-makers? Are they just as mobile here?

Absolutely. I think mobility is the name of the game and one should not confuse mobility with lack of principle or commitment. I think that as far as we're concerned, a producer is a person who ideally has lots of cash in the bank, a great idea and a script — everything else you tailor to suit the production. We don't see ourselves as a company with substantial investments in fixed assets and facilities — that's not the way we're moving.

Too much of a liability?

It may be, it's hard to say. It is just that we are not a service operation. We generate an awful lot of our own ideas in house and a lot are proposed to us: we have to run a pretty tight ship because otherwise again you don't have the mobility and flexibility that you need to go with something when it is really right. So I would say that the previous Ardmores didn't really make any substantial contribution to the creation of an Irish film industry, because an Irish film industry is about Irish people going out and making films and Ardmore was really about servicing international productions. Maybe the old Ardmore bred what I detected was an overwhelming provincialism. A service economy is really about people who very rarely have to take real responsibility for any creative or financial decisions.

I think ultimately an idea is stronger than a studio: if you put an infrastructure in place before there is a demonstrable ability to produce, then that is always dangerous. However, the new Ardmore, with the backing of MTM, seems to stand a better chance. And I think we can learn a lot from them.

What about your current projects? I believe you have bought the rights to Michael Farrell's novel, Thy Tears Might Cease: *is that going to go into production soon?*

We hope so. It needs one major investor, either a major broadcaster or a major portion of equity to put that into production. So it is well poised. We have developed a lot of projects; in almost all cases we have more than fifty per cent of the funds in place for any one of those projects. What we need, generally speaking, is the Irish component; if we don't get it we can probably sell off what we have to someone else but...well, we're reluctant to let go.

So is it becoming difficult for you to stick to your principles of being based in Ireland and insuring that you do something with strong Irish connections?

We've got many strong Irish connections which can generally produce a certain part of the investment required. I don't mean the nebulous amounts of £4000 here and there — one can't plan a production schedule on that basis. So we're doing whatever we can to create a change in the climate here. But by and large it is our preference to have some equity stake or carried interest in all the projects. Our job is to add value to ideas.

What about other projects — No Prisoners, *for instance?*

We're still reworking the script. One thing we've learned is that you really have to go to the market with very, very good scripts, otherwise you have no chance. Both John and I are heavily involved in the scripting and development process. People genuinely and understandably underrate the amount of very good material that does not get made and what you can't do is take something that is actually mediocre and, because it is Irish, expect people to jump up and down about it.

If anything, Irish material has to be brilliant and potential financiers might discount it even then. So that sets a very challenging target, particularly within a country that doesn't really have a history of screenplay writing, so we're very much encouraging that.

What about the television series on Parnell?

That is proceeding as planned. We've got some more scripts and it is likely to go into production in the next twelve months — that's ourselves and the BBC. That raises an issue which I think is worth considering: the extent to which Irish themes are taken up by overseas producers and the extent to which they solely develop the ideas, raise the production money and distribute or broadcast the end-result. Some would say, "We'd never have the money here to do something like that, so it is good someone is doing it." But without any Irish involvement in the project then you can find that in a curious way your own history is becoming colonised.

You certainly do have a very political — a very loose word to use, I know — attitude in that you're concerned that selling to the BBC is somehow continuing a kind of colonialism. How do you feel about that?

I think that it is an issue; it would be nice to think that we have resources ourselves to interpret our history to our own culture and then hope that that interpretation will find an international audience. To do that without any regard to what is internationally acceptable is foolhardy and based on a concept of state subsidy that simply does not exist in this kind of open economy. There are any number of middle ways through which you might not always get the best of both worlds, which is overseas money and a local Irish editorial control. The mere fact of being able to go in because you are part of the financing — and therefore your voice must be heard and if you were to pull out the project would stop — all this gives you leverage and influence.

What do you see as the main problem of the Irish film industry?

I think the major problem is that creative people are not working often enough. With every film that takes place one gets the feeling that the future of the Irish film industry (whatever that is) depends upon it, which is an unnatural pressure and it also leads to a very curious form of emotional blackmail. If the film is shit you can't actually say it, because maybe the guy mortgaged his house to make it. I

think people generally want to work and they could make a huge contribution if they were only allowed to. But I think that we're still not quite in the situation where production opportunities have opened up sufficiently.

I am also saying that if as a producer I can't produce something of quality for £15 000 then I am not a good producer. In other words I don't see my own success as in direct proportion to the budgets which are put under my control and those which I raise. I would regard it as possible failure on my part if I couldn't be objective enough to say, That's a good project, it's £15 000 and worth my while becoming involved." So I think it is important to maintain a feeling for scale.

What you do have is a general lack of confidence and suspicions between the independent sector and RTE. The country is too small for that. I think the Yeats line "Great hatred, little room,/Maimed us at the start" is unfortunately still true. And the question really is: did the hatred predate the claustrophobia or did the claustrophobia cause the hatred? Maybe because I'm an optimist I believe that the claustrophobia predated the hatred.

What about your relationship with RTE — is there a way you negotiate with them on scripts and directors and so on?

Yes, I think it's opening up a lot. We have a lot to learn from one another.

Do they regard you as a threat?

I hope so! Yes. I regard them as a challenge.

Did your experiences at the Arts Council and the Project Arts Centre give you the management skills necessary to run an operation such as this?

It has given me the emotional skills. I've always been fascinated by the relationship between art and the concept of value for money and also by the idea of trying to turn something which is an idea into a reality — be it a film, art exhibition, book or whatever — and then to see how these things actually exist in the world. And in some senses I went about it the other way — at the Arts Council I was very much an enabler and a deal-maker. So I started out on one side of the desk and then became more physically involved with putting my stamp on ideas.

So in a sense producing was a blindly obvious choice. I decided to go out myself and raise money and I'd never actually done that before. And I raised £150 000 to make *Pigs*, therefore I am a producer. It is as simple as that.

It has been said that whilst you were at the Arts Council you infuriated members of the literary establishment because you had a penchant for picking on some very talented unknown figures for awards. Would you care to comment on that?

Yes, I think that my taste at that stage was excellent; I just hope it will be as good again in the future.

So you don't have any qualms about what you did?

No I don't. I have a very clear conscience. I think at that stage our jobs were permanent and pensionable and we got them changed to short-term contracts. In other words, your own enthusiasms should count for something — if not, why are you employed? And enthusiasms have an effect and therefore the thing to do is to replace you with someone else who has got other enthusiasms.

One of the first people ever to get an award from the Arts Council was Neil

Jordan: as an unknown he got the biggest award granted in that year and there was outrage from the part-conservative, part-literary establishment. It was a great place to work in, I enjoyed it tremendously.

Do you have set criteria for taking on any film or television project? Is the small-budget, 'personal' film no longer a consideration?

It depends on the project. That project has to have integrity but it is also true that I am more aware now of more that is being done. I think that personal films are what it is all about ultimately — anything of any quality has to be motivated by vision, that's what you back and you back it all the way. I think there is always a bleak time in film production when everybody has fallen out of love with the project; at that stage you have to keep your nerve.

There are films that I admire greatly that I would never consider investing in because they simply don't make commercial sense. Some enthusiasm has to be tempered by the forces of commercial reality. I don't work for the Arts Council now. Is that the equivalent of saying that I sold out? I don't think so, I'm doing a different job.

The point is if the market here was large enough to support more than it is, then personal films could be justified against this market alone. That would make all sorts of things possible which are impossible now. But you cannot make a personal film for £1 million, because by the time you have raised that amount of money it is mediated by the investors' requirements. Great film-makers can maintain their vision even with those pressures. It is not necessarily any easier to make a film which costs £2 million than one which costs £1 million. There is never enough time, there are always problems, caused by lack of money or by the pressures and strings that money brings.

Can I draw you back to your Irish Film Theatre days by asking you why the IFT-distributed magazine Film Directions *was discontinued?*

Both Arts Councils felt there was a need for a film magazine. I became involved with it, and with the Irish Film Theatre. The IFT was independent of the Arts Council, without public subsidy of any kind. And we got a good board and a good guy in to run it. So questions started being asked: "Why should we be subsidising this magazine that we don't want to support?" And I said, "Fine, if that's your decision, that's your decision."

So I suppose one could work it all backwards and say, "Why didn't I fight and insist and say it would be embarrassing if the Arts Council decided to be seen not to support this magazine?" But I think the issue of independence is more important — if you set something up as an independent organisation, either *Film Directions* was paying its way editorially and in terms of its relevance to an IFT audience, or it wasn't.

The idea of a film magazine for Ireland...I don't know now. Having moved out of that area, I think I'm probably less impressed now with documentation than I was at the Arts Council.

Now you are a producer of a different kind?

Yes, more an enabler. If, say, a young band walked in here with a demo tape, if I thought it was the best one I had ever heard, I hope I'd have the courage to say, "Right, I'll manage you and I'll go on the dole for six months and back my hunch." If I didn't feel that I could do that, because it would be such a comedown for me in my new position or something like that, then I would be emotionally dead. If

something moved me, I would do it. At least I hope I would have the courage to do it.

Were you still around when the Irish Film Theatre demised?

I'd left the Arts Council but I was still connected with it. Basically the climate changed. We went through a slump in the early 1980s and audiences didn't have the disposable income. It was as simple as that. But I don't think people realise just how good it was when it was there, it was very exciting and very necessary. And the fact that it was put together so quickly and made such an impact in such a short time was a tribute to all the people involved.

Has the success of Eat the Peach *meant that future deals will be easier...?*

No... It's just a calling card. It shows what we are capable of.

Does each film have to be taken individually?

Absolutely. All the people will have changed by the next time around for a start! And the market will have changed. It has been a real experience to go out and try to sell your film.

Exchanging contracts for distributing Eat the Peach *in the United States must have been a major experience.*

Exchanging contracts isn't a problem, it's the follow-up, the marketing — telexes saying, "What about this?"...I got two more telexes today...Two things are wearing thin and one is my patience! I've fallen in love with the telex machine, I think it's great. It is the sound it makes, that insistent sound - "Read me, read me"!

What about the selling of your recent television series, When Reason Sleeps?

It was almost entirely funded by Channel 4 and RTE. Part of the idea was to give people new to television an opportunity. We had maybe eighty treatments; we commissioned about ten scripts and selected four.

What do you look for in a treatment?

A really interesting story. For television the big question you ask yourself is "So what?" It's a crippling question but it's one that is asked. I personally like material about people who are in extreme situations; in my view film captures that better than almost any other medium. Extreme, original, passionate — those are more important to me than whether the format is technically correct.

What about The Woman Who Married Clark Gable? *Was it difficult to get someone such as Bob Hoskins for such a short film?*

The co-producer on that film was Sally Hope, Bob Hoskins's agent. She was interested in becoming involved in feature film production and they had this project; Bob was attached to it and we were extremely lucky — the project came together in two months. Everyone admires the film and I hope that it will enable Thaddeus to get the break to make a feature.

Where do you see yourself going in the next few years? What other projects are you interested in?

I've just signed a three-year contract with Strongbow. I want to do something on Roger Casement — everyone has an Irish hero and I think Casement is much more interesting than Michael Collins. I'd love to make an Irish film outside Ireland. After that I'll just see. But I'm not only interested in film. I'd like to stay interested in all the arts. Film gives you an opportunity to maintain interest in all aspects of the imagination — writing, painting, music, theatre. It is a powerful combination and I'm lucky to be involved at this time in Ireland — at the birth maybe of something really exciting.

Interview with Cyril Cusack

Cyril Cusack was born in South Africa and raised in Ireland. He made his acting début, aged seven, first on stage and then on film in *Knocknagow* (1917). He rose quickly to become a major star at the Abbey Theatre and started his own company in 1945, producing Shakespeare, Shaw, Synge and O'Casey, as well as new Irish plays. He has won numerous awards during his long career and among his many film roles are *Odd Man Out, Shake Hands with the Devil* and *Poitín*. As a writer Cyril Cusack has staged his own Gaelic play at the Gate Theatre and has also published Gaelic poetry.

You had an early start to your film career as a child actor in Knocknagow, *I believe?*

Yes, I was seven, in 1917. At that time we were on tour in Tipperary. I was with my mother, who had been a chorus girl and graduated into the theatre and my stepfather, Brefni O'Rourke, who was a well-known actor and appeared in films much later on, mainly in England. Suddenly *Knocknagow* cropped up — out of nowhere it seemed at the time as a child — and away we went. We were working quite close to Mullinahone, about which it is said if you haven't been there you haven't travelled at all.

I think the name of the family was O'Brien. My film father was played by George Larchet who was brother to Doctor Jack Larchet, the maître d'orchestre in the Abbey Theatre for a considerable time. I can't remember who my film mother was. There was an eviction scene and we were turfed out of the cottage. It was set on fire and I remember being rather frightened. We then marched along the road, this abandoned and exhausted little family.

What I specifically remember is that we sat down on the grass by the roadside. I was wearing corduroy breeches which were rather torn and taller at the back than anywhere else and I sat down on a bunch of nettles. To my credit as a professional actor at that age I waited until the shot was over before I started to yell. In that scene we had the lady of the big house coming down to give us supper which consisted of hunks of homemade bread which I was to wolf and also a tumbler of bubbling, sunlit buttermilk: that's the loveliest drink I've ever had in my life.

There is a story told that it was shown to a deaf and dumb institute where they were able to read the lips. Of course it was a silent film and some of the language used was hardly romantic! Incidentally I was far from starving at that time, I was rather a fat little boy and I didn't look like a product of the famine at all. Nobody seemed to notice that — perhaps I acted so well!

Do you remember if the camera was moved during the shots?

No I can't remember that. Yet I must have seen the camera because when I saw the film a few years ago I was rather shocked at myself that I looked at the camera, so that's where the director must have been. I would say that it didn't move but was placed for each shot.

You then did a lot of theatre work until your next film, Guests of the Nation, *in 1935. How did you get that part?*

I think they were looking for someone to play a character rather like Kevin Barry, a university student who was hanged. Denis Johnston, the playwright, with whom I had struck up an acquaintance earlier, asked me to do it which I was very happy to do. It is a lovely short story, such a compassionate and luminous work. So we went to Kilmainham jail and there was a little scene there. Then we did some drilling up in the mountains and I had one chap with me, Sean Brady, who had actually been in the *old* IRA and handled his rifle very well.

You did a couple of films during the war. Can you tell me about those?

Yes. *Once a Crook* in 1941 and *Inspector Hornleigh Goes To It* in 1940. Gordon Harker played the leads in both and Alastair Sim was in the latter. In *Once a Crook* I played Gordon Harker's son which was very strange really since I was Irish and playing a Cockney. But I remember going to see it all on my own

one sunny afternoon in Shaftesbury Avenue and there were just two other people in the audience, I think there was one of the Darby and Joan Club sitting in front of me. Anyway I was watching myself with a little apprehension and I heard the woman turn to presumably her husband and say, "Oh I don't like the boy."

Going on now after the war to Odd Man Out, *do you remember how long the production period was?*

It was a quite a lengthy time because there was a hiatus for two or three months when we stopped filming. It was an interesting experience in that there was an avalanche of Irish actors who proceeded from there into films — Joseph Tomelty, Noel Purcell and so on. It was the first time I worked with James Mason, a very professional worker and very admiring of the Irish actors, one of whom of course had a great reputation, F J McCormick. Although he remained in Ireland, except for *Odd Man Out* and *Hungry Hill*, he had been spoken of as an actor of European stature, which I think he was. We worked in Belfast part of the time, then we did some of the exteriors in North London. The book by F L Green struck me as perhaps not a very well-written book, but certainly Carol Reed turned out a really good film.

What was Reed like towards actors?

He was excellent and I think the reason may well be that he was the son of a great actor, which is not generally known. He was, I believe, the natural son of Beerbohm Tree and Mrs Reed and with this background he had a relationship with actors which is very unusual. He was inventive, imaginative and had a good sense of the theatre and of film.

You worked with Kathleen Ryan in that film and again in Esther Waters *in 1948...*

Yes. Kathleen was chosen for *Odd Man Out* because of her looks, very beautiful. It was a kind of sombre, sad beauty perhaps, not an actress in the real sense but she certainly provided the feeling towards the story. I remember Carol Reed saying, "We'll have Kathleen there", the inference being that Kathleen did not act. My wife was also in it, she had a little scene. It was typical of the opportunism of the director, because my wife had a sty in her eye and we were worried about this. Carol said that when the character who wants to make love to her comes in she can say, "No, no, I've got a sty in my eye."

The other thing Reed said which is of some consequence I think was that acting is acting whatever the medium, and I agree with him. If one finds a sense of reality, it doesn't matter what the medium is.

You worked with another great director, John Ford. What was that like?

Being himself of Irish descent, Ford had very much in his nature a romantic idea of the Irish. But the material was there which steered him rather than his steering the material he had into a non-acceptable image of the Irish. He was a most attractive person with a sense of humour which I found very amusing. And he was very stimulating. He seemed formidable to a lot of people but I never thought that at all; I found him splendid to work with on *The Rising of the Moon* and I enjoyed that.

Here's a very funny story. An execution is about to take place and there were a number of Abbey actors, including Eileen Crowe, and John Ford wanted them to say the rosary. And then there were some fierce, brutal-looking people representing the Black and Tans, who had to look villainous at all costs on the top of a lorry. But most of them were locals. Ford said, "Eileen, look we've been through all this, we're not going to rehearse this at all. Just start off saying the rosary." So he says, "Action" and Eileen starts off and then suddenly he leaps forward and says, "Oh Jesus Christ! Cut, cut!" Here were the Black and Tans with their pistols cocked giving "Holy Mary, Mother of God"...they were finishing the rosary for her!

In Shake Hands with the Devil *you played with Cagney. How did you find that?*

We became very good friends. He worked with great dexterity and sympathy for the character he was playing. He had this amazing energy and at this time he did have many calls on his generosity — charities and so on. There was one occasion when he was entertaining until the small hours of the morning and then up at six o'clock to rehearse and film. Tremendous energy.

Shake Hands with the Devil *was made at Ardmore. What was Ardmore like in those days?*

It was a very pleasant and intimate studio to work in, although not very extensive.

A young Ray McAnally was also in that film.

Yes. I have great admiration for him as an actor. He is spoken of unfairly as being primarily a technician but there is much more to it than that. I went up once to congratulate him in a stage production of Friel's *Translations*. He has a strange, curt kind of humour and he said, "How can I be perfect when you're not perfect?"!

Did you know Orson Welles at all?

Not particularly well. I worked with him only once, in Greece in *Oedipus*. But I did see Orson in his very first performance here in Dublin at the Gate Theatre in *Jew Suss*. He didn't play the lead — Hilton Edwards did — but he was only about eighteen and had terrific stage presence. Then he was quite slim and angular in his movements, very impressive. I felt he overacted a bit; his personality overtook his acting.

After a long international career you came back to Ireland to do Bob Quinn's Poitín. *What attracted you to this?*

I have always been an enthusiast for the revival of the language — I've written a play and some poetry in Irish — so I was very pleased to get this script. I thought it had a strange, weird atmosphere which suggested Maupassant. Toibín and McCann were the nasty ones but not as nasty as I was!...It was liked here and also abroad — I had a very strange phonecall from a German man in Hamburg who had seen it there and was very enthusiastic about it.

What do you think are the reasons why the Irish cinema has not developed a sufficiently strong identity?

I think it is due rather to our mistrust of ourselves and that is very prevalent in Ireland; it manifests itself in another way sometimes by appearing to be very arrogant. That has been the drawback: that perhaps we didn't know how to go about it in the way of organisation. I do think our work should be essentially indigenous and native and that's another thing that we mistrust rather. If one is aware of the simple stories that emerge as lovely films or television pieces, such as the French and Italians have done, I think that is the kind of approach we should have. I don't think we need to imitate — I think Neil Jordan perhaps is influenced by some of the work that is done abroad that is considered avant garde.

What are your plans for the future?

Publication of my third, rather slim book of poetry. And several farewell performances!

Interview with George Fleischmann

George Fleischmann was born in 1912 in Austria. He qualified at the Film Academy in Berlin and worked in that city as a cameraman at UFA Film Studios. He won a Gold Medal at the Venice Film Festival in 1939 for his documentary, *Styria*. During the war he joined the Luftwaffe as a photographer on a reconaissance plane; on one mission he crash-landed in Ireland and was interned. After the war he remained in Ireland and formed Hibernia Films; in 1951 he photographed *Return to Glennascaul* and later was second-unit director on Huston's *Moby Dick*. He returned to Germany in 1959 to work on the Rank series, *Look at Life*, but came back to Ireland in 1966 and has since been active in making a number of commercial films.

How did you first get involved with camerawork and making films?

Actually I am a trained electrical engineer. I got a job with Siemens in Austria who at that time had a sister company, Siemens Klangfilm. They had the monopoly to install the sound system to convert silent cinemas to sound cinemas and I worked doing that. This equipment also had to be serviced — amplifiers were enormous then — and I began to get interested in the film side. I then went to Siemens in Berlin and became more involved with these sound systems and finally decided to go to the Film Academy in Berlin. This was in the early 1930s. The first sound films I ever saw were *White Shadows in the South Seas* in 1927 and of course Al Jolson's film. At that time the soundtrack was still on records played in the cinemas. The records were enormous, about 2½ feet in diameter. The record-player was mechanically locked to the projector to obtain synchronisation.

What were you taught at the Film Academy?

It was high tech really. The Academy was very much into the documentary field. We were told to go closer and from all angles and to dissect and explain it all that way. I then got a job with UFA; Dr Arnold Fanck was head of the documentary department. I learned a lot from him. There was a lot of theory as well as processing and sound and so on. We had scripts and split up: each unit had to make a section of the film.

You worked as a cameraman at the 1936 Olympics, I believe?

Yes. That was my first job, on Leni Riefenstahl's film of the Games, *Olympia*. It was very interesting because we made a lot of short films to show the technical details of how Jesse Owens started, for example. The amount of new equipment developed for these films was enormous: a chair was developed in the middle of the Olympic stadium so that you could follow the action 360 degrees right round, like a dentist's chair. It was a fascinating time. Riefenstahl was an extraordinary woman, very dictatorial but she had a vast knowledge. I was surprised that a woman should have that much power then. She was probably ahead of her time.

Then the war came. How did you eventually get into the airforce?

I was called-up to the army and had six weeks fundamental training in Potsdam. Really grilling! I thought it was lunacy to march for fifty kilometres in all your gear and then sing a soldier's song through your gas mask! I was very disillusioned. An Austrian friend of mine was the editor of a leading newspaper and he was in the airforce; I asked him if he could get me in. And so I was transferred to the Luftwaffe. UFA had newsreels, so I had a dual job of being a cameraman in an aircraft.

How did you arrive in Ireland?

We were flying over the Atlantic. We attacked a tanker and hit it and then made a second turn in order to film it — we shouldn't have done that as two spitfires arrived. They hammered us. We were on fire, the under-carriage on one side fell out and one of our crew was seriously injured. The last thing I remember was that the spitfire came along and just flew beside us. I could clearly see the pilot and suddenly he turned away and didn't do anything anymore. We managed to extinguish the fire but we knew we couldn't fly back to France; the dinghies were ruined and we couldn't land in the water. Then we saw

the Irish coast and made a belly-landing in a field. And there was nobody there, not a soul.

Eventually we found a farmhouse. A Church of Ireland minister came and then a local doctor. We had tea and bacon and eggs, and then suddenly we looked out of the window and saw the Irish army making a pincer movement with fixed bayonets, encircling the farmhouse and we were sitting there drinking tea! We were interned. Next door to us were British, Canadian and Polish airmen.

Then the next morning a fellow internee said that we'd better go shopping. He said that if you sign and give your word of honour that you won't escape, you can leave the camp and go shopping. So I did! Then they said you have to be mobile, so I bought a second-hand bicycle. This was all done on account. My camera was interned too but I insisted on having it back every six months to clean and polish and then it was taken away again. At the end of the war it was returned to me.

What was your reason for staying in Ireland after the war?

During the war I met a lot of people in Dublin — Michael Scott, an architect and a solicitor Roger Green — and they said, "A man like you is needed here in Ireland — let's form a film company." So we formed Hibernia Films. For my partners it was really only a hobby but I wanted to be professional.

The first film we made was on Michael Davitt. Then we made *The Silent Order* about Cistercian monks: it was the first time a film unit was allowed in a Cistercian monastery. I was involved in negotiating with the abbot. These people work extremely democratically and the abbot had to ask everyone but they finally agreed.

I built a small laboratory in Dublin to process the negative myself and made rush prints — the final prints were done in London. The film was distributed by MGM.

Then we made a number of government films — one was *Voyage to Recovery*, directed by Gerard Healy. Healy was of course an Abbey actor and was also very interested in film. He had experience of directing actors and so we worked closely together and made a number of films, road safety films and one for Irish shipping, *Lifeline*. Then I was contacted by Movietone in London and did stories in Ireland for them. In 1949 I left Hibernia Films and went on my own.

Then in 1950 you went to Rome to do a film. What was that about?

Ireland-Rome 1950. It was a film of the State visit of the Irish president. Of course there was great difficulty in getting the film made. Monsignor O'Flaherty, an Irishman, was in the holy office and was a very colourful character; I got to know him well.

I shall never forget I went to see him once in the morning; it was a hot day. "First things first, George", he said and put a bottle of Irish whiskey on the table. Nine o'clock in the morning...but I drank a glass because otherwise I'd fall out with

Cyril Cusack (with Patricia Plunkett) in The Art of Reception

him. He knew everybody, he was a real fixer. He rang the chief of the Vatican police and they smuggled me with the camera into the Sistine chapel, into the basilica.

Another Irishman who was in charge of Vatican radio gave me a live microphone line from the Pope's altar. I was found out at the end. This man — he must have been one of the Vatican detectives — came up and said, "You can film but you must not film the apostolic, the papal blessing from the altar." And he left one of his chaps to make sure I didn't. So I had my telephoto lens locked on the floor, focussed on the altar. When the apostolic came up, I knelt in deep devotion down by the tripod and I plugged in the battery and the film was away! It was the end scene: it was fabulous!

You photographed Return to Glennascaul *which received an Oscar nomination. What was Hilton Edwards like to work with?*

It was very tricky. Hilton Edwards was a theatre director. Peter Hunt will certify that there were endless arguments. He could never understand what 'Camera left' and 'Camera right' meant. He saw it as 'Stage left and right' which of course is the other way around. He couldn't grasp that. And then of course Hilton Edwards was always short of money — I had to buy the film and pay for the processing myself. In the end Louis Elliman, who at that time was the owner of all the main cinemas, rescued me and gave me my money back. But we're not talking about getting any salaries!

Hilton Edwards played in the Gate Theatre in the evening and then we started shooting when the play was over. The film was based on a ghost story which Micheál MacLiammóir was told by a police sergeant in County Kerry.

What about Orson Welles? What were your impressions of him at that time?

A fantastic, colourful character but most unreliable. When we did the final recording in London I had to book a studio. You know what that means in terms of time and money. Guess who didn't turn up? Orson Welles.

Some recent critics of Irish cinema have said that the documentarists of the 1940s period were over-reliant on government work?

Well, you couldn't do it otherwise. I have always made films to order; I've never made any other films. It's just not a viable experiment and I do the same today. I've just made two films - one last autumn and the other a few months ago, both to order. One is for the Irish Gas Board called *Natural Gas* and the other I worked on for eight years for the Electricity Board about the construction of Moneypoint Power Station, the coal-fired power station, called *Moneypoint — Power from Coal*. But it was a great achievement to make government films with actors. In *Voyage to Recovery* and so on we had real Abbey actors and a lot of humour. So they were not all dull, straightforward, government films. But all the films I produced got commercial distribution.

I've also done commercials but I hate them. I have to be near the bread-line before I do a commercial. I can't stand them. All these hangers-on and advertising agencies with thirty-five people for lunch, everyone eating fillet steak from the clapper-loader to the director. And every shot is taken ten times from different angles because no-one can make up his mind, or have a proper script written. It's awful.

You made a film about De Valera, Portrait of a Statesman. *What impression did you get of the man?*

De Valera was a very interesting character. He checked everything. He wouldn't say anything which could be proved afterwards wasn't true. I remember I sent the script to his secretary — he couldn't read anymore then; he was ill in Linden in Blackrock. One morning the phone rings and he said that his secretary had read the script — De Valera would never say that you were marvellous; the best you'd get was 'not bad' — and he asked me to come and see him to discuss a few small points.

One concerned the opening of the film. We show the skyline of Manhattan and then a steamer coming in to Cobh in the Cork harbour. Over this we say that De Valera was born in New York, the father died and the mother couldn't make a living and the boy was sent back to Ireland. And on this foggy, misty morning the liner pulled in and the boy De Valera returned to Ireland. Of course there are not so many liners coming in anymore!

So the only liner that came in I went down to Cork to film and it was a misty morning. De Valera said, "Look, I remember, it must have been eight-five years ago, and it was not misty, it was sunny." So I said, "Mr President, this is poetic licence. We couldn't say it was a sunny morning when in the camera the film says it is a misty morning."

I believe you also made another film about De Valera?

Yes. NBC made a series, *The Wise Men of Our Time.* The first film was about Bertrand Russell, the second about De Valera. The film was to be in an interview fashion and we had a professor from Trinity College asking questions. There were contracts and I think they paid $5000;

De Valera said he didn't want the money and that it should be given to schools here. The contract said, 'This is a contract between the National Broadcasting Company of America, hereinafter called the producer, and Mr Eamon De Valera, hereinafter called the performer' and so on.

Paddy O'Hanrahan, who was the Press Secretary to the Government, called me in and said, "Look, I don't know if you can save this but De Valera's not going to do it because of the wording of the contract."

So I had to go in and see him. De Valera said, "Do they think I am a tightrope dancer or what?" I explained that this contract was a standard form and written by an office girl who probably had no idea who you were! I suggested that he should get the Attorney-General's office to write a new contract on his terms, which I was certain would be accepted by New York, and to have a clause inserted that the film had to be approved by him, before transmission. So all went well and I still have this film.

But my greatest experience was to have worked with the late John Huston. I first met him when he directed *Moby Dick* and had the privilege to work as a second-unit on this film. To watch him direct was most interesting. He was not only a great director but a very pleasant man on set or privately. I later made a half-hour documentary about Ireland called *Return to the Island* and he kindly introduced the film and appeared in the opening sequence with his daughter, Anjelica. For the editing of *Moby Dick* he hired my movieola, so I had the opportunity of watching him direct the editing, which in itself was a fascinating experience.

Interview with Neil Jordan

How did you first become interested in writing film scripts?

I was writing novels and short stories that were very strongly influenced by film. I also read a lot of French novelists of the early 1960s — Alain Robbe-Grillet, Marguerite Duras and so on - who made a strong impression on me and I started to write scripts. I wrote three television plays; only one was made — *Night in Tunisia* by Pat O'Connor which was done quite beautifully. I wrote a television series on the life of Sean O'Casey and *Traveller* for Joe Comerford both of which I was very unhappy with because they didn't bear any relation to my scripts. So I began to direct because I wanted my scripts done correctly.

Your films have an obsession with the theme of unconventional love — Danny for the deaf mute, little red riding hood for the wolf and George for the high-class prostitute who turns out to be a lesbian. Would you agree with this?

I suppose the films are recreations of certain adolescent ideas about sensuality and emotion. They all have bruised innocent females, cripples in a way. They are all basically about the clash between the real world and the world of imagination and unreality, the conflict between dreams and reality. The constant concern is to do with realistic and surrealistic explanations of human behaviour and whether human beings answer to rational modes of thought or are inspired by things quite irrational and unknown to themselves.

Before John Boorman produced Angel, *you worked with him on* Excalibur *and directed a documentary about its making. What influence have his films had on you?*

Neil Jordan was born in 1951. He has written several novels and collections of short stories, including *The Dream of a Beast, Night in Tunisia and other stories* and *The Past*. His career in the cinema began with a documentary about the making of John Boorman's *Excalibur* in 1981; the following year he made his feature début, *Angel*. His next two films, *The Company of Wolves* (1984) and *Mona Lisa* (1986), were both further critical successes. We talked to him as he prepared his new film, *High Spirits*.

John was the only person in Ireland at the time who had any connection with serious narrative film-making and those were the kind of scripts I was writing and wanted to get involved with. I wouldn't say his films are a particularly strong influence on me; I think the level of the fantastic in his films and his insistence on a mystical and imaginary explanation of human behaviour are important.

In Angel *why did you avoid making any direct political comment?*

I wanted to make a film with the barest possible facts about Northern Ireland and concentrate on the most grotesque and simple of issues — what it means to kill another human being. I wanted to remove from the film any explanation of that fact which was beyond the fact itself. I wanted to make a film about the very unintellectual, mindless appeal of the destruction of human life. Danny becomes less feeling as he goes along and he turns into a clone, a numb person, a person without a soul.

A sense of landscape and location seems central in Angel. *Is this true?*

Yes. The whole film was shot around landscapes in Southern Ireland that I knew very well and had written about in my stories; the sense of place was very strong. In fact it's one of the main pieces of design of the film.

How important is the contribution of the cinematographer to your films?

It's very important. I look for a certain level of theatricality and for somebody who is willing to use colour and light and shade in a way that is consciously unrealistic.

Is it too simple to categorise The Company of Wolves *as a horror movie? Do you have strong generic distinctions when you start to make a film?*

I think one of the pleasures of film-making nowadays is that you can break the generic codes of movie-making. Each of my films has done that to a certain extent. I always conceived *Angel* as a musical — I wanted to light it like a musical, with the same type of colours. It should have certain elements in the design and photography that you connect with Stanley Donen musicals.

I like a certain tension between the genre within which one is working and what one is doing to it, and also between the film and the audience expectations of the genre — in a thriller they don't expect the central character to play the saxophone, for instance, or for it to be lit in candy-floss colours. Similarly in *The Company of Wolves* one doesn't expect in a horror film the lyricism of the young girl's emotional life.

Do you welcome script collaboration or do you find you have to make certain sacrifices?

It is something I'm trying to avoid more and more because as you make more films you realise the more collaborative they are on the script and the basic decisions of narrative structure, the less pure the films are. It just gets confused. It's not me talking to the producer, it's me and the other writers talking; they may not be there in the conversation but they are in the background.

High Spirits was written with three other writers and I find I get constantly persuaded to collaborate with others — in this case because there are so many main characters — and therefore different

American writers get involved and I end up rewriting a lot. There is a certain richness that comes through in the end but I'm getting a bit impatient with the method.

A sense of violence runs through your films. Danny's journey of vengeance is violent; violence is a constant threat in The Company of Wolves *and in* Mona Lisa, *where it punctuates the end of Simone's journey. Are you interested in representing violence?*

Yes. It's the thought of death and of the injury to others — the whole moral question of that is quite an obsession with me. There is also a certain kind of release in conceiving a violent act or in depicting violence. It's something that I find to my alarm I'm very good at. The sequence in *Mona Lisa* where Simone shoots everybody — we shot the entire scene in an afternoon. I find it very easy to generate the emotions in everybody and work out how to get the best effect from the shots and so on.

What I like to do is play with very extreme contrasts: I don't think that the sequence would have worked if she hadn't shot Michael Caine in the foot first. He hops backwards and he's laughing and it's ridiculous. The audience is laughing and the last thing they expect to see is for him to get really blasted.

Can you explain the significance of the white rabbit?

The white rabbit was put in because there was a certain hole in the story. Why has George come back? Why has he been away for ten years? What do these mates owe him? Did they do a bullion robbery together? To me the story wasn't about any of those issues yet there was a need to explain them. So I gave George a white rabbit and that was the starting-point and a link. It was a private joke in a way, a sort of MacGuffin.

You co-wrote Mona Lisa *with David Leland. How did you work together?*

David wrote the script before he wrote *Personal Services*. I was filming *Company* and hadn't time to write a first draft. I needed somebody to work with who knew the London environment well. David wrote a very hard, tough, angry script which was not what I had intended. I sat down with my original three-page outline and his script and wrote it.

In Mona Lisa *would you acknowledge the influence of Scorsese and in particular* Taxi Driver?

No, I wouldn't see that. I see it more like an operatic moral tale, more like *Carmen*. I was very nervous of the fact that it might be seen as a driver going round with some sort of obsession of immorality and that was something I didn't want to relate to in the film at all. *Taxi Driver* is a very complex movie and it's really about the absence of any moral paradigms. It's about a man who goes mad; I'd rather make a film about a man who was sane, saner than other people even though he was a simpleton. George is based on various criminal types I came across when I was doing manual and labouring jobs in London.

You are acting as an executive producer on Cityvision's The Courier. *What is that about and how did you become involved?*

It's a thriller set in Dublin and which is very local in its references and depictions; it's a bit like a piece of Italian Neorealism. It's a lovely script, so local and delightful and that's what will make it

Cityvision — Frank Deasy, Joe Lee and Hilary McLoughlin on the set of The Courier

work. The two directors, Frank Deasy and Joe Lee, were going to do it on 16mm on a budget of £200 000. They showed me the script, which I thought was great. I showed it to Stephen Woolley and Nik Powell at Palace and they got involved and we quadrupled the budget. The way I view it is that I have certain relationships that I have built up in England and contacts with avenues of finance that they and other Irish film-makers might not have. Because there was such aggression to me when I did *Angel*, I was anxious to do whatever I could to help.

Does it worry you that as you become more successful you will be forced into 'larger' films with bigger budgets and 'star' names?

In the best of all possible worlds I'd like to be able do both small-budget and big-budget films. But I'd be perfectly content to make small films the rest of my life: films that were released in London, New York, Los Angeles and two or three other big cities.

Do you regard your new film, High Spirits, *at $12 million as a small film?*

No, but if you want to deal with large canvasses and large, fantastic images and environments, you need a lot of money. And then you have to make a popular film that is going to work in a popular market place. But there's a small film I want to make at the moment called *The Miracle*, involving three actors which I would shoot at my house in Bray in Ireland. It would cost about £800 000 on a six-week shoot. I'd like to film my Michael Collins script which would cost about $20 million. Another film I want to do is called *Red Harvest* which would also cost about $20 million. But there are other films that I want to do which would cost nearly next to nothing. I'd like to make a series of films about Irish history and Irish politics.

What is High Spirits *about?*

It's a necrophiliac comedy with Peter O'Toole and Daryl Hannah. It involves a lot of effects and fantasy sequences. It's really a farce, a sort of large-scale Oscar Wilde or Feydeau or Molière farce, involving confusions between people, mismatched couples falling in love with other people — half the people they fall in love with are dead.

The film is set totally in Ireland and yet you are not making the film there. How do you react to accusations that you have abandoned the film-making scene in Ireland?

I wrote the script with the intention of actually making the entire picture in Ireland, hoping I would get some Irish and American finance. I'm now only doing a few locations there. Because I couldn't make any of the tax breaks work or get any financial involvement at all, I had to make progressively less and less of it there. If I get some finance that will enable me to make more of it there I will.

As for abandoning the Irish scene, well, I was kind of thrown out. The reason I went to England to make *Company* was because the reaction to my making *Angel* in Ireland was so vicious there, both from critics and from my peers. It's really odd; I couldn't understand it at the time. I think it was really that I had never directed a film before. It's something I just want to forget about and go back there and make films.

So no, I don't feel I've abandoned the Irish film scene at all. I see myself as an Irish film-maker and as an Irish writer. I'm very specifically Irish; I live there. One of the reasons I was so anxious to work with Cityvision on *The Courier* was to show that with a good script and a director who has got a visual eye and quite a lot of talent a small-budget movie can be put together very simply. I would love to help Irish directors put together the kind of financial packages they need to make movies. If a script like *The Courier* came along again I'd do exactly the same thing. It's just that I'm very intolerant of a certain kind of stupidity about Irish public life that goes on — in-fighting and factionalisation. I just have no patience whatsoever, so I don't deal with it. There's a particular viciousness in Ireland that you don't meet elsewhere.

Did the success of Angel *alienate you from people in Ireland?*

Yes it did, very much so.

Do you regret that?

No. Well, it's inevitable, what can I do? It's a tendency in Irish life which is a bit more extreme than it is in Britain.

How do you see the future of the Irish film industry?

There is a film industry there. Most of it is being financed and will continue to be financed by British television. Irish Governments have traditionally been penny-pinching and mealy-mouthed with regard to the arts. I don't think the Government's attitude towards film is any different than it is, say, towards theatre or music. It hasn't become more successful abroad because the films haven't been made. How many ninety-minute 35mm feature films that could be distributed abroad have been made in Ireland in the last ten years? Three? *Angel, Eat the Peach, Anne Devlin.* And now *The Courier* which I'm sure will be successful. I think there's every hope for Irish film-making as long as feature films are made.

Probably because I write scripts I've been able to cross the divide that most Irish film-makers haven't been able to do; I'd like to help other directors to do that because it is generally very easy to do. I think that once *The Courier* is released Joe Lee and Frank Deasy will have multiple opportunities to make films over the next few years. The tragedy is that they won't be able to work with enough freedom and financial backup in their native country.

Interview with Louis Marcus

Louis Marcus was born in Cork in 1936. After graduating from the National University of Ireland he became active in the Cork Film Society, and founded and edited *Guth na Scannán*, the periodical of the Irish Film Society. In 1967 his controversial pamphlet entitled *The Irish Film Industry* was published in the *Irish Times*. He began working professionally in films in 1958 and directed his first film, *The Silent Art*, in 1959. Since then he has made almost fifty documentaries which have won eighteen international festival awards including prizes at Berlin, Moscow, London and Chicago, as well as two Academy Award nominations. He was elected to the Academy of Motion Picture Art & Sciences in 1974.

At the start of your career you were involved in the early Irish Film Society. Can you tell me about that?

I first went to the Irish Film Society in Cork in the early 1950s when I was sixteen — lying that my age was eighteen — and the first film I saw there was *Stagecoach*. Then French classics, Japanese, Swedish and so on; I was completely bowled over. Then I very quickly joined the Film Society Committee and began to write articles about 'cinema'. I founded the journal of the Cork Film Society which became the Irish Film Society journal until it eventually folded.

The Cork Film Society was run by a fascinating group centered around intellectuals such as Sean Hendrick and Seamus Murphy, the sculptor. They were the intimates of Frank O'Connor and Seán Ó Faoláin, who had of course left the country at that stage. They were an independent, anti-establishment group at odds with the Church and with the very narrow conservatism of Ireland at the time. They were a highly stimulating group and I spent virtually all my spare time with them. They had discussion groups and were against pretentiousness.

There were also members such as Paudie Collins who had made amateur films of a good standard and I started to make 8mm films with them. I then went to university but spent summers in London. Through the Cork Film Festival I became friendly with a lot of film people, particularly the late Francis Koval, a film critic and a wonderful person, who took me to press shows in London.

Your first job was working with George Morrison on Mise Éire. *How did that come about?*

An organisation called Gael-Linn was

formed in the 1950s. It was a resurgence of the movement for the revival of the Irish language as the vehicle of Irish cultural identity. But unlike the earlier movements, such as the Gaelic League at the turn of the century, Gael-Linn was very modern and exciting in its outlook, a young university graduate organisation. It had commissioned George Morrison to make feature-length actuality documentaries of the incredible store of material on Ireland which he had discovered all over Europe. I was selected to be his assistant on *Mise Éire* and some of the preliminary editing of *Saoirse?*

I stayed from November 1958 until about April 1959, absorbing the excitement of working on 35mm. I also came into contact with Peter Hunt's recording studio, which was a real institution in Irish film-making for so many years, and where I learned so much.

What was Morrison like to work with?

He was a rather flamboyant creature whose expression was peppered with French phrases, a man of enormous musical knowledge and sensitivity, and a most accurate and melodious whistler! He had perfected a method of whistling inwards and outwards without any change in the tone colour so that he could whistle the whole of a Bach fugue without interruption. He belonged also to a generation of Trinity College students that were colourfully Bohemian, intellectual and European-minded.

I also came into closer contact at the end with Sean O Riada who was commissioned to write the music. I became very friendly with him and he subsequently wrote the music for a number of my films.

How did your first film as director come about?

I went back to Cork and realised that I would never be commissioned to direct a film unless I actually made one first. So I borrowed a camera from my Film Society friends, bought some black-and-white 16mm film through a chemist who got it for me wholesale and got £250 from my mother and made a film on Seamus Murphy called *The Silent Art*. I now shudder at its crudeness. I blew it up to 35mm, showed it at the Cork Film Festival in 1959 and subsequently got fairly good distribution around Ireland as a cinema short.

At the very start of 1960, *Mise Éire* was ready for commercial release and Gael-Linn wanted a trailer. George was out of the country and because I was familiar with the material and had made *The Silent Art*, I was asked to do it by Bob Mac Góráin at Gael-Linn. That led from one thing to another and I made some instructional films on hurling and Gaelic football: I felt that these sports were among the major passions of the Irish people and that they should not be made on 16mm for clubs but on 35mm for cinemas. That's how I got established.

You then left Ireland for a period. Why was that?

I was living in Dublin at the time and like very many young Irish people I felt a very, very severe need to get out of the country. Eventually, because I'm Jewish and because of my interest in the attempt to revive the Irish language, I went to Israel to learn Hebrew and to explore the Israeli film industry.

I was there from November 1963 to April 1964. While I was there, fortuitously, the Israeli Government had persuaded Carl Foreman, the American film-maker, to run an extensive course in scriptwriting for film and I was able to get into the course. It was fascinating: from that course has stemmed all that has happened in the Israeli film industry since.

I found it impossible, however, to get work in Israel and it was a very difficult industry to break into, especially for someone from overseas. Then I heard that Gael-Linn had raised the money through the Government for *Rhapsody of a River*, so I returned to Ireland.

What was your experience on that film?

It was a great disappointment. Sean O Riada had written the music which I had fallen in love with and which I had wanted to use for a film. It was going to be our idea of a very romantic, Richard Strauss-type of Cork which we had both experienced. It ended up under an inter-departmental committee under what was then the Department of External Affairs. It didn't work out since everyone had to have something: a bit of agriculture, a bit of electricity, a bit of industry and so on. Technically it is a beautifully shot film, the music is gorgeous and it allowed me to improve my editing skills. But it is totally and absolutely without heart.

That film was the first time you worked with cameraman Robert Monks. How did you meet?

Peter Hunt recommended him to me because he had just shot and edited *The One Nighters* which was a stunningly shot film. Bob is a man who hasn't sung his own praises in an industry where you are expected to do that and so he hasn't got the recognition he deserves. He is a most accomplished and versatile cameraman from whom I've learned an enormous amount. We've worked very closely and very well ever since.

In 1966 you made a film about the Easter Rising. How did you approach that?

Because the fiftieth anniversary of the 1916 Rising was imminent, I persuaded Gael-Linn that we should ask for film sponsorship from the 1916 Commemoration Committee which the Government had set up. At that time, before the present Northern "troubles", it was still respectable to celebrate Ireland's fight for freedom in a suitably ritualistic and sentimental fashion. When in the 1980s I came to do a centenary film on the birth of Pearse, the attitude had changed completely because of the grave ambiguities that "the troubles" in the North have now cast over this earlier and supposedly heroic period.

There was an annual grant available to Gael-Linn from the Department of the Gaeltacht which meant that for eight or nine years — until Gael-Linn lost the grant in the early 1970s — I was making a documentary a year. We started with *Fleadh Ceoil*, a film on the traditional folk music weekend festival, which won a Silver Bear at Berlin and three other awards.

Effectively the action lasted two and a half days. I wanted to capture the enormous spontaneity and enjoyment of the occasion. We needed three camera units. Bobbie Monks shot two thirds of the film, the synched and music material, while the other cameramen shot some of the social and human side. It was very intensive work, the editing was very complex but enjoyable and the end-result was successful.

Apparently at the Moscow Festival where we got a Certificate of Merit there was a great review in *Pravda*. It was most ironic to see ourselves being held up as an example to the Russian film industry of how to capture realistically the life of the people! We did a number of these films; two of them with English language versions got international distribution through United Artists — *Woes of Golf*, a comedy, was distributed with one of the Bond films in England.

How did you approach Pearse in the 1980s?

It was the last occasion that any Government in Ireland has celebrated any of these nationalistic centenaries at all — they just ignore them completely now. It was very difficult to make because one had to do something which was not the old chauvinistic, rhetorical rubbish, and which would not celebrate physical force and yet would be a fitting tribute.

I read everything that he wrote — a couple of million words. People who know Pearse only by his collected speeches — which were really the drum-beating, rabble-rousing recruiting speeches leading up to the Rising — don't know anything about the man. I discovered a man of broad vision, a liberal who clashed strongly with the Church and won on some crucial issues, one who had no time for chauvinism. He was not for an exclusivist, Gaelic Ireland but wanted independence in the sense of an ability to develop the best in this country and absorb the best in every other country — an ideal, I'm afraid, which everybody has fallen very far short of since.

I decided to let Pearse speak for himself; John Kavanagh played him, with lots of stills of the period interspersed. It had a very muted reception. Some critics even wondered whether Pearse could have said all these things: it didn't sound like the blood-thirsty, rabble-rousing Nationalist that he has now come to be seen as!

Can you tell me about Children at Work?

The idea for that film arose because my wife is a kindergarten teacher. It was a wonderful subject: audiences love children and it was utterly visual. We shot it in three schools: one upper class, one middle class and one in this wonderful school for itinerants or tinker children who were by far the most inventive. They used to create visual puns with the play equipment which were almost Chaplinesque. We put the tripod on wheels so we could move around inconspicuously. The first day we didn't put any film in the camera because we knew we were going to be the object of everyone's attention. After that we shot within about three or four feet of the kids and they took no notice at all.

What is your attitude towards Gaelic and English versions of your films?

The English versions were only for overseas distribution. We established a convention where we could use English on the soundtrack for an Irish audience provided it was 'actuality' English — ie the teacher in the playschool. I worked throughout with Breandán Ó hEithir who wrote the commentaries in Irish; he was marvellous. Certainly anyone who understood Irish got a big bonus from these commentaries. It was a great challenge to do that sort of thing; it forced you to be visual but it did restrict you to subjects which were virtually self-explanatory or self-justifying.

It was a yeasty period in Ireland — things were opening up, censorship was going out, ideas were flooding in, the economy was on a boom, and the interest in the past was great — it was a crest of a wave really for everybody. You couldn't produce that kind of film, or recreate the innocence and optimism of that period now. It was marvellous.

In 1967 you wrote a series of controversial and influential articles in the Irish Times. *You then served on the Irish Film Industry Committee under John Huston. What was Huston like to work with?*

All kinds of things were beginning to be discussed seriously, principally in the *Irish Times*. Michael Viney was doing all these tremendous investigative series. It was actually Robert Monks and Peter Hunt who suggested I write the film series. It was a period when you felt things were going to happen and Ireland was going to grow up and become a modern, sensible, adult community. I wrote the articles and then got a call from John Huston who asked me to come and see him. He was living in Ireland at the time and was an Irish citizen, and had acquired the mantle of the saviour of Irish film. He then made an appeal to Jack Lynch, having invited him to the set of his film at Ardmore, and the Irish Film Industry Committee was formed, with Huston as chairman. I was a member.

The story of that committee remains to be told and it is a fascinating one. Huston was terribly sentimental in his whole approach. His summing up of Ireland's potential for film was to say, "When you stop someone on the road for directions here, he gives you a story!" I don't want to knock Huston — he was a wonderful film-maker — but because he emerged from a highly organised Hollywood industry he hadn't the faintest idea about how to develop an industry infrastructurally and one which was in its infancy.

Huston's idea was that we would write a page in about three weeks, send it in to the Government and it was all over. We said that this was not what we had in mind: we were going to do research and put in a totally reasoned document. The crux came when Huston said, "If you're going to have any reference to documentaries, I'm resigning." And twelve of us on the committee said, "If there's no reference to documentaries, we're resigning first." So Huston caved in. After that we didn't see an awful lot of

him; I think he was shooting on the continent. He was going through a bad period: he had left America in the post-McCarthy atmosphere and he wanted to be an artist so he was making all these self-consciously artistic, 'European' films. I remember after he had visited Bergman in Sweden Huston came back and said, "There he was with a crew of sixteen and here am I shooting on a Wicklow hillside with 250 people." I didn't like to tell him that the kind of film he made required 250 people!

The committee's report came out, was accepted by the Government, had its first reading in the Dáil and was about to go through when the 1970 Arms Crisis occurred. In the musical chairs that followed, George Colley was moved as minister from Industry and Commerce and a new minister appointed; I don't know if he had ever seen the inside of a cinema. That was the end; I opted out of the campaign — with a sore head from hammering it against the brick wall. I couldn't afford the time and effort needed and I had fallen behind with my film projects.

Have things changed since the 1960s for the better and how do you see the present film-making climate?

It's so often a question of money. What is the ceiling for a full-length film? Bob Quinn says it's £100 000. But often it goes up to £250 000. Strongbow is the only real film production company in the ongoing sense, working for the outside market but not distorting Ireland. But that requires a kind of entrepreneurial and financial flair which John Kelleher and David Collins have. The example at the new Ardmore of Morgan O'Sullivan — a very energetic and capable businessman — of producing material for network and major television distribution in the United States is an

124

Louis Marcus filming The Heritage of Ireland

incredible achievement. But I don't think it's an example for anybody else to copy because it relies solely on the unique abilities of the man himself. I don't think he realises how unique and outstanding he is.

So you are left with the mass of fiction independents, with some wonderful young people coming up, such as Fergus Tighe who made *Clash of the Ash*, but they do not earn a living. They are usually without the large responsibilities of family and mortgages and they live most frugally; some of them earn money teaching, but it's an appalling existence and it relies totally on their devotion and commitment. I couldn't go into that now — there's no way I could pay the bills.

So while an awful lot has happened, all to the good and improving all the time, financially and infrastructurally we still have not reached a normal healthy situation. We are still in this awful predicament where we are an English-speaking country — which in cinema terms means aiming at the American majors — but we suffer from the old Irish

syndrome that you are a failure unless you make it in America. In any case, even the recent advances are now imperilled by the Government's abolition of the Film Board.

How do you see the documentary film-maker starting out now in Ireland?

The future is in television, where Radio Telefís Éireann is now commissioning much more work from independents, and the growing corporate area. Hopefully these will provide a breeding ground for the film-makers of the future. The sponsored film is still not being used in Ireland to anything like a fraction of what it should be compared to the rest of the world. What is happening now is an upsurge in video sponsorship — corporate video. There has been a mushrooming of companies producing these in Ireland, mostly here in Dublin, and some are very good and professional.

But I wouldn't recommend anybody to go into film. But if you're crazy about it, you'll ignore advice and go into it anyway. And if you're crazy enough, you might even succeed!

Interview with Robert Monks

Robert Monks is a Dubliner and began his film career in the National Film Institute of Ireland (now the Irish Film Institute). In 1955, after a period of training in England, he left to freelance, principally as a lighting cameraman. Since then he has worked on a wide variety of features, television series, documentaries and commercials in many parts of the world. He has worked closely with Louis Marcus, having photographed all his films since *Rhapsody of a River* in 1965. He received a Gold Camera Award for Photography at the 1975 United States Television Commercials Festival, is a Fellow of the Royal Photographic Society and a past Chairman of the Society of Independent Film-Makers and of the Film Producers Association.

When did you begin working in films?

I began 'dabbling' in films in the late 1940s. I was interested in still photography and amateur drama and through these I became involved in the Irish Film Society and the National Film Institute. There were various films made by these societies, all on 16mm and silent and usually in black-and-white. From time to time I was asked to help out on other people's films. I became very interested in camerawork and usually photographed or assisted the cameraman on these films. It was, of course, all amateur film-making; nobody got paid.

The *Little Willie* film is a good example of the kind of film-making in which I and many others were involved. A friend of mine, Donal Shanahan, was asked by a member of a fund-raising committee to make a film. The committee was endeavouring to raise money to build an extension to an orthopaedic hospital in Baldoyle run by the Irish Sisters of Charity, an order of nuns. One of the patients was a little boy named Willie and it was decided to feature him in the film, to show the kind of work the Sisters were doing and to show how donations would help him.

I wasn't involved in the photography; Shanahan was a very good cameraman. The film was intended to be shown in cinemas with a collection box in the foyer so that patrons could give something to the fund on their way out.

To show the film in cinemas meant it had to be on 35mm; we had only 16mm cameras so it was shot on 16mm and blown up to 35mm in English laboratories. It also needed a soundtrack, with music, effects and commentary, which was a problem. Peter Hunt Recording Studios may have had a tape recorder, I'm not sure. I do know that there were very few, even in the United Kingdom, and very expensive and even if Peter Hunt had had one we couldn't have afforded it, since all we were getting was the cost of materials. Shanahan also had a disc recorder, a Neumann I think, so we decided to do it on disc — all the effects and the music of a pipe and drum band.

Cyril Cusack had agreed to speak the commentary. The nuns of the hospital also had a school and they gave us the use of some classrooms. Since we were all working in other jobs, we went down to Baldoyle one Sunday and set up. We had a 16mm Bell and Howell projector for running the film. We had twin record turntables — for running the discs with the music and effects. And we had the Neumann Disc-Cutter. We set these up in one classroom and in an adjoining classroom we put Cyril Cusack. There was a door with glass panels between the two classrooms and he could see the projected picture through it.

Shanahan, who was operating the disc-cutting machine, ran a test and we were horrified to find that because the classroom was so big and high Cyril sounded as if he was in a cathedral. We borrowed some screens and blankets from the hospital which worked perfectly. (Years later I was to find that most proper recording studios had a somewhat improved version of this which they called a commentary booth. It goes to prove that you can sometimes hit on a correct solution to a problem by chance.)

The other problem was that the 10" discs running at 78 rpm gave only three minutes of recording time, so we had to divide a twenty-minute film into seven segments with 'natural' breaks. We did this and finally got everything running. I looked after the projector and changed the discs on the turntable which wasn't running. Someone else cued in the discs and faded them in and out, Shanahan

controlled the recording and Cyril watched from his tent and spoke the commentary as only he can. When one three-minute take was OK we went to the next section and so on. It was a long and nerve-wracking day.

When all this was finished, film and discs were sent to a London laboratory: the discs had to be transferred to optical track, the three-minute sections joined up so that the breaks weren't too obvious and also to be in synch with the picture. We were doing this kind of thing well into the 1950s, although by then we had tape recorders which would run much longer and would stay more or less in sync.

When you were working in this very ad hoc way did you feel that you were isolated? Did you have a vision of an industry taking off?

We didn't have a vision of a film industry; we had a vision of ourselves trying to do something we passionately wanted to do. I wanted to be a cameraman and to photograph films; therefore everything I did was that little bit more experience.

I think some of us realised that because of the small population and the cost of making films in those days (largely because, for a feature film, studios were essential then) we were never likely to have a native feature film industry. We were happy to settle for a documentary industry. But I certainly wasn't thinking that far ahead. I felt, if I gained experience and proved that I could photograph a film, somehow the opportunity would come and there I would be.

So how did you make a living at this time?

I was working in the statistics department at Dunlop Rubber - that was how I earned my living. I wasn't married; I was living with my parents. Living in Dublin was very cheap: seats in the Abbey and Gate Theatres cost one shilling and admission to cinemas cost the same. So I had a regular diet of theatre and cinema, kept dabbling at film-making whenever I had the opportunity and talked to like-minded enthusiasts about how we would do this scene or that and where and with what!

A job came up at the National Film Institute at the end of the 1940s and I got it. I was described as a technician: the principal job was to show 16mm films in schools and halls everywhere and anywhere. We had a van, a 16mm projector, screens and a small generator. The last was essential because many rural areas were without electricity. In addition I was to photograph any 16mm films that the Institute was making, lecture at courses for teachers on using audio-visual aids in education organised by the Institute, and contribute to a bulletin issued by the Institute.

Dr Noel Browne had become Minister for Health at this time and was very keen on using film as a medium for health education, and at one time we had four units from the Institute going around the country to schools during the day, and to a village hall at night, showing various films.

The Department of Agriculture, under James Dillon, also had a series of screenings of farming films to Young Farmers Clubs. Schools had educational film shows for pupils. The County Dublin Libraries Committee showed educational and cultural films in their libraries. Many priests, in an attempt to bring some form of entertainment — not to say culture — to their parishioners, ran film shows in the parish hall. One film that I frequently showed was *Man of Aran*, which made me somewhat critical.

What do you think of Flaherty's film?

I don't have any feelings as to the accuracy, honesty or integrity of it, just that it was about forty minutes too long! At about an hour, for the period and allowing for the problems they had, it would have been quite good. Most of it was shot on a Newman Sinclair camera which wasn't the most flexible of animals. It was clockwork driven and ran a 200-feet magazine of film, roughly two minutes. At the time the viewfinder seemed adequate but with the advent of cameras with the mirror shutter reflex system, such as the Arriflex or Cameflex, it was clearly primitive.

The camera was like a biscuit tin in shape and size but not in weight. The lens was in the centre of one of the narrow sides. The viewfinder was in the top right-hand corner, so straightaway there was a problem of parallax. This was overcome by having the viewfinder eyepiece mounted on a movable plate which could be set against a graduated scale to compensate for the parallax error. You guessed how far you were from the subject and adjusted the viewfinder and hoped for the best. You needed to allow an extra bit on the picture to cover any errors in calculation.

What about focussing?

The focussing was even worse. You could guess or measure the distance and set it on the lens calibration or you could use the reflex focussing attachment. Using this meant pushing a button to clear the shutter to a certain position, inserting a contraption like a small periscope, pushing it home, opening up the aperture, holding the camera steady, focussing and then repeating everything in reverse, in order to get the camera filming again.

How long were you at the National Film Institute?

For about seven years. I made a number of 16mm films for them, mainly I think on ceremonies. I filmed several ordination ceremonies of priests, reception ceremonies of nuns, commemorations of events such as the 1798 rebellion, Corpus Christi processions and the like. I also made some training films for use in the various courses given by the Institute.

I also spent a couple of weeks in Sligo with George Fleischmann when he was photographing *W B Yeats: A Tribute* in 1950. He had a 35mm Arriflex camera and he talked to me a great deal about it and his work. I also learned how to do a tracking shot at that time. He was shooting Yeats's grave in Drumcliffe churchyard and he wanted the headstones to move through the frame until the camera came to a stop on Yeats's headstone. We didn't have a dolly; I doubt if there was one in the country. Anyhow he was trying to do it as a panning shot and it was not working. There was another problem in that the sun was shining on the back of Yeats's headstone. It is a large stone and we really needed a large reflector.

Fleischmann was in despair when a friend of his, Kevin Murray, came along to see what we were doing. Kevin was a director in a timber and builders providers in Sligo. He had a light aircraft which he used to land on one of the beaches there. He had a 16mm Bolex camera which he regularly dismantled. He raced in trials cars. He also had a very big Ford car, enormous for those days — there were only about four of them in the country. He heard of our problems and said, "I may be able to help you, give me a few minutes".

Off he went and returned towing a four-wheeled trailer, several planks and a large sheet of aluminium. We laid the planks on the gravel, levelled them up and put the trailer on them with the tripod, camera and Fleischmann. Kevin Murray held the reflector, I pushed the 'dolly',

Fleischmann operated the camera and the tracking shot was done. Symbolic of the early Irish film industry!

What happened after 1955?

To explain that I have to go back a couple of years. Since 1948 the Film Institute had been making ten-minute films of the All-Ireland Hurling and Football Finals for cinema distribution. I was a sort of general assistant on one in about 1949 but I wasn't asked to work on any others, I don't know why. George Fleischmann was always one of the cameramen; various others were on the second camera, usually someone from London. However, in 1953 the then-secretary of the Film Institute, Sean O'Sullivan, had left.

George Fleischmann wasn't available and the job of organising the whole thing was tossed over to me at a week's notice. We had no 35mm cameras, except Fleischmann's in the country. He was using it, so cameras had to be got from London. I was very lucky, I got Brendan Stafford as second camera and although he was a Dublin man he had been living and working as a well-known feature lighting cameraman in London. He was available, would fly over and would hire and bring with him two 35mm cameras. I had known him slightly before this, but we became very friendly as I had to go to London with the film of the finals to have it processed, edited, commentary recorded and so on. He was impressed with my camerawork and asked why I didn't come to London for training.

There was no training school in the United Kingdom at that time and I couldn't see how I could be trained. He said that he might be able to arrange for me to go as an observer of film production on some future project. I told the chairman of the Film Institute of this and he put it to the council, who agreed that if they could be satisfied with the terms of such an arrangement they would send me to London for about six months.

In 1954 Brendan was working on a series called *Fabian of the Yard* at Alliance Film Studios, Twickenham and he organised the whole thing for me. So I studied with him, went to editing, sound recording, other studios, laboratories and began to get an inkling of what a film industry is all about. Of course I came back at the end of 1954 full of what I had learned and expecting to get some encouragement in film-making.

But it gradually became clear that the Institute, having kept its promise to send me for training, had no intention of doing anything further and if I remained I would spend the rest of my life doing what I had been doing for the last seven years. My wife and I talked it over; the 1950s were not the best time economically in Ireland.

Then I had a stroke of luck. Gordon Lewis had been the Pathé News cameraman in Ireland (as well as manager of Pathé Film Distributors). He died and his son, whom I knew, offered to sell me his father's Newman Sinclair 35mm camera. I borrowed the money and bought it. I told the new Secretary of the Institute in expectation that with a 35mm camera they would feel I should be making films on their behalf. Their answer wasn't encouraging, so I left. Strictly speaking, therefore, and after a long preamble I entered the industry as a freelance in 1955.

Have there been any political figures you have had to negotiate with over filming?

Yes. In the 1950s and early 1960s, before the advent of Radio Telefís Éireann and before politicians were aware of the proper power of television, Irish politicians were hesitant about appearing in front of the cameras. They didn't mind you filming them at some official function, most of the time, but they were slow to agree to be interviewed. One such time meant that for the only time in my life I was the reporter.

It happened in 1957 during a General Election. I was a "stringer" cameraman for CBS News and I was working with one of their London-based crews, Cyril Bliss and Frank Binney. The correspondent was Alexander Kendrick. We were doing the usual things — election meetings, posters, vox opos, interview with Eamon De Valera, who at that time was out of office and leader of the Opposition.

The Taoiseach was John A Costello of Fine Gael and we had been trying to set up an interview with him for days but he was proving very elusive. The crew was staying at the Gresham Hotel and one morning we had been filming around town, got back to the hotel for lunch, Kendrick had another appointment and went off to it. There was no word from Costello.

At about 2.30 a phone message came that Costello would be interviewed in his office at 3.00. We couldn't find Kendrick and in the end I got to do the interview — I wasn't on camera. I began by saying, "Mr Costello, if you get back to office, what do you propose doing about such and such?" He glared at me and said, "I would like you to rephrase that question before I answer it." Now he was a very eminent lawyer and I wondered what awful grammatical howler I had committed. So I said, "What do you mean?" To which he said, "Would you kindly say, 'When you get back... ' ".

Which Irish films have you most enjoyed working on?

I very much enjoyed working on the *Aisling Gheal* series for RTE but the most enjoyable film for me was *The Conquest of Light* on Waterford glass. It is a marvellous subject. I think that Louis came up with a marvellous treatment. I certainly could never have thought of it in those terms and I don't know of any other director who could. It gave me probably the greatest opportunity I have ever had to go to town on photography.

To what extent do you prepare your shooting style in advance?

If the director has told you of his ideas, you have discussed the style of photography and, hopefully, settled on it before shooting begins. But during the shooting it may not be possible for the director to be aware of what I am doing. For instance, I would describe *The Conquest of Light* as a very structured film, a very well prepared film. Each shot was carefully composed, lit and rehearsed. Louis Marcus could look through the camera and check the shot.

On other films, *Capallology* for example, which is an observation type of film, a lot of the time I was hand-holding the camera; while we could discuss what we hoped to do in the situation because we knew what was going to happen, at other times anything could happen and there was no way we could plan ahead.

On some of Louis's films I have been using very long focal lenses on, say, a football match and while Louis can look through the camera and see what the lens is like when setting up, during the match, because of distortion of perspective of the lens, I can see remarkable effects which are not apparent to the director's normal eyesight and view of the same event.

I am happiest when I have a measure of control over the lighting, weather conditions and camera position!

Interview with Michael Open

Michael Open was born in Kent, England in 1947. After leaving university, he came to Northern Ireland in 1969 to run Belfast's Queen's Film Theatre and, apart from a spell away in the mid-1970s, has been Administrator ever since. He has also been Film Officer for the Arts Council of Northern Ireland, edits *Film Directions*, Ireland's only regular film magazine, and is the author of *Fading Lights, Silver Screens*, an affectionate history of Belfast cinemas.

You arrived at the Queen's Film Theatre in Belfast in 1969. Why did you come to Belfast from England?

Unfortunately there is nothing glamorous about that. At university I worked for the British Film Institute during the summer vacations and got to know a lot of people there. It was a different organisation then — much smaller, more cohesive and unified, and everybody seemed to be going along in the same direction. I hoped that there would be a job for me there when I left university but there was no expansion in the Institute.

The first job that came up in serious film was this one. In fact I had met Andrew Douglas Jones, who opened the QFT, at a British Film Institute party and he said that he was leaving his job. I said I was interested and he said that I was much too inexperienced. But I got the job. Probably he was right, I was too inexperienced!

1969 to 1972 was a bad time generally in Belfast and I believe the Film Theatre had a financial crisis. Is that right?

Yes. We had a perception of what the QFT was supposed to be doing and we had seasons with primarily foreign-language films. There is no doubt that people didn't go to see foreign-language films — they had no history of doing that in the cinema context. We tried hard to persuade people that this kind of film was as stimulating and entertaining as any other, but the QFT had a deficit of £6000 after three full years of operation, at the end of the 1970/71 season.

The University naturally said that they couldn't contain losses like that indefinitely. The decision was taken to close the QFT but we were given six months to try to make amends. With slightly less idealistic programming we actually made a profit in that period and luckily were given a reprieve. I think I was idealistic then in a different way than I'm idealistic now.

So in 1972 the Arts Council felt that the QFT was a viable venture?

Yes. They always backed us in that they gave us their blessing but they hadn't really become involved in it. They had to look hard at their constitution and check whether they were allowed to spend money on it, which it turned out they were — and in fact had a duty to do so. When the QFT was set up it was sold to the University as a profit-making venture; and so when you then make losses, people expect you only to make more losses. When the Arts Council came in and said that they'd take care of the losses, they were thinking on a very small level.

At that time the equivalent organisations in Britain were getting about £30 000 a year subsidy; we were getting nearly £3000. It has been rather like that ever since, with different stepping stones. We have a lot of overheads and large fluctuations in income from week to week. It's very volatile and that is really the problem.

In your book, Fading Lights, Silver Screens, *you talk of the QFT as "a new kind of cinema, uncomfortable, difficult to find, rather unprofessional". This is obviously not your attitude now but do you still find some aspects frustrating?*

No...What I find frustrating much more is the industry's attitude towards us. The fact is that most distributors would much rather wait and see if they can persuade one of the other two cinemas in Belfast to show something that they don't really want to show (thereby losing any kind of publicity momentum that there is in the release of a film) than say, "This is a film that ought to go to the QFT" — because it is that type of film, more thoughtful, more subtle.

So are your relationships with the Curzon and the Cannon cinemas good?

They are two very different sorts of organisations. Our relationship with the Curzon is pretty good I think, given that obviously we're in competition to some extent. It is worthwhile for me to have a creative dialogue with them because they are their own masters. The Cannon get what they are given and basically we tend to see that very much as part of the sausage machine. It is fairly irrelevant for us to have a relationship with them although I get on well enough with the individuals concerned.

There are several creative things that could be done as co-operation between the cinemas which I have suggested on occasions, such as having an all-Belfast cinema poster. They're not interested mainly because it is going to cost money and they think they've figured out best what their approach is.

All I have ever tried to do is to make the QFT the best cinema. I always think: if I was somebody in Belfast who loves cinema, what type of cinema would I most like to have? Then I modify that with the knowledge that if I was the quintessential cinéphile there would be a lot of films I would want to see that hardly any other people would want to see. For a long time the problem was a physical one: we had an uncomfortable cinema with good but old and dilapidated equipment. When people came it looked like a second-rate place; now it doesn't.

The one part of my heady idealism that I really retain is that I much prefer the QFT to be frequented for its excellence rather than for its trendiness. As far as I am concerned, the people I am serving are not the people of Belfast, not the Arts Council, not the university, but the film-makers. I'm getting their films to the people they make them for: that's the underlying philosophy.

You left in 1974 and spent some time in England. When you came back in 1978 you took over from Robert Caldicott. Had the QFT changed much?

It got a new screen — I think I had already ordered it when I left. The refurbishment last year was the first major overhaul. So it was basically the same. What is interesting about my coming back is that it corresponded with the dreadful day when the three longest-surviving central cinemas were fire-bombed. In a way that was the ideal time to come back — when I left, the job I went into was a hornet's nest whereas when I came back it was a feather bed. With all these other cinemas — especially the ABC — out of action, a whole series of films, which would normally have gone there, became available to us. We showed an awful lot of films — *Days of Heaven*, *The Chant of Jimmie Blacksmith*, those kind of films - and they were a huge success.

Had the policy changed substantially?

No. It had become slightly more populist. The audience level was very, very low when I arrived back. The total box-office income was around £10 000; it's now over £100 000.

Can I ask how you became involved with the magazine Film Directions?

I actually started it just before I left but it was a very insubstantial little news-sheet. I was interested in it but Caldicott wasn't

so it had only three issues and four other issues in the years I was gone. The two Arts Councils decided that they wanted to do a joint venture on *Film Directions*. Basically David Collins and Brian Ferran from the Arts Councils and myself and Ronnie Saunders all got together as I was about to come back and it was agreed that the magazine would start off in a major new way.

It was suggested that Ronnie Saunders and myself should jointly edit it. But Ronnie Saunders said he wasn't interested; it would be distributed through the IFT but he wasn't having any part in editing it. So David Collins was co-editor. It fell more on my shoulders than it did on David's largely because I was coming back and wanted to get in on things. It started out and was pretty successful with a 7000 circulation, 4500 via the IFT and the rest through subscription.

Were the political and editorial tensions partly why the IFT stopped distributing it?

I think there was an element of that. Basically the whole film scene in Dublin got very politicised. What I found particularly annoying was that the IFT had every opportunity to be an equal partner in the editing of the magazine; they chose not to. The feedback was that most of the people in the IFT who were getting it seemed to quite like it but perhaps not many of them really wanted to go out of their way to get the magazine. Once the break had been made with automatic subscription, the demand declined.

Was there anything specific that the IFT disliked?

They said that they didn't think it was of high enough quality, that the articles were not sufficiently well-written, which I would consider rather lame and unpointed

134

objections. It was an alliance among people who didn't have much in common except their dislike for *Film Directions*.

The Arts Council in the Republic were caught in a squeeze because they had on the one hand the Arts Council of Northern Ireland who were backing the magazine, and on the other their clients and heavyweight debaters who were demanding something that the Arts Council in the North wouldn't allow. So the reply of the Republic's Arts Council was to withdraw and pass the whole project over to the North. I think the detractors were delighted with that because they imagined the magazine would simply fold. But it didn't: we got advertising, introduced colour, joined it up with the QFT programme and went fairly heavily upmarket, which all worked out very nicely.

There must be some regret that the North and South couldn't agree over a film magazine?

Yes, absolutely. I think it was bloody silly. I didn't feel any guilt on my part. One of the arguments was that there wasn't sufficient Irish content: we did a count and found that over a third was about Irish cinema. Given the output of the Irish cinema, this was grossly disproportionate anyway! If we had more manpower we could distribute the magazine quite successfully. It has been redesigned and updated and it is looking quite exciting; we're going to try for a bigger market. But only three people run QFT and *Film Directions* combined!

How do you see the future of film and film-making in Northern Ireland? What about a Belfast Film Festival, for example?

I'd like that but it really is a question of manpower: if we did that we would be

stretching what are already very thin resources. I do want the Film Theatre to be run well. I would like to see more film-making in Northern Ireland. The Arts Council used to have a policy which encouraged film-makers but they don't get any specific money from the Government for film whereas in all other regions of the United Kingdom there is specific money set aside for film. Video is quite big now: there is a big video workshop in Derry, funded by Channel 4. It's very politicised, doing items on tenants' rights and strip searching and so on. It is not what I would call very creative use of video but it's fine.

Interview with Morgan O'Sullivan

Morgan O'Sullivan was born and educated in Dublin. He began his career in broadcasting with RTE and then went to Australia to work in various production management capacities. He also acted in a broadcasting capacity on television and radio as an on-air announcer. Returning to Ireland three years later, he rejoined RTE and established himself as a major on-air celebrity with a weekly interview show broadcast on radio. He has produced a movie of the week for NBC, a drama special for Mobil Corporation and acted as a production consultant on the television series, *Remington Steele*, for MTM and on *The Mansions of America* mini-series for ABC.

He is Managing Director of Tara Productions Ireland Limited who are currently developing a five-hour mini-series for Home Box Office. He now heads the re-opened film studios in Bray, Co. Wicklow, which operate under the name of MTM Ardmore Studios.

I would like to start by asking your opinion of the cause of the Ardmore studios' closure in 1982.

The problem with the National Film Studios of Ireland was that it wasn't properly capitalised by the State. The State wrote letters of guarantee for the company to the banks and the banks advanced the funding. The interest rates were so high and the amount of funding so large it was extremely difficult to beat that. What also mitigated against them was that Ireland had no film policy. The Government of Ireland still hasn't made a decision about that — probably because there are no votes in it — or about whether they want to be in the international entertainment industry.

You have to go in not on a local level but on an international one and you have to provide some sort of tax investment programme that will allow growth. I would say that it's particularly pertinent that the Government of Ireland should be addressing that issue now because Ireland has never shown such success as it has shown in the last couple of years. We're producing real talent now in film, television and music.

How do you see the new Ardmore avoiding a similar fate?

I worked for some time in Australia and was there when the Australian film industry was started. The Government of Australia decided that they wanted an industry; they had the political will. The reason a momentum has gathered force here is due mainly to Channel 4. If you look at the films that have been made, most of them have been funded by Channel 4. Had they not come into being we wouldn't have any semblance of an industry.

When we set up Tara Productions in

1977 we had a policy that we would make material only on a commission basis; we were not speculators. We would also pre-sell to end-users and our budget would be one hundred per cent covered. We managed to do that but knew we could only do that in the American market.

Our market was the American majors, the American television networks — ABC, NBC and CBS — and HBO. Nothing below Home Box Office can pay us enough money to produce. You're into highly speculative money and an artificial tax structure to do it any other way. Out of that came a growth: we were the first company in Europe to get an order directly from an American television network.

We thought that if we are making films for America we have to understand America: there were elements that were missing. So we brought in seven key personnel from the United States and we understudied them with Irish people. Then over a period of time we phased out the Americans and moved the Irish into the key roles.

This had a dual effect on Tara. Firstly, it made us cost-effective; secondly, we were putting together the semblance of an Irish film unit. By 1981 we became fairly self-sufficient and were more atuned to the American way of creating the product. That impressed American companies who saw that we understood their approach to things.

You also used the word 'cost-effective' in one of your submissions to the Public Hearing of the Irish Film Board in 1982. You emphasized the need for the producer and it seemed that you skirted around the Irish element. Is this a fair comment?

We've made an investment in people, technical and creative people. That is the Irish element. A good example is Michael Feeney Callan whom we've believed in for

years. It's very hard to sell a European writer to American television. He's now writing a six-hour mini-series for us called *The Negotiator*. We are cautious about being loud about those sort of things but I believe he'll make a director at the end of the day. There are other people Tara believes in here.

So I would take issue with the charge that I haven't paid attention to developing that kind of talent. If there was a governmental policy towards film-making we would take risks if it was that determined to set up an industry. We're not asking the Government to underwrite the film industry; we're asking for a benign tax environment. But we're not going to stop going out and making the pre-sales!

How did MTM's involvement come about?

I did my training in the United States with Leonard Freeman in the early 1970s; he was very kind to me. I used to go over there for periods of time to learn the business. A lot of his senior personnel went to work for MTM. When *Remington Steele* was being made in Europe they contacted me. They knew I had made for American television and they knew I knew what was required for an American television series. So they literally asked me how to go about it in Europe.

I told them to base it outside Ireland, shoot an episode here and we'd send the Irish crew with them to mainland Europe. It was a gigantic success.

I said to MTM that I'd love to see them doing more in Europe: they were setting up shows in the South of France, London and Norway; I was peripherally involved in terms of advice. It was at this stage that MTM made a commitment to carry out a study of the studio.

When we set up Tara one of the things I had learned and wanted to bring from

The way this studio will be a success is if it attracts an international television series, one that is bought by one of the American networks, between 22 and 26 episodes a year. To produce that amount a year you must have flexibility in working and be able to produce the material at a certain rate.

The studio is run as a four-wall operation; it really has no employees except security. The production company, Tara Productions or MTM Enterprises, comes in and rents the facility from MTM Ardmore. The union contract is between Tara, MTM Enterprises and the group of unions. To attract and induce producers into this country we've got to be (a) efficient and deliver the product to the network within certain specifications and (b) competitive: not cheaper but less expensive than other countries.

What did you find when you moved in here in October 1986?

The place was in shambles. One of the good things the liquidator did was to keep the security. But no money was spent so as it ran down it was just left. We did a complete study, every nook and cranny, and drew up plans. We knew that in the first quarter we had to get the basics working. We took it over on a Thursday; we had it full by the Monday. A complete telephone system was in very quickly. Everything needed a thorough clean. And in six weeks we were ready: we finished on a Friday and *Remington Steele* came in on the Monday.

We've got *The Courier* here at the moment, a lot of commercials, then Littlebird are coming in with *Troubles*, then Radio Telefís Éireann — they're going to shoot *Glenroe* here.

What are the main facilities here?

Exterior, Sound Stage A, MTM Ardmore Studios

the United States was that the Americans had an attitude of mind: you can teach anybody optics but it's the attitude you have to learn. The American industry has an attitude of mind; that constant tradition developed the film industry and it is now the leader in the field and we must learn from the best.

They are good at the *management* of motion pictures. It is very highly structured but it has its own enormous flexibility. There is very good organisation, a sense of security — once a show is greenlighted it is really green-lighted. There's no fudging or funny money — here's the money, go and do the show. It's very, very pleasant to work in that kind of environment. It has hassles but these are different from European hassles.

Ardmore suffered in the past from poor management-union relationships. You have made some progress in that area, have you not?

138

We have four sound stages, one of 15 000 square feet, two of 8000 square feet and one of 3000 square feet. There is also office space, a restaurant, workshop facilities, cutting rooms and preview theatres.

Do you think that the problem with Ireland is that it is not making the right sort of product for the right market?

I cannot knock popular entertainment. I go to the movies and I want to escape and to be entertained. *Crocodile Dundee, E.T....* great fun, great entertainment. I think Steven Spielberg is a genius — *Jaws, Close Encounters*: some of the best work ever done — but I also like Ingmar Bergman. But I think Bergman is a popular entertainer and he operates almost with the music hall tradition in mind; there's theatre in his films.

I find a lot of the material we produce in this country is dour and... depressing. What's wrong with a little bit of entertainment? There is one sector in this industry — not just in Ireland but worldwide — where it is unfashionable to enjoy popular entertainment.

There is a great theatrical tradition in Ireland but yet this hasn't spawned a film industry in the way that perhaps Sweden, for example, has done. Why is this, do you think?

I don't think we're visually strong. We're strong in the word. In fact we're wordy: we'd put two people in a room and they'd talk. An American director and writer would want to break it out. They would maybe try to use pictures to advance the narrative. We need a visual education if we are going to succeed. However, the greatest asset anybody can have is the will to succeed. This is too big for any one individual; it's got to be done by a group all pulling together with the State behind us.

Setting up the Film Board was a start but it needs much more: we were a group of people sitting behind a table with our hands tied behind our backs. You've got to fund it properly: you either go into it properly or not at all. There's no point doing things by halves. It's a terrible thing to say but I feel as an industry we are really not wanted.

Shooting a rock video in Sound Stage A at MTM Ardmore

Interview with Thaddeus O'Sullivan

Thaddeus O'Sullivan was born in Dublin and has lived in London since 1966. He worked at odd jobs for three years before attending Ealing School of Art and the Royal College of Art. He made a number of experimental films between 1972 and 1980 and worked as a stills photographer. His work as a lighting cameraman includes *Anne Devlin*, *Pigs*, *When Reason Sleeps* and *Traveller*, whilst he has recently directed the highly acclaimed *The Woman Who Married Clark Gable*, starring Bob Hoskins and Brenda Fricker.

You left Dublin immediately after school. Why did you come to England?

I was interested in photography then but I had no intention of doing anything in particular except getting away from Dublin. Schooling in Dublin in the mid-1960s was so awful and when I got to London it was just wonderful. It was a foreign country; I felt very remote and independent. I did labouring work and then went to art school, and then film school from 1972 to 1975.

So your interest in photography was not something that came from school in Ireland?

No it wasn't. You weren't encouraged to be anything. It wasn't ever mentioned anywhere that you could consider yourself worthy of expression, visually or in any other way! I enjoyed making films at art school. Later, when I went to the Royal College of Art, there was a strong emphasis on theory (structuralism was popular) and the instinctive part of film-making, which I liked, was very unfashionable. I made a series of short films, some about being Irish in London, ending with *A Pint of Plain*. This was made in a very 'relaxed' style — improvised acting, no script — but within a formal structure of shots and camera movements. I think it pretty well summed up my experiences at film school.

Did you get involved with the Irish community in London?

No, not really. The Irish in London never had a proper community. There was the older, inward-looking and very nostalgic emigré community and I didn't want to get involved with that. There wasn't anything else. When I first came here a lot of people I knew were going to university in Ireland so they would call for the summer, scoff at the meanness of your lifestyle and run back to Dublin.

The British Film Institute were involved in financing On a Paving Stone Mounted. *How did that come about?*

I applied to them — everybody applied every year. There was no Channel 4 then, there was nothing really. I had projects in for two or three years running and my number came up, much to my surprise. I had sent in five pages of thoughts about being an emigrant in this country and how one would express that visually and in a personal way. They financed it with £14 000. So I got a production manager who was a close friend, a sound man, I was the cameraman and off we went to the West of Ireland and had a great time. It was a mixture of documentary and drama, we had very good actors both here and for the sequences shot in London. The finished film was a pretty good reflection of what I felt living in this country at that time.

In 1981 you made a film about the painter Jack B Yeats. What inspired you to make that?

I was fascinated by the classic struggle — the artist and his work, his inspiration and how he translates it. For Yeats the inspiration was Ireland. As I saw it, there were two significant periods or events in Yeats's life. One was the period when his work became much more expressionist in style. He was fifty then and it coincided with his return to Ireland after living for years in the quiet Devon countryside. Then there was the 1916 Rising; he was terribly affected by that and suffered a nervous breakdown around that time. Central to the film is that change in his style and the political events of the time — the period from 1916 to 1922, Irish

Independence and what it meant to him. His pictures of the period reflected his feelings. I also used archive material in the way I had always wanted to try — much more subjectively, more emotionally, rather than used as something to describe a real event, which it can never do.

Do you prefer working as a director or as a lighting cameraman?

I like both. Obviously, I have to say there is more satisfaction in directing. However, lighting is an aspect of directing in the sense that it is part of the mise-en-scene and so your contribution can be significant. There is a kind of after-image or 'memory-picture' which stays with you long after you've seen a good film. The strength of that image is a measure of the success of the lighting design. I'm talking about a film which is useful to the imagination that has experienced it. If it is worth remembering then it is cinema and I've contributed to it and I'm satisfied. Unfortunately there aren't any worth remembering.

How do you feel when you are directing and supervising another cameraman as, for example, on The Woman Who Married Clark Gable?

When we did *Clark Gable*, Jack Conroy and I discussed how it should look and subsequently spoke very little about it while we were shooting. I thought he'd be good for the film; he was probably closer to black-and-white than many others — he was older and had worked as a gaffer on some films in the 1950s and so on. I think he did a good job.

You have recently shot the television series When Reason Sleeps. *How do you approach television work?*

I've shot drama on 16mm but they were all movies. But that's the first time I've done drama for television and it was a real nightmare to watch those three programmes. I was very disappointed with them, especially with the effect of television on my contribution. With lighting for television a lot of it is lost: I was lighting things that are just not seen. *Out of Time* would be quite stylish on a big screen; *A Summer Ghost* not so much because it has a lot of video effects in it.

You have been working on Birchwood. *Will that be made now?*

I don't think so. Working with John Banville on that screenplay has been one of the most satisfying things I've ever done and that's why I don't feel too bitter about it not being made. I think it is a terrific screenplay. The problem is that it's just not considered commercial at all at the moment. At a budget of just under £1 million it would just be possible but over that it's priced out of the market. But it needs to be done in a certain way or it won't be right.

How do you find working with actors?

Actually it is what I enjoy most. I like finding a location; I feel that when I've done that I know that it will be represented visually because it's just a question of where to put the camera. But the real kick is working with an actor and making it come alive. I love going through a bit of dialogue with an actor and finding the best way to do it, where the emphasis is, the resonance it can give to other scenes or to other moments either side of that moment. Each movement in the frame is part of a montage. With every single movement there is an echo within the frame which means that every shot is working to further the idea. In a way part of the actor's job is to orchestrate this since he's the one you're looking at. He doesn't need to know this (he couldn't act if he did!) but the director should.

You worked with Pat Murphy on Anne Devlin. *Do you feel that it is difficult for her as a feminist director to be working in Ireland with its restrictions towards women?*

There is a lot of prejudice towards women in the film industry in England. I don't see any reason why it should be any different in Ireland, though I can't say I was aware of any difficulty that Pat had on *Anne Devlin*. Crews are friendlier and more supportive there, perhaps that atmosphere makes it a bit easier for women in Ireland. On the face of it women should make more efficient film-makers than men anyway: they're certainly better at dealing with both the emotional and practical problems...at the same time! And they are more persistent and more patient. Women are better at all that, men of course know this...

Pat and I used to talk a lot about the difficulties of living and working in Ireland. I'd say to her, "Get out, don't live here." But it's her centre. I've been away too long, my centre is in the 'crack' — somewhere between the two cultures. Living in Dublin can be bad, I think, in the sense that it's possible to develop a false sense of your own importance and achievement. There's something about making films in Ireland which is good because there's a terrific collaborative feeling but bad because it is allowed to get too important for what it is. What is produced becomes overly significant because there is so little of it because there's so little money around. More energy goes into talking about money and production difficulties than thinking about what the film is or should be. But I don't suppose any of that is peculiar to Ireland.

Interview with Bob Quinn

Bob Quinn was born in Dublin but is now settled in Connemara, Co. Galway, from where he runs his film and video company, Cinegael, formed in 1973. His career as a film-maker began after a wide variety of jobs, including teacher and commercial representative, and a not altogether agreeable period at RTE. In 1975 he made the highly original and successful *Lament for Art O'Leary* and soon after continued to establish his reputation with *Poitín* (1978) and the multi-part *Atlantean* (1984), which explores the relationship between the Gaelic and Arab worlds. His most recent film is *Budawanny*. Bob Quinn is a member of Aosdána, the Academy of Irish artists and has written several books.

When did you first become interested in film-making?

I was interested in and enjoyed film way back, as a child of course. Interest in film-making grew out of television where I was working in about 1964; I was employed by Radio Telefís Éireann. There was a course on documentary film-making and they showed a selection of films, two of which were made by John Boorman when he was at Bristol BBC, which I thought were magnificent. I felt that I hadn't seen anything like them before and they intrigued and fascinated me.

Also at the same time on Ulster Television was a series presented by John Grierson and he showed some marvellous documentary films. Also I became pretty sick of the television studio strait-jacket and so it was liberating to have a camera and go out and have a less obtrusive effect on ordinary people — I wasn't particularly interested in actors or professional performers, or people in suits or with nice accents. I found that the film camera disturbed and inhibited ordinary people less than when they were brought into a studio.

And so gradually I concentrated on film, even though at one time I was doing all the output for the religious affairs department at RTE. What kept me sane was that every five weeks I had to produce a documentary film on any subject I liked — it was the only department in television where I had total freedom.

What was RTE like in the early 1960s?

It was completely new and it was delightful and free; you met people who had open minds and it was very exciting.

In fact it was the best job I ever had in my life. I loved working in television until I started thinking about its effect on society and the control of it by the commercial ethos.

That was the reason why I left — I didn't want my work supporting that ethos. Of course as it happens eventually television is the main outlet for one's work in this country.

So you became fully independent as a film-maker in 1972?

Yes. I moved out finally in 1969 and came down here to Connemara, County Galway but it took a couple of years before I got back into making films because I had more or less turned my back on that entire world.

I would like to discuss Caoineadh Airt Uí Laoire/Lament for Art O'Leary, *completed in 1975. Kevin Rockett said that it was a breakthrough in formal and thematic terms. Do you agree with him?*

Yes. I think it is a revolutionary film; certainly in this country it was completely revolutionary. Its background — and the reason I started making films that year — was a tiny attempt to counteract the images of ourselves portrayed on national television. I was living in a community of people, Gaelic-speaking, whose image and self-image did not in the least correspond to that being presented as the sensible human being in Ireland.

So I started what was really a closed-circuit television service from here, making video documents and travelling with them around the halls and pubs to show people themselves on television. It was an attempt to demystify the idea that if you appear on television there is something special and wonderful about you; to show that really the best material for images on screens is ordinary people.

In the film you have various reconstructions of the past. You mention the area of contemporary cultural theory: the idea that each version is a deconstruction of believed mythology. Do you see the film-maker as a deconstructer?

I suppose that there is a cussedness about my approach to any subject: if something is believed by everybody then I assume it is wrong. If it is popular and profitable I am against it! When this happens I smell a rat and so I look for the obverse. The film was trying to deconstruct a monolithic approach to Irish culture and the Irish language. And theological: one of my objects of course has been to distinguish between Irish culture and language and its theological connotations and its hijacking by particular religious clans.

So the film was trying to separate off the respectable, middle-class, urban interpretation of Gaelic culture, which is boring and which has damn near destroyed the whole thing in the last sixty years, and try to counterpoint what I perceive to be a vibrant and living expression of this, which is where I live, that people speak it, they don't philosophize about it, they don't even discuss it, they just speak it and live energetic lives.

What I also wanted to do was to try to show the background to the very beautiful ballad, *Caoineadh Airt Uí Laoire.* I think it is one of the finest pieces ever written in any language and it still moves me. So I wanted to show that poem — and in a way revise it. In doing so I insulted everybody of course because I chopped it up into bits and that irritated people terribly. But I thought it was worth it.

Is there a deeper political reason why you prefer 16mm to 35mm?

It is mainly financial. If I could afford, or someone would give me money to shoot on 35mm I'd certainly shoot on 35mm. But I know that the conditions on which you are given the money to make a 35mm film, certainly in our culture, preclude the freedom that I find necesssary to make films. I do know that the entire process of writing the script — adapting it to the requirements of distributors, exhibitors, film boards, television investors and so on — must water it down to the point where the exercise is pointless in the first place.

It is analogous to the relationship here between Irish and English. You can write, print or say anything in the Irish language in this country, even the most subversive or vulgar thing and you will get away with it. You can't do that in English.

In the same way you can do things in 16mm that you can't do in 35mm. For instance, the film I've just made, *Budawanny*: the title means the monk's prick; you couldn't say that in English. And to reverse fifty years of cinematic history by making a film in silent black-and-white is also outrageous. You couldn't do that in 35mm and get away with it. Maybe I haven't got away with it...

It was shown at Cannes...

I really have no interest in that. The only reason why it was brought to Cannes and Berlin was that the executives of the Irish Film Board needed an excuse to go to Cannes and Berlin and all these places and it was the only film they had. Indeed the only reason it was made was that twelve months ago the Film Board looked around and said, "Holy God we've no film being made!" and they rang me up and said, "We'll give you £50 000. Are you ready to go?" I said, "Sure. I'm going anyway, with the £15 000 I have."

I don't care whether the films are shown abroad or not; I'm only concerned that they're shown in this country.

That does raise the problem of distribution. Some years ago it was suggested by Joe Comerford and yourself that a company could have been formed to enlarge 16mm films to 35mm to get better distribution or an organisation set up to mobilise halls and various other places for showing 16mm films. How has your thought developed since then?

I don't really see either of those things coming about. What I've seen happening is that Irish film-makers have been seduced by the great big world outside and have been led to believe that they can become international cinema figures by aiming outside the country all the time. I am of exactly the opposite point of view. I think there are not sufficient film-makers interested in the idea of showing their films in and around this country.

At the moment I'm showing a film in a small theatre here. It is not being shown through an exhibitor or distributor; I'm doing the whole thing myself. I'll be standing on the street there next week handing out leaflets. It's not perverse — I'm really interested in keeping the whole process at human levels. I just can't handle that big world of people talking in millions, I admire them and envy them actually for their confidence and talent, but I can't swim in that air, I choke.

I think it is much more preferable to make one small film a year than every four years to gather sufficient money to make a 35mm cinema film that might flop anyway.

Statistically I can't understand the logic of the fact that eight or nine out of ten Hollywood films don't make money. So where is the incredible confidence and arrogance that make us think we can break into this big international market and make money out of it? I have a sneaky little theory that this is not a decision of the film-makers at all. This is a decision of the new breed of producers who realise that if you have £1 million to play around with on a film, you can shave more for your office expenses, trips abroad and for your lifestyle than you could if you were making a film for £100 000 — I'm really sure that's the basis of it.

Is it a question of telling a simple story and being satisfied with that?

Yes it is for me. It is odd that I seem to have come full circle from the convolutions of *Caoineadh Airt Uí Laoire*; my object in *Budawanny* was to be as simple and pure as possible and to contrast that against the pyrotechnical convolutions of modern editing techniques and all the complications of getting a film made. Trying to be simple turned out to be a much more complex process than anything else could be!

So to be subversive in 1974 was to be technically difficult, whereas today it is to avoid that and to tell stories simply...

That is subversive. Absolutely. That's a very good point.

I would like to turn to Cloch, *about the stone cutter's art. It seems that you are suggesting in the film that here is an art form that offers an alternative culture or way of life. Is that a fair comment?*

That may be suggested but it wasn't one of the most conscious aspects about it. The main aspect that interested me was the physical relationship between a person and inanimate material. I wanted to suggest that it is a very sensual activity. The clue I got for that was a sculptor who said to me, "I love to see people touching my sculptures." That is why in the film

there is a little boy and he touches the breast of a female sculpture and it was that sensuality of stone — cold, awful stone — but it was sensual and physical. That's why I introduced the voiceover where a woman is saying "Fuck me" in Irish, when the sculptor is chiselling in slow-motion.

What about Poitín? *How important is it for you to make films with Gaelic-speaking actors?*

It is very important. I don't know why a big thing is made of this because Ray makes them in Indian, Bergman in Swedish...what is the objection, what is the problem? They can be subtitled. A film is supposed to be about pictures so what's the problem about the words?

Given the 'Northern problem', is it not that people are very conscious about language?

It is a response to Dublin more than to the North. I think I see Dublin as the enemy, not the North!

What is your attitude to the new Ardmore?

I think it's great, a pure business activity which is not confused with the national film industry. Morgan O'Sullivan is an excellent and energetic businessman and he's direct and honest: he doesn't make himself out to be Irish and cultural first, he is primarily a businessman. I respect people who don't confuse their objectives.

You wrote once in an IFT newsletter that any written material prejudices a response, perhaps even more so material written by the director. Is that your attitude now? Would you rather just show your films without introducing them?

Yes I would. At the time I was asked to

write that article I was concerned about the defining of the image by sounds. I was trying to get away from the idea that film is purely about beautiful pictures and to emphasize that it is now a business of sound and image combined.

I would like to ask you about the Atlantean *series. You wrote a book to go with the series and were criticised for the approach you took...*

I didn't actually get criticism for either the films or the book: the film was praised to the skies and won a Jacob's Award. So far there has been practically no criticism in black-and-white anywhere about the book. Recently there have been two reviews. One of the fascinating things that has been proved by the book is that it has not been confronted at all; it has been greeted with the greatest defence of all, silence. It is a very powerful weapon. Any Irish book that comes out is reviewed because there are so few. This one has not been reviewed at all. It's very odd.

As I say in the book, it was necessary for us to achieve respectability to counter us against the British Empire; that we were part of an ancient and magnificent empire or imperial ethos called the Celts. What intrigues me is that I know it would offend people who believe in the Celtic, Aryan, central-European, mainstream idea. What I don't quite understand is that people who don't believe that have not really come out in support of it, except privately.

To conclude, what was the background to the making of Budawanny? *How did you go about it?*

I got the book five years ago and immediately wrote to the priest, Pádraic Standúin, who had written it and said that I'd love to make a film of it sometime. He wrote back and said, "You can have the film rights for a penny because I'd like to tell my grandchildren that a film was made from my book."

Eventually I filleted the book, writing down in order all the characters and incidents. And when I'd read this it suddenly occurred to me — why does this need words? The story is here, why have a babble of voices? Why not do a black-and-white film with subtitles. I had my options of doing it either in Irish or English.

Then I read Standúin's second book in which the priest becomes a bishop. So I wrote a monologue for this bishop. I showed it to Standúin and he said, "I couldn't have done it better myself." So I contextualised the simple story with this bishop speaking, that was the aim. Unfortunately the leading actor suffered...some inconvenience and I had to drag in the character who played the bishop in the inner story and get him to do this bishop part, thus destroying much of the irony of the film.

I could have waited another twelve months but I decided to stick with what I had. However, most of the irony of the film is gone. But the story is good and enjoyable, people weep at it.

I'm a bit of a puritan and what I wanted to do was to make people earn the pleasure of this beautiful, sad story by forcing them to think with this very aesthetic monologue by the bishop where there are some very complex issues explored.

It didn't take long to make — twelve days on Clare Island, County Mayo. Then half of the negative was destroyed so I had to go back and reshoot several scenes.

It is an amazing film really because it was the first film that I ever insured in my life and it was the first film where dreadful things happened on it. Terrible things: props and cameras stolen; the leading actor locked up for a night; one of the stars of the film, our pet dog, killed. If I was superstitious I'd be very worried about it.

Interview with David Shaw-Smith

David Shaw-Smith was born in Dublin in 1939. Well-known as an independent producer of documentaries, he has made a large number of films on Irish traditional crafts which have been seen all over the world and have won many awards including the Golden Harp for Ireland in 1984. Of these he is best known for the long-running series, *Hands* and *Patterns*. Many of his films are in the collections of the Museum of Modern Art and the American Museum of Broadcasting. He is married to the illustrator Sally Ann Shaw-Smith, with whom he collaborated on the book, *Ireland's Traditional Crafts*, published by Thames and Hudson in 1984.

How did you first become involved in photography and film-making?

Indirectly, it began through the influence of my mother who was an artist. I was born in County Dublin and we lived between Dundrum and Sandyford, which was countryside at that time. My father had a nursery garden called Ballawley Park. Throughout my childhood my mother was constantly drawing my attention to the natural beauty that surrounded us — red berries on a tree; the way low sunlight struck the fields; the Dublin mountains behind us — I also think children are fascinated by the small details of nature which become important to them. So I grew up with a strong visual awareness and a genuine love and appreciation of the countryside.

My secondary education was at Gordounstoun in Morayshire, Scotland. When I left school I studied agriculture at the North of Scotland College of Agriculture in Aberdeen. Then I started travelling. I went to Norway, France, the United States and Canada, working as a student, not just short trips — 6 months at a time. I wanted to record the places I'd been to, so I bought an Agfa 120 camera and soon started exploring the visual possibilities of taking pictures. In 1959 I emigrated to America and worked for the Virginia Polytechnic Institute for a year. I took a lot of photos during this period and began to study the great photographers — Steichen, Penn, Avedon, Cartier-Bresson.

I came back to Ireland in 1961 and tried to get a job in Galway with the Department of Agriculture. It required a working knowledge of Irish which I had never learned. I didn't get the job; it was a bad time for work — lots of young people were emigrating — and I thought I might become a maltster. So I joined a company that malted barley for Guinness and I've never been so bored in all my life!

Then I began taking photos on a freelance basis and supplied the Dublin newspapers — the *Irish Times*, the old *Evening Mail* and others. I was covering a story once about the live export of horses from the Dublin docks when a man chased and attacked me: I took a quite dramatic series of photos.

At this time Telefís Éireann were looking for trainees for the new television service that was shortly to go on the air. I was granted an interview, took along my photographs and was subsequently selected with twenty-six others to train for the opening of the service in 1962. It was a very exciting time. I always used to joke that there were twenty-five Roman Catholics, I was the token Protestant and Louis Lentin the token Jew!

Has your religion ever been a problem?

Absolutely not. At no stage in my career working with Radio Telefís Éireann or at any other time have I ever felt discriminated against because of my religion — in fact at times I think it is an advantage.

What did you train as in RTE?

I trained to become a floor-manager and then spent about five years working on a whole range of shows. They were exciting days, we worked very hard, there was a tremendous amount of live television. Then I spent a year in lighting which I found beneficial but very boring. I really wanted to become a film cameraman but there were no vacancies.

I was not happy in a large organisation. I felt that to be successful one had to learn to play internal politics and I was definitely not interested in doing that. I am really more of an individual and a loner.

At that stage Gerrit van Gelderen, a Dutchman making wildlife films in

Ireland, was looking for an assistant. I talked to him and he asked me to join him. I was twenty-eight, married with three children and the RTE job was pensionable...I left RTE much to the amazement of my colleagues. I spent two very happy, interesting and exciting years working for Gerrit. He shared a series with Éamon de Buitléar called *Amuigh Faoin Speir*. When we were on transmission we had to produce a programme every two weeks for RTE. That meant going out with a Bolex camera, shooting one week and editing the next, on a Murray viewer. The shots were all individually hung. We worked in black-and-white negative. The films were made on very limited resources. Very quickly I found myself shooting entire programmes with the help of Sally, my wife.

Since then Sally and I have always worked very closely together with our film-making. For years she was the only female sound recordist and dubbing-mixer in the Irish Transport and General Workers Union. She is a superb judge of film but likes to distance herself from the editing, only viewing rushes and coming in to give welcome advice at the rough cut stage.

Then my thirtieth birthday came up and I thought that if ever I was going to do my own thing, it should be now. So I left Gerrit in September 1969 and started David Shaw-Smith Productions, which was Sally and myself. We immediately set about making films. Our first film was *Connemara and Its Ponies* which took about nine months to shoot. I think it was the first time that anybody had ever recorded the birth of a Connemara foal out in the open. We filmed two births. The first, the mare, had it in the middle of the night and we tried to film it with a tilly lamp. That was no good so we went back with a sun gun, sat out waiting for a whole week and managed to film the birth of a second foal.

If I could make films as successful as that one was I would have had few career crises and financial worries! It seemed to come at the right time and it had a sort of romance to it. It was shown in Sweden, Denmark, France, Canada, the United States and eventually worldwide.

After that I made two commercial documentaries for Aer Lingus in 1972, one on the promotion of fly-drive holidays, the other about students coming to Ireland for the summer to learn English. In 1973 we bought a van, rented our house and drove off to Greece. We ended up on Corfu where we had stayed years before, spending an idyllic six months there until the money ran out! We made three documentaries commissioned by RTE, one on the life of our village, one a history of the island, and one about the wildlife there, all seen through the eyes of our children who narrated the commentaries.

The films were edited by Marlene Fletcher, a first-rate film editor who now lives in Toronto. Her husband, John, who sadly has just died, was Director of Studies at the London Film School and closely involved with the ACTT. They stayed with us in Ireland on several occasions and gave us lots of good advice about the value of good research and the structuring of documentaries.

Can you tell me about the World of Houses *series?*

I was commissioned to make six films for RTE for the European Architectural Heritage Year in 1975. I felt particularly strongly about presentation of cultural and educational material to a television audience; at that time the average architectural programme was presented in a far too intellectual, almost élitist manner. I felt that this approach was not suitable for a television series for European Architectural Heritage Year, as the whole

aim was to make the public at large more aware of the good architecture around them and conscious of the dreadful things that were being done in the name of modern development.

So we went for the more popular approach and asked Mike Murphy to present them. Mike up to that time had been involved in light entertainment programmes. The critics did not like him presenting the programmes — I suspect because he came from a non-academic background. One actually commented on the clothes he wore rather than on the content of the programme — what rubbish. I think he did a very good job and they reached an audience which would otherwise have switched off.

One programme called *The Country Seat* was about the non-defensive architecture of the great country houses of Ireland, starting with Elizabethan, Georgian and so on to the present day. We also made one on fortified dwellings and another called *Our Towns*, which drew attention to towns such as Kilkenny and how the centres were being ruined by the unsympathetic sightings of supermarkets and the spoiling of roof lines, and how attractive the old buildings, shop fronts and hand-painted signs were. I think the programmes achieved their aim in that the man in the street enjoyed them.

The series was naïvely ambitious and in the end I think we lost £2000. We travelled endlessly up and down the country, sleeping in our van in the depths of winter to save money. This is something you will always find with the independent film-maker - he will put his last penny and all his effort into his film because he feels fiercely about the end-result. To a large extent I feel that independent film-makers in this country have been exploited by organisations such as RTE. They may not have been aware of it but they certainly did exploit us. They did little or nothing to encourage independent production companies. We were a thorn in their side. It is only recently that a complete policy change has taken place.

After you made the series you went through a bad spell, I believe.

Yes, a terribly bad spell: we got absolutely no commissions. My mother suggested I became a window-cleaner or a market-gardener! We ran up debts at the bank and it was really looking grim. On more borrowed money I went into Kodak and bought film and made a series of seven to ten-minute films, mildly educational, of my daughter, Sophie, who was six at the time. I suppose one would call them fillers but they were small cameos — aspects of childhood, how a child could occupy and amuse herself in the summer holidays when boredom sets in. They were nearly all filmed outside in available light. One was called *Sophie Combats the Flies*. We filmed the births and the puppies' antics until they left us. None of the sound was synched — all wildtrack. We recorded Sophie's voiceover later.

How did the Hands *series first come about?*

In 1976 I decided that I would give the film-making business another three months; if after that I failed to get any work I really was going to consider doing something else — I owed it to my family. I felt that the area of traditional crafts was one that had to be recorded so I started looking for money in all directions — to no avail. Then one day I bumped into the late Jack White who was Controller of Programmes at RTE. I told him about the difficulty of raising money and our situation in general and he asked me to come and see him; subsequently RTE

decided to fund an initial six programmes. We shot them in 1977 and they were first transmitted in 1978. Then we made another six, another six and another six. We have now made over thirty. Had it not been for Jack White and Muiris Mac Conghail I think my career would have foundered.

How do you go about shooting?

The first thing I do is sit down with the craftsman and get him to tell me all about his craft, which we record wild. I learn a great deal from this conversation about his or her own personality and particularly about the craft. They won't ever again describe their craft to me in the same way. Having filmed the work, they will know that I know a good deal more about it. Always at the end of the shoot I do another interview which is totally different — they are relaxed then and the details are much more personal. The combination of the two recordings forms the basis for the commentary script — a bonus if I can use his or her voice and a gold mine of information. I base my camera script on the first interview which emerges very quickly.

I visualise in my mind's eye each shot I want to get and a style — or more correctly — the atmosphere I want to create. Very often I can build a whole sequence out of the natural sound effects that I can hear and I have done this many times. So I now know the sort of scene or shot I want, which camera angles are going to help me achieve this and then I start shooting.

I also make continuous notes throughout filming and try to keep as flexible as possible so if an event takes place during the shoot — such as the swarming of a hive of bees — I'm ready to film it. I love getting loose film (recording unscheduled events). Sometimes it is quite difficult trying to assess whether there is enough material, or rather content, for a programme. We quickly discovered that the narrower the focus and the simpler the subject matter, the better the film. We have often made programmes about people who would never have been considered for normal television programmes, particularly if they practise a dying — I hate that word, it's so final — craft.

Cavan Cooper from the Hands *series*

The films are very personal, both as a statement and the way they are made. One builds up an intense relationship on a one-to-one basis. At the start of the filming the craftsman is often not sure of you; they don't know what to expect — maybe they're nervous or I'm unrelaxed because I have had to do a lot of persuading. The hardest shot to take in a documentary is the first one! But soon the craftsman or woman forgets about the paraphernalia of cameras and lights. They realise I have a genuine interest in what they are doing and an immense respect for their craft and I want to make a good and interesting film of their work. Then the relationship really takes off and when this happens it is very exciting.

Whenever possible I like to use the craftsman's voice for the commentary because I feel it brings out the person's character. I often film synched conversations between people as part of the story but one has to be particularly careful that the sequences do not appear to be contrived and stagey. I really strive for naturalness. To achieve this one either has to 'grab' the moment because it is happening and the people are unaware of you filming or it is carefully thought out and set up — these people are not actors. I think the Irish temperament lends itself to performance and talk.

Sometimes dialect is a huge problem: in *Bees and Bee Skeps*, which was made in West Cork, there is a conversation between two old men and several times there were odd words even I couldn't understand because of the accent. I could have used subtitles but it would have spoiled the delightful naturalness of the conversation. The way they spoke was like a piece of music and I wanted people to listen to it as such. Éamon de Buitléar said to me that grammatically they were still speaking Irish although Irish had not been spoken in that location for over a hundred years — very interesting.

How do you find the light in Ireland?

The light is nearly always superb but unless one is looking for a certain effect — strong cross-lighting on stone, for example - it's probably a good policy to shoot regardless of the weather. You can get some marvellous effects on a wet, miserable day, particularly with the new fast negative film rated at 320 ASA. The light in Ireland has a wonderful translucency — a lack of pollution, I expect — winds straight off thousands of miles of Atlantic Ocean.

The weather in Ireland is so unpredictable — if I know I have to get certain scenic shots for a programme and the weather is good when we arrive, I get the shots fast for tomorrow it's bound to be pouring. I use a lot of back-light when shooting interiors, but try to keep my lighting very simple. Back-light can be very artificial but it works well, used skillfully, when one is filming a craftsman at work and wants to separate him from a confusing background.

Could you tell me about the Patterns *series?*

Patterns evolved quite logically. During the filming of the programmes on traditional crafts I met young craftsmen who did not fit into that particular slot. I realised that there were some interesting documentary films to be made about young people, most of them highly skilled and educated, who hated the thought of a white-collar job, who wanted to use their skills and who desired a better lifestyle for themselves and their children. The films were meant to act as a catalyst and hopefully influence young people leaving school, showing them that there was an alternative to a factory or office job or the dole queue.

Don't you feel it is a great irony and shame that the crafts you have recorded will eventually disappear and that the absence of a national film archive means that in turn your films will disappear?

Yes I do. Most of the traditional crafts will undoubtedly disappear and my programmes may well disappear too. I don't have copies of all of my films and I'm now trying to get videos of them. It costs money. A national film and video archive is absolutely vital; it is astonishing that there isn't one. So much of our recent history is on film and there are many famous Irish films, a few indeed where only one print exists!

The unsung hero has to be Liam O'Leary who has worked tirelessly on the history of the Irish cinema, unearthing valuable old films, collecting bill posters and other memorabilia together with information on defunct cinemas around the country. He has called for a national film archive many times — a voice crying in the wilderness. It is easy to say the government of the day should create an archive — and so it should — but we, the film-makers, could also try and do more about it. Finance is always a problem, as well as time.

You have recently been elected to Aosdána, the Irish Academy of Artists. I believe you and Bob Quinn are the only film-makers to have been elected?

Paddy Carey was elected at the very beginning and rightly so, he is a superb film-maker. It's a very great honour. There is always the argument as to whether film-making is an art or a craft. I would say it is an art with craft aspects to it.

You have also been given a honorary degree by Trinity College, Dublin. How do you feel about that?

It really surprised and baffled me, I don't know who put my name forward. It is flattering that people think your work is good enough to reward in this manner but I refuse to let it go to my head. You win the award, you get a degree, you shake people by the hand and say "thankyou very much" but then you put it aside and get on with the next project.

I suspect the time I spent at Gordounstoun was more formative than I realised. The school operates on the trust system instead of the more traditional English school system of monitors and prefects. One took personal responsibility and was trusted to carry out the various school duties and in some cases punished oneself. This has continued into my adult life and can be applied directly to my film-making. At the end of the day, when there is still work to be done, one is tempted to say, "Oh, to hell with it, let's go home, we've got enough material." But one is only cheating oneself and the film loses out. As they say in the industry, one is only as good as one's last film. I am never totally happy with my films, nor should I be. I know that they can always be better.

What are your plans for the future?

To make a feature. People have said to me that my documentaries are rather like feature films in the way the action and conversations between people take place. Just at the moment it would mean a big change of direction for me. I am always busy and would have to create a space, as I have a number of documentaries on the go. In a way it is a shame that features carry such kudos at the expense of the documentary which is often far more demanding to shoot and edit and equally - or perhaps more — important. I get great personal satisfaction and fulfilment from my film-making, as there is always something tangible at the end. I will never be short of ideas!

Interview with Niall Toibín

Niall Toibín began his professional acting career in 1953 with RTE's radio repertory. He remained there until 1967 when he joined the Abbey Theatre. He has since performed at London's National Theatre, on New York's Broadway and in Ireland's main theatres. His famous one-man show is on tape and he was a personal friend of the Irish playwright, Brendan Behan, whom Toibín later played in *The Borstal Boy*. His television roles have included *Brideshead Revisited* and *Tales of an Irish RM*, whilst amongst his film work are parts in *Wagner, The Outsider* and *Eat the Peach*.

You have had a long career on the stage but when was your first film part?

The first film I was really involved in was the Disney film, *Guns in the Heather*, which was made here in Ireland in 1968, — it was released theatrically under some other title I think. I played a sort of East European spy, one of four running around the countryside with practically no lines. It was a semi-comic piece, a boy's adventure story really. Then *Ryan's Daughter* in 1969: I spent ten and a half months on that and had quite a decent part, but as they shot I think 11½ screen-time hours and cut it down to 3½ hours I finished up with practically nothing. I was also in *Flight of the Doves* in 1971, playing a sergeant of the guards.

I have come across references to Michael...

Yes — that was subsequently released as *The Outsider* which had Craig Wasson and Sterling Hayden in it. That was a very good film, directed by Tony Luraschi. I had a very, very good part, probably the best part I've ever had in a straightforward film. I played the Provo Commander in the Short Strand. It was a very good film except for the beginning and the end: Sterling Hayden was superimposed on it as an Irish-American grandfather, sort of tagged on as a postscript and an intro: it didn't really work.

What about To the Western World*?*

That was a private film made mainly for university use by a girl called Margy Kinmonth. I played a Connemara boatman. The film described a journey through Connemara by J M Synge and Jack Yeats, the painter. It was a series of articles for the *Manchester Guardian* written by Synge and illustrated by Yeats; she based the film on that journey.

And Tristan and Iseult?

That was an unfortunate film...

There has to be one!

Oh there are several! *Tristan and Iseult* was one along with another, *The Sleep of Death* or *The Inn of the Flying Dragon*. In *Tristan and Iseult* by some unexplained process which shall never now be known they managed to talk Richard Burton into playing King Marc. Nicholas Clay played Tristan and I played the baddie, Andred. I advised the King and poisoned his wine. That was made here in Ireland; I never saw the completed version. It was shown at the Cork Film Festival and in Boston somewhere and was then lost, deliberately lost, you know. Someone told me it was available on video which I hope is untrue.

What about The Sleep of Death?

That is based on a very good story by Sheridan Le Fanu and could have been a good film. It had a marvellous cast — Patrick Magee, Curt Jürgens, that very stark Swedish actor, Per Oscarsson, Brendan Price. I played the comic relief. That never got released but it wasn't bad at all. It ran out of money and they finished it on a shoelace; there were a lot of complications.

You worked with Bob Quinn in Poitín *which was wholly in Gaelic. You have also narrated in Gaelic for Patrick Carey's and Louis Marcus's films. How did you find the experience of* Poitín?

I'm a native Gaelic speaker anyway so I don't find there is any difference really. But I found the making of *Poitín* a very interesting experience because it was made by what was basically a family film

unit. Apart from the camera crew, Bob and his wife did everything as a family, even the catering. Lots of local people who were not professional actors played the parts: the only three pros in it were myself, Cyril [Cusack] and Donal McCann. It worked very well.

I am interested in how you met people such as Bob Quinn, Patrick Carey and Louis Marcus.

They had come across me mainly in radio and television. I knew Louis and Bob personally anyway. I had done a lot of work for Gael-Linn, who made the Marcus films. Bob Quinn worked in television where I was so that is how we came across each other.

Can you tell me about your part in Wagner, *the Tony Palmer ten-hour epic?*

That was made in various locations, including Vienna, Northern Italy, parts of Switzerland, Bavaria, Hungary. I played a Government Minister in King Ludwig's cabinet; Burton played Wagner. It had everybody: it was the only time that Gielgud, Olivier and Richardson were ever seen on-screen together in a film and I had the distinction of being the fourth man in that shot. I didn't get a knighthood though as a result!

And Eat the Peach, *which I believe you enjoyed very much?*

Yes I did. You'll notice that the script credits are pretty sparse and in fact I wrote all my own script. It was very much a case of making it up as we went along. I don't know whether that shows or not but there is a certain spontaneity about it. I was more or less allowed to develop the character from Day One before we even started to shoot. I was asked, having been given the basic script which was subsequently thrown out of the window anyway, as always happens, whether I wanted to play this part. I was offered one of two parts — the Mafia godfather part or Boots. I'd played the other role before, particularly in television. But Boots was totally fresh and I found it very diverting in a way to be able to think what I was going to do tomorrow that would be different and yet retain the character.

Recently you have worked with Kieran Hickey. How was that?

I played the Irish priest in *The Rockingham Shoot*, the John McGahern piece. It is a lovely scene, beautifully written. You wouldn't live anyway if you tried to rewrite anything McGahern wrote! It would not be tolerated, I can assure you. I loved working with Kieran Hickey, he's a smashing director, good for actors again, an absolute joy to work with.

Which method of acting do you like best?

I would love to have a bit of freedom to invent or extemporise within a strict framework as I go along, especially when it comes to dialogue. One of the television pieces I did was *Murphy's Stroke*. After the first half-day the director, Frank Czitanovich, said, "Why don't you rewrite your dialogue to suit yourself?" So I wrote ninety per cent of it myself.

Finally, what is the key difference for you between film work and television and theatre work?

I love film work. There is the subtlety — you can take your time on it and every possibility is explored, which is not the same with television. Also as a lazy person you feel once you've done it you've done it. But with the theatre I've got to go on tonight and tomorrow night and so on!

Chronology of Irish cinema

1800: Act of Union creates United Kingdom of Great Britain and Ireland.

1803: Robert Emmet's Rising in Dublin.

1829: Roman Catholic Relief Act.

1846: Beginning of severe winter and gales which lead to famine.

1857: Fenian Association formed in New York supporting the overthrow of the English government in Ireland.

1858: Irish Republican Brotherhood formed in Dublin by James Stephens.

1869: Disestablishment of Church of Ireland.

1879: Irish National Land League formed.

1882: Irish National League formed.

1886: Gladstone's first Home Rule Bill (defeated).

1893: Defeat of Gladstone's second Home Rule Bill (defeated in House of Lords). Douglas Hyde founds the Gaelic League; first meeting arranged by Eoin MacNeill.

1896: First screening of a film in Ireland at Dan Lowrey's Star of Erin Music Hall, Dublin (20 April).

1898: Dr R A Mitchell films a yacht race in Belfast Lough — the first Irish film.

1899: W B Yeats, Lady Gregory and others form the Irish Literary Theatre (later called the Abbey Theatre).

1900: Irish Animated Pictures Company formed to exhibit and distribute films.

1904: Louis de Clerq makes the first Irish documentary, *Life on the Great Southern and Western Railway*. Formation of the first production company, Irish Animated Photo Company.

1905: Sinn Féin founded.

1907: J M Synge's *The Playboy of the Western World* first performed on the Dublin stage. Melbourne-Cooper's *Irish Wives and English Husbands*. Troubles in Belfast filmed.

1909: James Joyce opens the Volta in Dublin, Ireland's first cinema (20 December). Filmophone shown in St George's Hall, Belfast. Fianna Éireann founded.

1910: Canadian Sidney Olcott makes the first of the Kalem company's many films in Ireland, *The Lad From Old Ireland*.

1911: Sidney Olcott makes over fifteen films, including *Rory O'More*, *Arrah-na-Pogue*, *The Colleen Bawn*, *The Irish Emigrant*, *Ireland 50 Years Ago* and *Ireland the Oppressed*.

1912: Ulster Covenant signed. J Theobald Walsh's *The Life of St Patrick*. First screening of colour films at the Grand Opera House, Belfast (1 April).

1913: Irish Volunteers founded (later becomes Irish Republican Army — IRA). Formation of Ulster Volunteer Force and Irish Citizen Army.

1914: Walter MacNamara and P J Bourke's *Ireland — A Nation*; Sidney Olcott's *Robert Emmet, Ireland's Martyr* and *For Ireland's Sake*. Irish Theatre Company formed by John MacDonagh, Joseph Plunkett and Edward Martyn. Third Home

Rule Bill passed but is suspended. Kinetophone films shown in Belfast Picture House.

1915: F J McCormick's *Fun at Finglas Fair*, destroyed in the Easter Rising the following year. Gordon Lewis and Norman Whitten film the funeral of Sinn Féin's O'Donovan Rossa (1 August) at which Patrick Pearse gives a famous speech.

1916: Easter Rising in Dublin; Irish Republic proclaimed. The Film Company of Ireland formed. J M Kerrigan directs eight films, including *O'Neill of the Glen*, *The Food of Love* and *Widow Malone*. 150 cinemas and halls in Ireland are showing films.

1917: *Knocknagow* produced (released 1918). *Irish Events* newsreel begins. General Film Supply Company founded by Norman Whitten. William Power sets up the Celtic Film Company. Fred O'Donovan's *When Love Came to Gavin Burke*, *Rafferty's Rise* and *A Passing Shower*. Norman Whitten and Gordon Lewis film the funeral of Thomas Ashe.

1918: Last all-Ireland elections.

1919: Declaration of Irish Republic by Sinn Féin; armed struggle for Irish independence begins. Norman Whitten's *Sinn Féin Review 1 & 2*.

1920: Bloody Sunday (21 November); deaths of Kevin Barry and Terence MacSwiney. Government of Ireland Act. John MacDonagh's *Willie Reilly and His Colleen Bawn*; William Power's *Rosaleen Dhu*; Norman Whitten's *In the Days of St Patrick*.

1921: Anglo-Irish Treaty: agreement on creation of Irish Free State and on establishment of Boundary Commission to review North-South border. George V opens Northern Ireland Parliament. Rex Ingram makes *The Four Horsemen of the Apocalypse*.

1922: Civil war begins between pro- and anti-Treaty parties in the South. Deaths of Arthur Griffith and Michael Collins. W T Cosgrave heads the new government. John MacDonagh's *The Casey Millions*, *Cruiskeen Lawn* and *Wicklow Gold*. James Joyce's *Ulysses* first published in Paris.

1923: End of the Civil War (May). Censorship of Films Act. Opening of the Classic Cinema in Belfast. James Montgomery appointed film censor.

1925: Report of Boundary Commission suppressed; new Anglo-Irish Treaty confirms six-county border. Sean O'Casey's play, *Juno and the Paycock*, produced at the Abbey. Dr Eppel produces *Irish Destiny*.

1926: Michael Curran presents a 'sound' show using the DeForest Phono Optical Sound-on-Film System at the Lyceum, Belfast. First Irish radio station (later becomes Radio Éireann). Fianna Fáil founded. John Ford's *The Shamrock Handicap*.

1928: Censorship of books established. Gate Theatre founded by Hilton Edwards and Micheál MacLiammóir. Galway Gaelic Theatre opens (afterwards called the Taibhdhearc Theatre).

1929: Sound cinema established in Ireland with *The Singing Fool* and screening of sound recording of Catholic Emancipation Centenary celebrations at Capitol Cinema, Dublin. Arthur Robison's *The Informer*.

1930: Frank Borzage's *Song of My Heart*; Alfred Hitchcock's film version of *Juno and the Paycock*.

1931: *Irish Press* founded.

1932: Colonel Victor Haddick makes Ireland's first sound travelogue film, *The Voice of Ireland*. Eamon De Valera in power as President of Executive Council and Minister of External Affairs. Food riots in Belfast.

1933: Henry Edwards's *General John Regan*; Harry Lachman's *Paddy the Next Best Thing*. United Ireland Party founded, later known as Fine Gael. Formation of Communist Party of Ireland.

1934: First Irish sound fiction film, Brian Desmond Hurst's *Irish Hearts*. Robert Flaherty's *Man of Aran*. Cinema admissions in Ireland total 36 million.

1935: Sectarian riots in Belfast. John Ford's version of *The Informer*; Lloyd Bacon's *The Irish in Us*; Brian Desmond Hurst's *Riders to the Sea*.

1936: Irish Film Society and Belfast Film Society founded. Irish Ciné Group set up. Tom Cooper's *The Dawn*; Denis Johnston's *Guests of the Nation*. Richard Hayward and Donovan Pedelty's *Irish and Proud of It*. Brian Desmond Hurst's *Ourselves Alone*. IRA declared illegal. Aer Lingus founded.

1937: Harold Schuster's *Wings of the Morning*; John M Stahl's *Parnell*; Jeff Musso's *Le Puritain*. New Irish constitution adopted.

1938: Tom Cooper's *Uncle Nick*; Harry Hughes's *Mountains o' Mourne*; Alex Bryce's *My Irish Molly*.

1939: Ireland declares neutrality in World War Two; Northern Ireland involved in war. IRA campaign in Britain.

1940: Max Kimmich's *The Fox of Glenarvon/Der Fuchs von Glenarvon*; Norman Taurog's *Little Nellie Kelly*. Periodical *The Bell* first published. Dr Richard Hayes appointed film censor (November).

1942: Children's Film Committee formed. Irish Film Society's *Tibradden*, *Zones*, *They Live By the Sea* and *Aiséirghe*.

1943: Formation of the National Film Institute. Publication of *Irish Cinema Handbook*.

1944: 240 cinemas in the Republic; 110 cinemas in Northern Ireland.

1945: Brendan Stafford and John D Sheridan's *A Nation Once Again*. Liam O'Leary publishes *An Invitation to the Film*.

1946: Frank Launder's *I See a Dark Stranger*; Liam O'Leary's *Dance School*; Brian Desmond Hurst's *Hungry Hill*.

1947: Carol Reed's *Odd Man Out* and Frank Launder's *Captain Boycott*.

1948: Irish Free State becomes a Republic and leaves British Commonwealth. George Fleischmann's *Who Fears to Speak of '98?* and *The Silent Order*. Liam O'Leary makes *Our Country*, *Mr Careless Goes To Town* and *Safe Cycling*.

1949: William Moylan's *Lifeline*; George Fleischmann and Ronald Ream make *March of a Nation*. Government of Ireland Act affirms Northern Ireland as part of United Kingdom; Éire formally becomes a republic and leaves the Commonwealth.

1950: George Fleischmann's *W B Yeats — A Tribute*. British National Film Finance Corporation founded.

1951: Liam O'Leary's *Portrait of Dublin*; Paul Rotha's *No Resting Place*. Hilton Edwards makes *Return to Glennascaul* and *Hamlet at Elsinore*.

1952: Basil Dearden's *The Gentle Gunman*; John Ford's *The Quiet Man*; Gerard Healy's *A Voyage to Recovery*. Irish Film Industry Committee formed.

1953: Gael-Linn founded. Hilton Edwards makes *From Time to Time/A Stone in the Heather/Cross My Heart*. Gerard Healy's *Art of Reception*.

1954: Dr Martin Brennan appointed film censor (January).

1955: Ireland joins United Nations. Irish Tourist Board/Bord Fáilte established. Rank buys all Irish Theatres and Curran circuits based in Northern Ireland. 278 cinemas in the Republic, of which 49 are in Dublin.

1956: First Cork Film Festival (May). Liam O'Hora appointed film censor (July). Approximately fifty million cinema attendances a year: half the Irish population attend the cinema once a week.

1957: John Ford's *The Rising of the Moon*.

1958: Ardmore Studios opened (May). Fielder Cook's *Home is the Hero*; Paul Rotha's *Cradle of Genius*.

1959: Radharc Film Unit formed by Reverend Father Joseph Dunn. George Morrison makes *Mise Éire*. Michael

Anderson's *Shake Hands With the Devil* and Muriel Box's *This Other Eden*.

1960: Irish Film Finance Corporation founded. Broadcasting Authority Act. Tay Garnett's *A Terrible Beauty*.

1961: Radio Telefís Éireann set up; first transmission 31 December. George Morrison makes *Saoirse?* Colm O Laoghaire's *Our Neighbour's Children*.

1962: Brian Desmond Hurst's film version of *The Playboy of the Western World*; Colm O Laoghaire's *Fior Uisce/Water Wisdom*.

1963: Peter Collinson's *The One Nighters* and Desmond Davis's *The Girl With Green Eyes*.

1964: Dr Christopher Macken appointed film censor (April).

1965: Desmond Davis's *I Was Happy Here* and George Morrison's *The Irish Rising 1916*.

1966: Radharc's *Turkana*; Louis Marcus's *An Tine Bheo* and Colm O Laoghaire's *This Most Gallant Gentleman*.

1967: Louis Marcus publishes series of influential articles in the *Irish Times* and makes *Rhapsody of a River* and *Fleadh Ceoil*. Film Industry Committee set up, with John Huston as chairman. Kieran Hickey's *Faithful Departed* and Joseph Strick's version of *Ulysses*.

1968: Film Industry Committee publishes report (July). Queen's Film Theatre opens (October). Peter Lennon makes *Rocky Road to Dublin*. Patrick Carey's *Yeats Country*, Radharc's *The Restless Knives*. Civil rights campaign begins in Northern Ireland.

1969: Radharc's *Night Flight to Uli* and Don Sharp's *The Violent Enemy*. British troops deployed in Derry and Belfast.

1970: Film Industry Bill introduced in the Dáil for the establishment of a board to be known as An Bord Scannán. Patrick Carey's *Oisín* and David Lean's *Ryan's Daughter*. Toronto Film Society stages a season of Irish films.

1971: David Shaw-Smith's *Connemara and Its Ponies*; RTE's *A Week in the Life of Martin Cluxton*. Introduction of internment.

1972: Robert Altman's *Images*; Kieran Hickey's *The Light of Other Days*; Thaddeus O'Sullivan's *Pint of Plain*. Marcel Ophuls makes *A Sense of Loss*. All major cinemas in Belfast bombed. Dermot Breen appointed film censor (June). Northern Ireland Parliament suspended and direct rule introduced.

1973: United Kingdom and Republic join the EEC; new Northern Ireland Constitution Act; elections for Northern Ireland Assembly. Change of government results in the Film Industry Bill not being proceeded with. Ardmore Studios purchased by the Government. Wolf Mankowitz's *Hebrew Lesson* and John Boorman's *Zardoz*.

1974: Power-sharing Executive established; Ulster Workers Council strikes lead to collapse of Executive and dissolution of Assembly. Joe Comerford's *Withdrawal*.

1975: Northern Ireland Convention established. Government establishes The National Film Studios of Ireland at Ardmore Studios (June). Louis Marcus's *Conquest of Light* and Bob Quinn's *Caoineadh Airt Uí Laoire/Lament for Art O'Leary* and *Cloch*. Deirdre Friel makes the *Victims* trilogy for RTE. Don Sharp's *Hennessy* and Stanley Kubrick's *Barry Lyndon*.

1976: Cathal Black's *Wheels*. Corporation Tax Acts.

1977: Joseph Strick makes *A Portrait of an Artist as a Young Man*. Joe Comerford's *Down the Corner*. Arts Council establishes Film Script Award. Irish Film Society replaced by Irish Film Theatre.

1978: Tommy McArdle's *The Kinkisha*; Bob Quinn's *Poitín*; Kieran Hickey's *Exposure*; Thaddeus O'Sullivan's *On a Paving Stone Mounted*; Joe Comerford's *Traveller*; Patrick Carey's *Errigal*.

1979: Irish Film Board Bill introduced in the Dáil by the Minister for Industry. Tony Luraschi makes *The Outsider*. Frank Hall appointed film censor.

1980: Anglo-Irish Intergovernmental Council established at Haughey/Thatcher summit. Tommy McArdle's *It's Handy When People Don't Die* and Kieran Hickey's *Criminal Conversation*.

1981: The Irish Film Board/Bord Scannán na hÉireann established. Cathal Black makes *Our Boys*. Neville Presho's *Desecration* and Armand Gatti's *The Writing on the Wall*. Pat Murphy and John Davies direct *Maeve*.

1982: Northern Ireland Assembly reconvened. National Film Studios closed down by government; public hearing on the proposed work of the Irish Film Board (April). Neil Jordan's début, *Angel*. Robert Wynne-Simmons's *The Outcasts*.

1983: New Ireland Forum established. Kieran Hickey's *Attracta*; Donald Taylor Black's *At the Cinema Palace — Liam O'Leary*; Bill Miskelly and Marie Jackson's *The Schooner*; Pat O'Connor's *The Ballroom of Romance*.

1984: New Ireland Forum reports; Thatcher/Haughey summit. Cathal Black's *Pigs*; Pat Murphy's *Anne Devlin*; Bob Quinn's *Atlantean*; David Shaw-Smith's *Bees and Bee Skeps*.

1985: Anglo-Irish Agreement signed between Thatcher and Fitzgerald. Donald Taylor Black's *Remembering Jimmy O'Dea*; Thaddeus O'Sullivan's *The Woman Who Married Clark Gable*; Pat O'Connor's *Cal*.

1986: Peter Ormrod's *Eat the Peach*; Joe Lee and Frank Deasy's *Sometime City*; Kieran Hickey's *Short Story: Irish Cinema 1945-1958*; Bill Miskelly and Marie Jackson's *The End of the World Man*; Colin Gregg's *Lamb*; David Hammond's *Steel Chest, Nail in the Boot, and the Barking Dog*. Sheamus Smith appointed film censor. National Film Studios sold to a consortium including MTM Enterprises, Tara Productions, National Development Corporation and others (October).

1987: Abolishment of the Irish Film Board. Siobhán Twomey's *Boom Babies*; Fergus Tighe's *Clash of the Ash*; Bob Quinn's *Budawanny*. Strongbow produce series *When Reason Sleeps*, directed by Robert Wynne-Simmons and Tony Barry. John Huston's *The Dead*, Jack Clayton's *The Lonely Passion of Judith Hearne*, Mike Hodges's *A Prayer for the Dying* and Joe Lee and Frank Deasy's *The Courier*.

1988: Louis Marcus makes six programmes on contemporary Irish life for RTE with the series title *The Entertainers*; Joe Comerford's *Reefer and the Model*. Irish Film Directors forum meets at Sense of Ireland festival in London (May). Irish Film Institute opens venue periodically for plays. Action Committee formed to lobby for a state agency responsible for film.

Filmography of Irish films

These filmographies give concise information on Irish films and films with an Irish theme or interest. It is not our aim to be comprehensive in such a small space, but Flicks Books are compiling the *Directory of Irish and Irish-related Films* which will attempt to be the most complete reference work on Irish cinema, including features, documentaries, animation and shorts from the last eighty years.

A   animation
ad   art direction
CF   children's feature
d   director
D   documentary
DF   documentary feature
DS   documentary short
F   feature/drama
G   in Gaelic
GV   Gaelic version
m   music
md   musical direction
n   novel
narr   narrator
ph   photography
pl   play
prod   production
S   short
s   story
ss   short story

Aiséirghe
Ire 1942 30m silent b/w D
wd, ph Liam O'Leary

An Tine Bheo/The Living Flame
Ire 1966 45m col D
d Louis Marcus *ph* Robert Monks *m* Sean O Riada

An tOileanach a dFhill/Return of the Islander
Ire 1970 25m col F
wd James Mulkerns *ph* Val Ennis, Alan Blowey *m* Noel Kelehan *narr* Richard Harris
Michael Connely, Maire Burke.

Angel
Ire/GB 1982 92m col F
USA title: Danny Boy
wd Neil Jordan *ph* Chris Menges *m* Keith Donald, Paddy Meegan, Verdi
Stephen Rea, Honor Heffernan, Veronica Quilligan, Alan Devlin, Peter Caffrey, Marie Kean, Ray McAnally, Donal McCann.

Anne Devlin
Ire 1984 124m col F
wd Pat Murphy *ph* Thaddeus O'Sullivan *m* Robert Boyle
Brid Brennan, Bosco Hogan, Des McAleer, Gillian Hackett, Ian McElhinny, David Kelly, Chris O'Neill, Niall O'Brien.

Art of Reception
Ire 1954 F
d Gerard Healy *ph* George Fleischmann
Cyril Cusack, Liam Redmond, Anna Manahan.

At the Cinema Palace — Liam O'Leary
Ire 1983 53m col D
prod Poolbeg Prods *wd* Donald Taylor Black *ph* Sean Corcoran *m* Bill Whelan
Liam O'Leary, Michael Powell, Lindsay Anderson, Cyril Cusack, Kevin Brownlow, Denis Forman, Sean MacBride.

Atlantean
Ire 1984 3 x 53m col D
prod Cinegael *wd* Bob Quinn *ph* Seamus Deasy, Sean Corcoran, Thaddeus O'Sullivan, Joe Comerford, Nick O'Neill, Abdelhadi Tazi *m* Roger Doyle *narr* Alan Stanford

Attracta
Ire 1983 55m col F
prod BAC Films *d* Kieran Hickey *w, ss* William Trevor *ph* Sean Corcoran
Wendy Hiller, Kate Thompson, Joe McPartland, John Kavanagh, Kate Flynn, Deirdre Donnelly, Cathleen Delaney.

The Ballroom of Romance
Ire 1982 52m col F
prod RTE *d* Pat O'Connor *w, ss* William Trevor *ph* Nat Crosby
Brenda Fricker, John Kavanagh, Cyril Cusack, Niall Toibín.

Bank Holiday
Ire 1930 silent b/w DS
d Mary Manning

The Best Man
Ire/GB 1985 85m col F
wd Joe Mahon *ph* Terry McDonald *m* Eamon Friel
Seamus Ball, Máireéad Mullan, Denis McGowan, Jean Flagherty, Mickey McGowan.

Blarney
Ire 1938 66m b/w F
d Harry O'Donovan
Jimmy O'Dea, Ken Warrington, Julie Suedo, Noel Purcell, Rodney Malcolmson, Hazel Hughes, Myrette Morven.

Boom Babies
Ire 1986 34m col F
wd Siobhán Twomey *ph* Nicholas O'Neill *m* John and Neil McGrory, John Ryan
Aisling Toibín, Andrew Connolly.

Brendan Behan's Dublin
Ire 1966 29m col D
d Norman Cohen *w* Carolyn Swift *ph* Robert Monks *m* The Dubliners *narr* Ray McAnally

Budawanny
Ire 1987 79m part silent b/w and col F
prod Cinegael *wd* Bob Quinn *n* Pádraic Standúin *ph* Seamus Deasy *m* Roger Doyle
Donal McCann, Maggie Fegan, Tomas O'Flaharta, Peadar Lamb, Freda Gillen, Sean O'Colsdealbha.

By Accident
Ire 1930 60m silent b/w F
wd J N G Davidson
C Clarke-Clifford, Olive Purcell, Mary Manning, Paul Farrell.

Cancer
Ire 1976 63m col F
prod RTE *d* Deirdre Friel *w* Eugene McCabe *ph* Stuart Hetherington
J G Devlin, Louis Rolston.

Caoineadh Airt Uí Laoire/Lament for Art O'Leary
Ire 1975 56m col F
prod Cinegael *wd* Bob Quinn *ph* Joe Comerford *m* M Finn
Séan Bán Breatnach, Eibhlín Nic Dhonncha, John Arden.

Capallology!/Horse Laughs
Ire 1968 17m col D G
d Louis Marcus *w* Louis Marcus, Breandán O hEithir *ph* Robert Monks *m* Gene Martin *narr* Niall Toibín

The Casey Millions
Ire 1922 silent b/w F
d John MacDonagh
Jimmy O'Dea, Barrett MacDonnell, Chris Sylvester.

A Cattle Drive in Galway
Ire 1908 silent D
d Robert Paul

Caught in a Free State
Ire 1983 56m col F
prod RTE/C4 *d* Peter Ormrod *w* Brian Lynch *ph* Eugene McVeigh *m* Seoirse Bodley
Gotz Burger, Benno Hoffman, Peter Jankowsky, John Kavanagh, Barry McGovern, Niall Toibín.

A Child's Voice
Ire 1978 30m col F
prod BAC Films *d* Kieran Hickey *w* David

Thomson *ph* Sean Corcoran *narr* Valentine Dyall
T P McKenna, Stephen Brennan, R D Smith, June Tobin.

Christmas Morning
Ire 1978 7m col F
wd Tiernan MacBride *ph* Seamus Corcoran *m* traditional arranged by Paul Brady
Paul Bennett, Paul Erskine, Godfrey Quigley, Don Foley, Paddy O'Neill.

Christy Ring
Ire 1963 23m col D
d Louis Marcus *ph* Vincent Corcoran

Clash of the Ash
Ire 1987 53m col F
wd Fergus Tighe *ph* Declan Quinn
Liam Heffernan, Vincent Murphy, Gina Moxley, Alan Devlin.

Cloch
Ire 1975 26m col D
prod Cinegael *wd, ph* Bob Quinn *m* Roger Doyle
James McKenna.

Connemara and Its Ponies
Ire 1971 28m col D
d, ph David Shaw-Smith *w, narr* Michael Killanan *m* Donal Lunny, Drowsy Maggie

Conquest of Light
Ire 1975 12m col D
wd Louis Marcus *ph* Robert Monks *m* Vic Flick *narr* Denis Brennan

The Courier
Ire 1987 85m col F
prod Cityvision *d* Joe Lee, Frank Deasy *w* Frank Deasy *ph* Gabriel Beristain *m* Declan MacManus and others
Gabriel Byrne, Cait O'Riordan, Padraig O'Loingsigh, Ian Bannen, Andrew Connolly.

Cradle of Genius
Ire 1958 20m b/w D
d Paul Rotha *w ph* Wolfgang Suschitzky bsc
Sean O'Casey, Barry Fitzgerald.

Criminal Conversation
Ire 1980 60m col F
prod BAC Films *d* Kieran Hickey *w* Kieran Hickey, Philip Davison *ss* Philip Davison *ph* Sean Corcoran
Emmet Bergin, Deirdre Donnelly, Peter Caffrey, Leslie Lalor.

Cruiskeen Lawn
Ire 1922 silent b/w F
d John MacDonagh
Jimmy O'Dea, Fay Sargent, Tom Moran, Kathleen Armstrong, Barrett MacDonnell, Chris Sylvester, Fred Jeffs.

A Cuban Breeze
GB/Ire 1984 33m col DF
prod IFB/NFTVS *d* Colm Villa *w* Colm Villa, Sean Hinds *ph* Graham Dixon

Dance School
Ire 1946 10m silent col and b/w D
d, ph Liam O'Leary

The Dawn
Ire 1936 b/w F
d Tom Cooper
Tom Cooper, Brian O'Sullivan, James Gleeson, Eileen Davis, Donal O'Cahill, Jerry O'Mahony, Bill Murphy, Marion O'Connell.

Dementia 13
aka: The Haunted and the Hunted
USA/Ire 1963 81m b/w F
wd Francis Coppola *ph* Charles Hannawalt *m* Ronald Stein
William Campbell, Launa Anders, Bart Patton, Patrick Magee, Mary Mitchell, Eithne Dunne.

Desecration
Ire 1981 52m col F
d Neville Presho *w* Breandán O hEithir, Declan Burke-Kennedy *ph* Godfrey Graham *m* Jolyon Jackson
Tom Hickey, Johnny Murphy, Eamonn Keane.

Devil's Rock
Ire 1938 55m b/w F
d Germain Burger, Richard Hayward
Geraldine Mitchel, Richard Hayward.

Down the Corner
Ire/GB 1978 60m col F
d Joe Comerford *w, n* Noel McFarlane *ph* Adam Barker-Mill *m* Liam Weldon, Roger Doyle
Joe Keenan, Declan Cronin, Kevin Doyle, Christy Keogh.

Down There
Ire 1973 col D
d Gerry Murray, Ted Dolan

Dubliners — Sean Agus Nua/Dubliners — Then and Now
Ire 1971 23m col D
d Louis Marcus *ph* Robert Monks *m* Gene Martin

Eamon De Valera
Ire 1975 58m b/w D
d, ph George Morrison *w* George Morrison, Robert Kee *narr* Robert Kee

Eamon De Valera: Portrait of a Statesman
Ire/GB 1968 30m b/w and col D
d George Fleischmann *w* Peter O'Reilly *ph* George Fleischmann, archive

The Early Bird
Ire 1936 b/w F
d Donovan Pedelty, Richard Hayward

Eat the Peach
Ire 1986 95m col F
d Peter Ormrod *w* John Kelleher, Peter Ormrod *ph* Arthur Wooster *m* Donal Lunny
Stephen Brennan, Eamon Morrissey, Catherine Byrne, Niall Toibín, Joe Lynch.

Eh Joe
Ire 1986 38m col F
prod Yellow Asylum Films *d* Alan Gilsenan *w* Samuel Beckett *ph* Peter Butler
Tom Hickey, Siobhán McKenna (voice).

Emtigon
Ire 1977 14m col
d Joe Comerford *m* Roger Doyle

The End of the World Man
Ire 1985 82m col CF
prod Aisling Films *d* Bill Miskelly *w* Marie Jackson *ph* Seamus Deasy *m* John Anderson
John Hewitt, Leanne O'Malley, Claire Weir, Maureen Dow, Michael Knowles.

Errigal
Ire 1970 14m col D
d, ph Patrick Carey *m* Brian Boydell *narr* Brian Carey (English version), Niall Toibín (Gaelic version)

Exposure
Ire 1978 48m col F
prod BAC Films *d* Kieran Hickey *w* Kieran Hickey, Philip Davison *ph* Sean Corcoran *m* Beethoven
Catherine Schell, T P McKenna, Bosco Hogan, Niall O'Brien.

Faithful Departed
Ire 1967 10m b/w D
prod BAC Films *d* Kieran Hickey *w* Des Hickey *ph* Sean Corcoran, Roland Hill *songs* from *Ulysses narr* Jack McGowran

Fear of the Dark
Ire 1986 53m col F
d Tony Barry *w* Robert Wynne-Simmons
ph Breffni Byrne *m* Tim Doherty
Hugh O'Connor, Aisling Toibín, Owen
O'Gorman, Donal O'Kelly.

Fleadh Ceoil/Folk Music Festival
Ire 1967 23m b/w D G
d Louis Marcus *w* Breandán O hEithir *ph*
Robert Monks *m* traditional *narr* Chris
Curran

The Food of Love
Ire 1916 silent b/w
d J M Kerrigan

Foolsmate
Ire 1940 20m b/w F
d, ph Brendan Stafford *w* Geoffrey Dalton

From Time to Time
aka: A Stone in the Heather/Cross My
Heart
Ire 1953 b/w F
d Hilton Edwards

Fun at Finglas Fair
Ire 1915 silent b/w
d F J McCormick *w* Cahal McGarvey

Guests of the Nation
Ire 1936 50m silent b/w F
d Denis Johnston *w* Denis Johnston, Frank
O'Connor, Mary Manning *ss* Frank
O'Connor
Barry Fitzgerald, Cyril Cusack, Shelah
Richards, Fred Johnson, Denis O'Dea,
Hilton Edwards.

Hamlet at Elsinore
Ire 1951 b/w F
d Hilton Edwards *ph* George Fleischmann
Micheál MacLiammóir.

Hands series
Ire 1977-88 27m col D

d, ph David Shaw-Smith *w, narr* Maurice
Craig, Mairead Dunleavy, Con Houlihan,
Benedict Kiely, Eamonn MacThomais,
Brid Mahon, Conor McAnally, Ray
McAnally, Seamus O'Cathain, Andy
O'Mahony, Diarmid Ó Muirithe, Timothy
O'Neill, Gillian Somerville-Large, Maxwell
Sweeney *m* Brian Boydell, Roger Doyle,
Jolyon Jackson, Terry Odlum

*Basket Making, Bees and Bee Skeps,
Carley's Bridge Potteries, Carriage
Building, Cavan Cabinetmakers, Cavan
Cooper, Curraghs, Donegal Carpets,
Donegal Weavers, Dublin Bookbinder,
Dublin Candlemakers, Dublin Silversmith,
Dublin Work Horses, Fermanagh
Country, Hurley Making, Irish Lace, Irish
Patchwork, John Surliss: Chairmaker, Pipe
Works, Rush Work, The Saddler,
Shoemaker, Stone, Stoneground, Tailor,
Wexford Thatcher, Wool Spinning,
Woollen Mills.*

Harp Of My Country
Ire 1986 76m col D
prod Anner Communications *d* P J Barron
w Timothy Patrick Coogan *ph* Gerrard
MacArthur
Niall Murray, Suzanne Rhattigan, James
Barkley.

The Hebrew Lesson
Ire 1972 25m col F
wd Wolf Mankowitz
Milo O'Shea, Patrick Dawson, Harry
Towb, Alun Owen.

Heritage
Ire 1976 col F
prod RTE *d* Deirdre Friel *w* Eugene
McCabe *ph* Stuart Hetherington

The Heritage of Ireland
Ire 1978 6 x 50m col D
d Louis Marcus *ph* Robert Monks *m* Sean
O Riada

Home is the Hero
Ire 1959 80m b/w F
d Fielder Cook *w* Henry Keating *pl* Walter
Macken *ph* Stanley Pavey *m* Bruce
Montgomery
Walter Macken, Eileen Crowe, Arthur
Kennedy, Joan O'Hara, Marie O'Donnell.

Images
USA/Ire 1972 101m col F
wd Robert Altman *ph* Vilmos Zsigmond *m*
John Williams
Susannah York, Rene Auberjonois, Marcel
Bozzuffi.

In the Days of St Patrick
Ire 1920 silent b/w
d Norman Whitten *ph* Gordon Lewis
Ira Allen.

Ireland — Rome 1950
Ire 1950 15m b/w D
d, ph George Fleischmann *w* Bart Bastable

Irish and Proud of It
Ire 1936 72m b/w F
d Donovan Pedelty *w* David Evans,
Donovan Pedelty *s* Dorothea Donn Byrne
Richard Hayward, Dinah Sheridan, Gwen
Gill, George Pembroke.

Irish Destiny
Ire 1925 93m silent b/w F
d George Dewhurst *w* Dr Isaac J Eppel *ph*
Joe Rosenthal
Brian Magowan, Frances MacNamara,
Patrick Cullinane, Cathal McGarvey.

Irish Hearts
aka: Norah O'Neale
Ire 1934 b/w F
d Brian Desmond Hurst *n* Dr J Johnston
Abraham

**Is There One Who Understands Me?/The
World of James Joyce**
Ire 120m col D
prod RTE *d* Seán Ó Mórdha

The Islandman
aka: West of Kerry
Ire 1939 48m b/w F
d Donal O'Cahill
Cecil Ford, Eileen Curran, Brian
O'Sullivan, Gabriel Fallon.

It's Handy When People Don't Die
Ire 1980 100m col F
d Tom McArdle *w, ss* John McArdle *ph*
Ciaran Tanham *m* Mícheál Ó Súilleabháin
Garret Keogh, Bob Carlyle, Brendan
Cauldwell, Catherine Gibson, Barbara
McNamara.

John, Love
Ire/GB 1983 34m col F
prod NFTVS *wd* John Davis *ph* Sue
Gibson
Nuala Hayes, Niall O'Brien, Tony Hyland,
Carmel Callan, Danny Cummins, Martin
Dempsey.

Jonathan Swift
Ire 1967 30m b/w D
prod BAC Films *d* Kieran Hickey *w* David
Thomson *ph* Theo Hogers *narr* Cyril
Cusack, Alan Badel, Patrick Magee,
Siobhán McKenna

Kilian of Wurzburg
Ire 1982 27m col D
prod Radharc Films

The Kinkisha
Ire 1977 65m col F
d Tom McArdle *w* John McArdle *ph*
Ciaran Tanham *m* Mícheál Ó Súilleabháin
Barbara McNamara, John McArdle,
Catherine Gibson, David Byrne.

Knocknagow
Ire 1918 60m 8 reels silent b/w F
d Fred O'Donovan *n* Charles J Kickham *ph*
William Moser
Brian Magowan, Kathleen Murphy, J M
Carre, Alice Keating, Charles Power,
Dermot O'Dowd, Cyril Cusack.

Land of Her Fathers
Ire 1924 silent b/w F
d John Hurley *ss* Dorothea Donn Byrne
Micheál MacLiammóir, Frank Hugh
O'Donnell, Phyllis O'Hara, Barry
Fitzgerald, Tom Moran, F J McCormick,
Maureen Delaney.

The Late Dr Plunkett
Ire 1975 25m col D
prod Radharc Films

Life on the Great Southern and Western Railway
Ire 1904 silent D
d Louis de Clerq

Lifeline
Ire 1949 b/w D
d William Moylan *ph* George Fleischmann

The Light of Other Days
Ire 1972 50m sepia D
prod BAC Films *d* Kieran Hickey *w* Des
Hickey *ph* Sean Corcoran *m* arranged by
John Beckett *narr* Colin Blakely, Marie
Kean

London to Killarney
Ire 1907 silent b/w F
d Arthur Melbourne Cooper

Luck of the Irish
Ire 1935 79m b/w F
d Donovan Pedelty *w, n* Colonel Victor
Haddick
Richard Hayward, Kay Walsh, Niall
McGinnis, J R Mageean.

Maeve
Ire/GB 1981 110m col F
d Pat Murphy, John Davies *w* Pat Murphy
ph Robert Smith *m* Molly Brambeld and
the Country Four and others
Mary Jackson, Brid Brennan, Mark
Mulholland, Trudy Kelly, John Keegan,
Nuala McCann

March of a Nation
Ire 1949 b/w D
ph George Fleischmann, Ronald Ream

Mise Éire/I Am Ireland
Ire 1959 90m b/w D G
d George Morrison *w* George Morrison,
Seán Mac Reamoinn *ph* archive footage,
Vincent Corcoran *m* Sean O Riada

The Miser's Gift
Ire 1916 silent b/w
d J M Kerrigan
Fred O'Donovan, John MacDonagh

Mists of Time
Ire 1969 28m col D
wd, ph Patrick Carey *m* Brian Boydell *narr*
Tom St John Barry

Moneypoint — Power from Coal
Ire 1987 35m col D
d, ph George Fleischmann *w* Paul Moran

Mr Careless Goes To Town
Ire 1949 10m b/w D
wd Liam O'Leary *ph* George Flesichmann

Nano Nagle
Ire 1976 35m col D
prod Radharc Films

A Nation Once Again
Ire 1945 b/w D
d, ph Brendan Stafford, John D Sheridan
w John D Sheridan

Natural Gas I
Ire 1983 20m col D
d, ph George Fleischmann *w* M Murray

Natural Gas II
Ire 1988 20m col D
d, ph George Fleischmann *w* Michael
Boyle *ph* Robert Monks

Night Flight to Uli
Ire 1969 30m b/w D
prod Radharc Films

Night in Tunisia
Ire 1983 52m col F
prod RTE *d* Pat O'Connor *w* Neil Jordan
ph Peter Dorney
Michael Lally, Ciaran Burns, Jill Doyle, Jim
Culleton.

Now I Know
Ire 1988 col F
prod Now I Know Film Partners/
Strongbow *d* Robert Pappas *ph* Jack
Conroy
Matt Mulhern, Maeve Germaine.

Oidhche Sheanchais/A Night of Story-telling
Ire 1935 15m b/w G
d Robert Flaherty
Tomas O Diorain, Maggie Dirrane, 'Tiger'
King, Patch Ruadh, Michaeleen.

Oilean Eile/Another Island
Ire 1985 135m col D GV
prod RTE *wd* Muiris Mac Conghail *ph*
Breffni Byrne *m* Gerard Victory

Oisín
Ire 1970 17m col D
d, ph Patrick Carey

One Day Time
Ire 1982 30m col DF
prod Cityvision *d* Joe Lee *w* Joe Lee, Frank
Deasy *ph* John Malachy Coleman, Joe
Mulholland *m* Resisdance, John
McMenamin
Gregg Gough, Siobhán McCluskey,
Vincent McCabe, Garrett Keogh, Helen
Roche.

The One Nighters
Ire 1963 48m b/w D
wd Peter Collinson *ph* Robert Monks *m*
The Royal Showband *narr* Frank Hall

One of Ourselves
GB/Ire 1983 50m col F
d Pat O'Connor *w, ss* William Trevor *ph*
Kenneth MacMillan *m* Trevor Jones
Cyril Cusack, Niall Toibín, Frances Quinn,
Stephen Mason, Bill Paterson.

O'Neill of the Glen
Ire 1916 3 reels silent b/w
d J M Kerrigan *w* W J Lysaght *ss* M T
Pender
J M Kerrigan, Fred O'Donovan, J M Carre,
Nora Clancy, Brian Magowan.

Oscar Wilde: Spendthrift of Genius
Ire 1986 58m col D
prod RTE *d* Seán Ó Mórdha *w* Richard
Ellmann *ph* Cedric Culliton *m* Alan
Seavers
Voices: Denys Hawthorne (narrator), Alan
Stanford, Barbara Brennan, Seamus Forde.

Our Boys
Ire 1980 40m b/w DF
d Cathal Black *w* Dermot Healy *ph*
Thaddeus O'Sullivan *m* Bill Somerville-
Large
Mick Lally, Vincent McCabe, Archie
O'Sullivan, Seamus Ellis.

Our Country
Ire 1948 8m b/w D
wd Liam O'Leary *ph* Brendan Stafford
Seán MacBride, Noel Hartnett, Noel
Browne.

Our Neighbour's Children
Ire 1960 10m b/w D
wd Colm O Laoghaire *ph* Jim Mulkerns
narr Ray McAnally

Out of Time
Ire/GB 1987 53m col F
prod Strongbow Films *d* Robert Wynne-
Simmons *w* Ronald Frame *ph* Thaddeus
O'Sullivan *m* Roger Doyle
Sian Phillips, Phyllis Logan, Kate
Thompson, Oliver Maguire.

The Outcasts
Ire/GB 1982 100m col F
wd Robert Wynne-Simmons *ph* Seamus
Corcoran *m* Stephen Cooney
Mick Lally, Mary Ryan, Cyril Cusack, Don
Foley, Brenda Scallon.

Páisti Ag Obair/Children at Work
Ire 1973 10m col D G
wd Louis Marcus *ph* Robert Monks *m*
Gene Martin

A Passing Shower
Ire 1917 silent b/w F
d Fred O'Donovan

Pathetic Gazette
Ire 1930 silent b/w DS

Patterns series
Ire 1979-83 27m col D
d, ph David Shaw-Smith *w, narr* Conor
McAnally, Tom McGurk, Brendan
O'Hehir, Hilary Orpen *m* Brian Boydell,
Roger Doyle, Jolyon Jackson

Young craftsmen and craftswomen:
Ken Thompson — Stone carver
Keith Leadbetter — Glass blower
Eugene Lamb — Pipe maker of Fanore
Nick Moss — Potter
Norman and Veronica Steele —
Cheesemakers of Beara
Danny Osborne — Sculptor of birds in
porcelain
Joseph Hogan — Basket maker of Lough
Nafooey
Alison Erridge — Ballycar design
Fred Carroll — Rock collector
Edmund and Carmen Chesneau —
Craftsmen in leather.

Paying the Rent
Ire 1920 silent b/w F
d John MacDonagh *ph* Brian Magowan
Arthur Sinclair.

Peil/Football
Ire 1962 23m col D
d Louis Marcus *w* Breandán O hEithir *ph*
Vincent Corcoran *m* Artane Boys' Band
narr Pádraig Tyers, Micheál O hEithir

Pigs
Ire 1984 79m col F
d Cathal Black *w* Jimmy Brennan *ph*
Thaddeus O'Sullivan *m* Roger Doyle
Jimmy Brennan (also narrator), George
Shane, Maurice O'Donoghue, Liam
Halligan, Kwesi Kay, Joan Harpur.

The Playboy of the Western World
Ire 1962 100m col F
wd Brian Desmond Hurst *pl* J M Synge *ph*
Geoffrey Unsworth *m* Sean O Riada
Siobhán McKenna, Gary Raymond,
Elspeth March, Liam Redmond.

Poc ar buile/The Woes of Golf
Ire 1973 8m col D G
d Louis Marcus *ph* Robert Monks *m* Gene
Martin *narr* Niall Toibín

Poitín/Poteen
Ire 1978 65m col F G
prod Cinegael *d* Bob Quinn *w* Colm
Bairead *ph* Seamus Deasy
Cyril Cusack, Niall Toibín, Donal
McCann, Máireéad Ní Conghaile.

Portrait of Dublin
Ire 1952 20m b/w D
wd Liam O'Leary *ph* Brendan Stafford

The Prisoner
Ire 1982 12m col A
wd Tim Booth *poem* W B Yeats *ph* Seamus
McInerney *m* Dr Strangely Strange *narr*
Tara Merry

The Promise of Barty O'Brien
Ire 1951 49m b/w F
d George Freedland *w* Seán Ó Faoláin *ph*
Brendan Stafford
Eric Doyle, Harry Brogan, Eileen Crowe.

The Purple Taxi
orig title: Un taxi mauve
Fr/It/Ire 1977 120m col F
d Yves Boisset *w* Michel Déon, Yves
Boisset *n* Michel Déon *ph* Tonino Delli
Colli *m* Philippe Sarde, Schubert
Fred Astaire, Charlotte Rampling, Peter
Ustinov, Philippe Noiret, Agostina Belli.

Rafferty's Rise
Ire 1917 silent b/w F
d Fred O'Donovan *ph* William Moser
Fred O'Donovan, Brian Magowan,
Kathleen Murphy.

Reefer and the Model
Ire 1988 93m col F
d Joe Comerford *w* Joe Comerford,
Eoghan Harris *ph* Breffni Byrne *m* Johnny
Duhan
Ian McElhinny, Carol Scanlan, Sean
Lawlor, Ray McBride.

Remembering Jimmy O'Dea
Ire 1985 52m col D
prod Poolbeg Prods *wd* Donald Taylor
Black *ph* Sean Corcoran
Maureen Potter, Ursula Doyle, Rita
O'Dea, Noel Purcell, James Plunkett,
Connie Ryan, John Jordan.

The Restless Knives
Ire 1968 26m b/w D
prod Radharc Films

Return to Glennascaul
Ire 1951 22m b/w F
wd Hilton Edwards *ph* George
Fleischmann *m* Hans Gunther Stumpf
Orson Welles, Michael Laurence, Helena
Hughes, Shelah Richards.

Return to the Island
Ire/UK/Germ/USA 1963 27m col D
d George Fleischmann *w* Reg Coast

Revival
Ire 1980 75m col D
d Louis Marcus *ph* Robert Monks
John Kavanagh.

Rhapsody of a River
Ire 1965 12m col D
d Louis Marcus *ph* Robert Monks *m* Sean
O Riada

Riders to the Sea
Ire 1935 40m b/w F
d Brian Desmond Hurst *pl* J M Synge *ph*
Eugen Schüfftan
Ria Mooney, Denis Johnston, Kevin
Guthrie, Sara Allgood, Shelah Richards.

Riders to the Sea
Ire 1987 46m col F
d Ronan O'Leary *pl* J M Synge *ph*
Wolfgang Suschitzky bsc *m* Ian Llande,
Michael Hewer
Geraldine Page, Amanda Plummer, Barry
McGovern, Joan O'Hara, Micheal
O Briain, Sachi Parker.

The Rising of the Moon
aka: Three Leaves of a Shamrock
Ire/USA 1957 81m b/w F
d John Ford *w* Frank Nugent *s* Frank
O'Connor, Malcolm J McHugh, Lady
Gregory *ph* Robert Krasker *m* Eamonn
O'Gallagher
Tyrone Power (narrator), Noel Purcell,
Cyril Cusack, Jack McGowran, Jimmy
O'Dea, Donal Donnelly, Maureen Delany,
Maureen Connell, Eileen Crowe.

Rituals of Memory
Ire 1977 17m b/w D
d Pat Murphy

The Rockingham Shoot
N Ire 1987 60m col F
prod BBC N Ireland *d* Kieran Hickey *w*
John McGahern *ph* Philip Dawson *m*
Mozart

Bosco Hogan, Niall Toibín, Tony Rohr, Marie Kean, Oliver Maguire.

Rocky Road to Dublin
Ire 1968 75m b/w D
wd Peter Lennon *ph* Raoul Coutard Georges Liron *m* The Dubliners, Luke Kelly
Seán Ó Faoláin, Conor Cruise O'Brien, John Huston, Jim Fitzgerald.

Rosaleen Dhu
Ire 1920 4000' silent b/w
d William Power
William Power

Safe Cycling
Ire 1949 10m b/w D
wd Liam O'Leary *ph* George Fleischmann

Sam Thompson: Voice of Many Men
Ire 1986 53m col D
prod Poolbeg Prods *wd* Donald Taylor Black *ph* Thaddeus O'Sullivan *m* Bill Whelan
Stephen Rea.

Samuel Beckett, Silence to Silence
Ire 1984 80m col D
prod RTE *d* Seán Ó Mórdha *w* Richard Ellmann, Declan Kiberd *ph* Peter Dorney *m* based on Schubert
Billie Whitelaw, Jack McGowran, Patrick Magee; poems read by David Warrilow.

Saoirse?/Freedom
Ire 1961 90m b/w D G
d, compilation George Morrison *w* George Morrison, Seán Mac Reamoinn *ph* archive footage, Vincent Corcoran *m* Sean O Riada *narr* Liam Budhlaeir, Pádraig Ó Raghallaigh, Aindreas O Gallchóir

The Scar
Ire/GB 1987 53m col F
d Robert Wynne-Simmons *w* Robert Wynne-Simmons, Tom Gallacher *n* A V Mellor *ph* Thaddeus O'Sullivan *m* Stephen Cooney
Ken Colley, Gerard McSorley, Olwen Fouere, David Heap.

The Schooner
Ire 1983 53m col F
prod Aisling Films *d* Bill Miskelly *w* Marie Jackson *ss* Micheál McLaverty *ph* Seamus Deasy *m* Van Morrison
Lucie Jamieson, Michael Gormley, Johnny Marley, Ann Hasson, Barry Lynch.

A Seat Among the Stars series
N Ire 1984 6 x 26m col D
prod Ulster TV *wd* R S Brien *narr* R Maxwell

A Second of June
Ire 1984 40m col F
prod RTE *d* Francis Stapleton *w* Francis Stapleton, Fergus Manifold *ph* Nick O'Neill *m* Roger Doyle
Lisa Birthistle, Dermot King, Mary Stokes, Derek Molloy.

Self Portrait with Red Car
Ire 1977 16m col F
prod Cinegael *wd* Bob Quinn *ph* Joe Comerford *m* Roger Doyle
Brian Bourke.

Sheila
Ire 1985 23m col S
prod Yellow Asylum *wd* Alan Gilsenan *ph* Peter Butler *m* various
Anne Enright, Jean Trench.

Short Story: Irish Cinema 1945-1958
Ire 1986 62m b/w and col D
prod BAC Films *wd* Kieran Hickey *ph* compilation footage *narr* Bosco Hogan

Siege
Ire 1976 col F
prod RTE *d* Deirdre Friel *w* Eugene McCabe *ph* Stuart Hetherington

The Silent Art
Ire 1959 12m b/w D
wd Louis Marcus *ph* Robert Monks *m*
Bernard Geary, Declan Townsend *narr*
Dan Donovan

The Silent Order: Cistercian Monastery Roscrea
Ire 1948 15m b/w D
d, ph George Fleischmann *narr* Richard
Massingham

Sinn Féin Review 1 & 2
Ire 1919 silent b/w
d Norman Whitten

Sometime City
Ire 1986 37m col F
prod Cityvision *d* Joe Lee, Frank Deasy *w*
Frank Deasy *ph* Seamus Deasy *m* Michael
Holohan
Michele Houlden, David O'Meara, David
Nolan, Mary Ryan, Joe Savino.

Steel Chest, Nail in the Boot and the Barking Dog
Ire 1986 54m col D
d David Hammond *ph* David Barker *m*
John Anderson

A Summer Ghost
Ire/GB 1987 53m col F
d Robert Wynne-Simmons *w* M J
Fitzgerald *ph* Thaddeus O'Sullivan *m* John
Buckley
Susan Bradley, Dearbhla Molloy, Brian
McGrath, Alison McKenna.

This Most Gallant Gentleman
Ire 1966 16m col DS
wd Colm O Laoghaire *ph* Colm
O Laoghaire, Nick O'Neill *m* Paddy
Moloney and The Chieftains

This Other Eden
Ire 1959 80m b/w F

d Muriel Box *w* Patrick Kirwan, Blanaid
Irvine *pl* Louis d'Alton *ph* Gerald Gibbs *m*
W Lambert Williamson
Leslie Phillips, Niall McGinnis, Harry
Brogan, Paul Farrell, Geoffrey Golden,
Audrey Dalton, Norman Rodway.

Three Funerals
Ire 1975
prod RTE *d* John Kelleher, Joe Mulholland

Tibradden
Ire 1942
d John White

To the Western World
Ire 1982 32m col DF
wd, narr Margy Kinmonth *ph* Ivan
Strasburg *m* Richard Harvey
Niall Toibín, Patrick Laffan, Tom Hickey,
Brendan Cauldwell.

Top of the Morning
Ire 1935 18m b/w

Turkana
Ire 1966 32m b/w D
prod Radharc Films

Uncle Nick
Ire 1938 b/w F
d Tom Cooper
Jerry O'Mahony.

An Unfair Love Affair
Ire 1916 silent b/w
d J M Kerrigan
J M Kerrigan, Fred O'Donovan, Nora
Clancy.

The Voice of Ireland
Ire 1932 49m b/w F
d Colonel Victor Haddick *songs* Richard
Hayward

Voyage to Recovery
Ire 1952 b/w DF

d Gerard Healy *ph* George Fleischmann
Marie Kean, Joe Lynch.

W B Yeats — A Tribute
Ire 1950 27m b/w D
d, ph George Fleischmann *w* John D
Sheridan *m* Eamonn O'Gallchovhair
Cyril Cusack, Siobhán McKenna, Micheál
MacLiammóir.

Waterbag
Ire 1984 15m col
d Joe Comerford *ph* Thaddeus O'Sullivan

A Week in the Life of Martin Cluxton
Ire 1971 70m col F
prod RTE *d* Brian MacLochlainn *w*
Caoimhin O Marcaigh, Brian
MacLochlainn *ph* Stuart Hetherington
Laurie Morton, Bill Foley, Dearbhla
Molloy, Jimmy Bartley, Derek King.

Whaling Ashore and Afloat
Ire 1908 silent D
d Robert Paul

Wheels
Ire 1976 18m col S
d Cathal Black *w, ss* John McGahern
Brendan Ellis, Paul Bennett, Tom Jordan.

When Love Came to Gavin Burke
Ire 1917 6 reels silent b/w F
d Fred O'Donovan
Fred O'Donovan, Nora Clancy, Stephen
Gould, Brian Magowan, Valentine
Roberts.

Wicklow Gold
Ire 1922 silent b/w F
d John MacDonagh
Jimmy O'Dea, Chris Sylvester, Ria
Mooney, Kathleen Carr.

The Widow Malone
Ire 1916 silent b/w F
d J M Kerrigan

Willie Reilly and His Colleen Bawn
Ire 1920 silent b/w F
d John MacDonagh *n* William Carleton
Brian Magowan, Frances Alexander, Jim
Plant.

Willie Scouts while Jessie Pouts
Ire 1918 silent b/w F
d William Power *ph* Matt and Bob Tobin

Withdrawal
Ire 1974 27m col F
d Joe Comerford *w, n* David Chapman
Mark Quinn, Marian O'Loughlin.

The Woman Who Married Clark Gable
Ire/GB 1985 28m b/w F
d Thaddeus O'Sullivan *w* Andrew
Pattman *ss* Seán Ó Faoláin *ph* Jack Conroy
m John Buckley
Bob Hoskins, Brenda Fricker, Eamonn
Kelly, Peter Caffrey.

Woman's Wit
Ire 1917 silent b/w
d J M Kerrigan
J M Kerrigan, Fred O'Donovan, Kathleen
Murphy.

A World of Houses series
Ire 1975 6 x 27m col D
wd, ph David Shaw-Smith
Presenter: Mike Murphy.

The Year of the French
Ire 1982 6 x 52m col F
prod RTE *d* Michael Garvey *w* Eugene
McCabe, Pierre Lary *n* Thomas Flanagan
ph Ken Murphy *m* Paddy Moloney
Jeremy Clyde, Oliver Cotton, Jean-Claude
Drouot, Keith Buckley.

Yeats Country
Ire 1965 18m col D
wd, ph Patrick Carey *m* Brian Boydell
narr Niall Toibín, Tom St John Barry

Filmography of Irish-related films

Acceptable Levels
GB 1983 100m col DF
d John Davies *w* Gordon Hann, Kate McManus, Ellin Hare, John Davies, Robert Smith, Alastair Herron *ph* Robert Smith *m* Nick Garvey
Andrew Rashleigh, Kay Adshead, Sally McCafferty, George Shane, Peter Dean, Tracey Lynch.

Arrah-na-Pogue
USA 1911 3 reels 3000′ silent b/w F
d Sidney Olcott *w* Gene Gauntier *pl* Dion Boucicault *m* Walter Cleveland Simon
Jack Clark, Gene Gauntier, Sidney Olcott, Agnes Mapes, Arthur Donaldson, Robert Vignola.

Ascendancy
GB 1982 85m col F
d Edward Bennett *w* Edward Bennett, Nigel Gearing *ph* Clive Tickner *m* Ronnie Leahy
Julie Covington, Ian Charleson, John Phillips, Susan Engel, Philip Locke.

Barry Lyndon
GB 1975 187m col F
wd Stanley Kubrick *n* W M Thackeray *ph* John Alcott *md* Leonard Rosenman
Ryan O'Neal, Marisa Berenson, Patrick Magee, Hardy Kruger, Marie Kean.

Boy Soldier
Wales 1986 98m col F
d Karl Francis
Richard Lynch, Emer Gillespie, Bernard Hill.

Cal
GB 1984 102m col F
d Pat O'Connor *w, n* Bernard Mac Laverty *ph* Jerzy Zielinski *m* Mark Knopfler
Helen Mirren, John Lynch, Ray McAnally, Donal McCann, John Kavanagh, Tom Hickey.

Captain Boycott
GB 1947 93m b/w F
d Frank Launder *w* Wolfgang Wilhelm, Frank Launder, Paul Vincent Carroll, Patrick Campbell *n* Philip Rooney *ph* Wilkie Cooper *m* William Alwyn
Stewart Granger, Kathleen Ryan, Alastair Sim, Robert Donat, Mervyn Johns, Cecil Parker, Noel Purcell, Niall McGinnis.

The Cause of Ireland
GB 1983 107m col D
prod Platform Films *d* Chris Reeves *w* Geoffrey Bell *ph* David Glyn, Steve Sprung *narr* Anne Lamont

The Colleen Bawn
USA 1911 3 reels 3000′ silent b/w F
d Sidney Olcott *w* Gene Gauntier *pl* Dion Boucicault
Sidney Olcott, Gene Gauntier, Jack Clark, Robert G Vignola, J P McGowan, George H Fisher.

The Company of Wolves
GB 1984 95m col F
d Neil Jordan *w* Neil Jordan, Angela Carter *s* Angela Carter *ph* Bryan Loftus *m* George Fenton
Sarah Patterson, Angela Lansbury, David Warner, Micha Bergese, Stephen Rea, Graham Crowden, Brian Glover.

The Country Girls
GB 1983 103m col F
d Desmond Davis *w, n* Edna O'Brien *ph* Denis Lewiston *m* Francis Shaw
Maeve Germaine, Jill Doyle, Sam Neill, John Kavanagh, Niall Toibín.

Curious Journey
GB 1979 50m col DF
d Gareth Wynn Jones *w* Kenneth Griffiths *ph* Gareth Owen, Mike Reynolds *m* The Chieftains
Maire Comerford, Joseph Sweeney, Sean

Cavanagh, John O'Sullivan, Brigid Thornton, Sean Harling, Martin Walton, David Nelligan, Tom Barry.

The Dead
GB/USA/W Germ 1987 83m col F
d John Huston *w* Tony Huston *ph* Fred Murphy
Anjelica Huston, Donal McCann, Dan O'Herlihy, Donal Donnelly.

Every Picture Tells a Story
GB 1984 85m col F
d James Scott *w* Shane Connaughton *ph* Adam Barker-Mill *m* Michael Storey
Phyllis Logan, Alex Norton, Leonard O'Malley, John Docherty, Mark Airlie, Paul Wilson, Willie Joss.

Excalibur
USA 1981 140m col F
d John Boorman *w* John Boorman, Rospo Pallenberg *ph* Alex Thomson *m* Trevor Jones
Nigel Terry, Helen Mirren, Nicol Williamson, Nicholas Clay, Cherie Lunghi.

The Fishermaid of Ballydavid
USA 1911 silent b/w F
d Sidney Olcott

Flight of the Doves
USA 1971 101m col F
wd Ralph Nelson *n* Walter Macken *ph* Harry Waxman *m* Roy Budd
Ron Moody, Dorothy McGuire, Helen Raye, Dana, Jack Wild, Stanley Holloway, Niall Toibín.

For Ireland's Sake
USA 1914 silent b/w F
wd Sidney Olcott
Sidney Olcott, Gene Gauntier, Jack Clark.

The Fox of Glenarvon
orig title: Der Fuchs von Glenarvon
Germ 1940 col F
d Max W Kimmich
Ferdinand Marian, Olga Tschechowa, K L Diehl.

The Gentle Gunman
GB 1952 88m b/w F
d Basil Dearden *w, pl* Roger MacDougall *ph* Gordon Dines *m* John Greenwood
John Mills, Dirk Bogarde, Elizabeth Sellars, Barbara Mullen, Eddie Byrne, Joseph Tomelty, Gilbert Harding, Robert Beatty, Liam Redmond, Jack McGowran.

Gipsies in Ireland
USA 1911 1 reel silent b/w F
d Sidney Olcott

The Girl of Glenbeigh
USA 1917 silent b/w F
d Sidney Olcott

Guns in the Heather
GB 1968 90m col F
d Robert Butler *w* Herman Groves *n* Lockhart Amerman *ph* Michael Reed *m* Buddy Baker
Glenn Corbett, Alfred Burke, Kurt Russell, Patrick Dawson, Niall Toibín.

Hennessy
GB 1975 104m col F
d Don Sharp *w* John Gay *s* Richard Johnson *ph* Ernest Steward *m* John Scott
Rod Steiger, Richard Johnson, Lee Remick, Trevor Howard, Eric Porter, Peter Egan.

Hungry Hill
GB 1946 92m b/w F
d Brian Desmond Hurst *w* Daphne du Maurier, Terence Young, Francis Crowdy *ph* Desmond Dickinson
Margaret Lockwood, Dennis Price, Cecil Parker, Michael Denison, F J McCormick, Dermot Walsh, Jean Simmons, Eileen Herlie, Siobhán McKenna, Eileen Crowe, Dan O'Herlihy.

The Informer
GB 1929 83m silent b/w F
d Arthur Robison *w* Benn W Levy, Rolfe E Vanlo *n* Liam O'Flaherty *ph* Werner Brandes, T Sparkuhl
Lars Hanson, Lya de Putti, Warwick Ward, Carl Harbord.

The Informer
USA 1935 91m b/w F
d John Ford *w* Dudley Nichols *n* Liam O'Flaherty *ph* Joseph H August *m* Max Steiner
Victor McLaglen, Heather Angel, Margot Grahame, Preston Foster, J M Kerrigan, Una O'Connor.

Ireland: Behind the Wire
aka: Behind the Wire Ireland
GB 1974 110m b/w D
prod Berwick Street Collective

Ireland 50 Years Ago
USA 1911 silent b/w D
d Sidney Olcott

Ireland — A Nation
GB 1914 5 reels silent b/w
d Walter MacNamara
Barry O'Brien.

Ireland the Oppressed
USA 1911 1 reel 1000' silent b/w
d Sidney Olcott *w* Gene Gauntier
Jack Clark, Gene Gauntier, Sidney Olcott, Robert Vignola.

The Irish in Us
USA 1935 84m b/w F
d Lloyd Bacon *w* Earl Baldwin *ph* George Barnes *md* Leo F Forbstein
James Cagney, Pat O'Brien, Olivia de Havilland, Mary Gordon, Frank McHugh.

Irish Wives and English Husbands
GB 1907
d Arthur Melbourne-Cooper

Jack B Yeats: Assembled Memories 1871-1957
GB 1980 37m col F
wd, ph Thaddeus O'Sullivan *m* John Tams, Graeme Taylor
Bosco Hogan, Sebastian Shaw.

Juno and the Paycock
GB 1930 85m b/w F
d Alfred Hitchcock *w* Alfred Hitchcock, Alma Reville *pl* Sean O'Casey *ph* Jack Cox
Sara Allgood, Edward Chapman, Marie O'Neill, Sidney Morgan, John Laurie.

The Lad from Old Ireland
USA 1910 10m 1009' silent b/w F
d Sidney Olcott *w* Gene Gauntier *ph* George Hollister
Sidney Olcott, Gene Gauntier.

Lamb
GB 1985 110m col F
d Colin Gregg *w, n* Bernard Mac Laverty *ph* Mike Garfath *m* Van Morrison
Liam Neeson, Harry Towb, Hugh O'Connor, Frances Tomelty, Ian Bannen, Ronan Wilmot.

Little Nellie Kelly
USA 1940 100m b/w F
d Norman Taurog *w* Jack McGowan *pl* George M Cohan *ph* Ray June *songs* George M Cohan, Roger Edens, Lew Brown, Arthur Freed
Judy Garland, George Murphy, Charles Winniger, Douglas McPhail, Arthur Shields, Forrester Harvey.

Lost Belongings
GB 1987 6 x 60m col F
d Tony Bicat *w* Stewart Parker
Catherine Brennan, Gerard O'Hare.

Man of Aran
GB 1934 76m b/w D
d, ph Robert Flaherty *w* Robert and Frances Flaherty *m* John Greenwood
Colman 'Tiger' King, Maggie Dirane.

Mona Lisa
GB 1986 104m col F
d Neil Jordan *w* Neil Jordan, David Leland
ph Roger Pratt *m* Michael Kamen and others
Cathy Tyson, Bob Hoskins, Michael Caine, Robbie Coltrane, Clarke Peters.

Mountains o' Mourne
GB 1938 85m b/w F
d Harry Hughes *w* Gerald Brosnan *s* Daisy L Fielding *m* various
Niall McGinnis, Rene Ray, Jerry Verno, Betty Ann Davies.

Naming the Names
GB 1986 86m col F
prod BBC TV *d* Stuart Burge *w* Anne Devlin *ph* Michael Williams *m* Simon Rogers
Sylvestra le Touzel, Mick Ford, James Ellis, Michael Maloney, Eileen Way.

No Resting Place
GB 1951 77m b/w F
d Paul Rotha *w* Paul Rotha, Colin Lesslie, Michael Orrom *n* Ian Naill *ph* Wolfgang Suschitzky bsc *m* William Alwyn
Michael Gough, Noel Purcell, Jack McGowran, Eithne Dunne, Brian O'Higgins.

Odd Man Out
GB 1947 115m b/w F
d Carol Reed *w* F L Green, R C Sheriff *n* F L Green *ph* Robert Krasker *m* William Alwyn
James Mason, Robert Newton, F J McCormick, Cyril Cusack, Kathleen Ryan, Dan O'Herlihy, Denis O'Dea, Maureen Delany, Joseph Tomelty.

On a Paving Stone Mounted
GB 1978 96m b/w D
wd, ph Thaddeus O'Sullivan *m* Christy Moore

Annabel Leventon, Stephen Rea, Miriam Margoyles, Mannix Flynn, Gabriel Byrne.

Ourselves Alone
aka: River of Unrest
GB 1936 70m b/w F
d Walter Summers, Brian Desmond Hurst *w* Dudley Leslie, Marjorie Jeans, Dennis Johnstone *ss, pl* Dudley Sturrock, Noel Scott *ph* Walter Harvey, Bryan Langley
John Lodge, John Loder, Antoinette Cellier, Niall McGinnis, Maire O'Neill.

The Outsider
aka: Michael
Neth 1979 128m col F
wd Tony Luraschi *s* Colin Leinster *ph* Ricardo Aronovitch *m* Ken Thorne, Matt Molloy and others
Craig Wasson, Sterling Hayden, Patricia Quinn, Niall O'Brien, T P McKenna, Niall Toibín, Ray McAnally.

Paddy the Next Best Thing
GB 1923 7200' silent b/w F
d Graham Cutts *w* Herbert Wilcox, Eliot Stannard *n* Gertrude Page *ph* Rene Guisart
Mae Marsh, Darby Foster, Lilian Douglas, George K Arthur.

Paddy the Next Best Thing
USA 1933 75m b/w F
d Harry Lachman *w* Edwin Burke *n, pl* Gertrude Page *ph* John Seitz
Janet Gaynor, Warner Baxter, Walter Connolly, Harvey Stephens, Margaret Lindsay.

Parnell
USA 1937 115m b/w F
d John M Stahl *w* John Van Druten, S N Behrman *pl* Elsie T Schauffler *ph* Karl Freund *m* William Axt
Clark Gable, Myrna Loy, Edmund Gwenn, Edna May Oliver, Alan Marshal, Donald Crisp, Billie Burke.

Passages from James Joyce's *Finnegans Wake*
USA 1965 97m b/w F
d Mary Ellen Bute *w* Mary Manning, Mary Ellen Bute *pl* Mary Manning *n* James Joyce *ph* Ted Nemeth *m* Elliot Kaplan
Martin J Kelly, Jane Reilly, Peter Haskell, Page Johnson, John V Kelleher, Ray Flanagan.

The Patriot Game
Fr 1978 97m b/w D
wd Arthur Mac Caig *ph* Arthur Mac Caig, Théo Robichet *m* Horslips and others *narr* Winnie Marshall

A Pint of Plain
GB 1972 40m b/w D
wd Thaddeus O'Sullivan, Derrick O'Connor *ph* Dick Perrin
Tony Haygarth, Tony Rohr, Toby Salaman, Anthony Trent.

A Portrait of the Artist as a Young Man
GB 1977 92m col F
d Joseph Strick *w* Judith Rascoe *n* James Joyce *ph* Stuart Hetherington *m* Stanley Myers
Bosco Hogan, T P McKenna, John Gielgud, Rosaleen Linehan, Maureen Potter.

Le Puritain
Fr 1937 87m b/w F
d Jeff Musso *s* Liam O'Flaherty *ph* C Courant *m* J Dollin, Jeff Musso
Jean-Louis Barrault, Viviane Romance, Pierre Fresnay, Mady Berry, Jean Tisier.

The Quiet Man
USA 1952 129m col F
d John Ford *w* Frank Nugent *s* Maurice Walsh *ph* Winton C Hoch, Archie Stout *m* Victor Young
John Wayne, Maureen O'Hara, Barry Fitzgerald, Victor McLaglen, Ward Bond, Francis Ford, Sean McClory, Jack McGowran.

Reflections
GB 1984 100m col F
d Kevin Billington *w, n* John Banville *ph* Mike Molloy *m* Rachel Portman
Gabriel Byrne, Harriet Walter, Donal McCann, Fionnula Flanagan.

Robert Emmet, Ireland's Martyr
USA 1914 silent b/w F
d Sidney Olcott
Jack Melville.

Rory O'More
USA 1911 1 reel 1000' silent b/w F
d Sidney Olcott *w* Gene Gauntier *n* Samuel Lover
Jack Clark, Gene Gauntier, Arthur Donaldson, Robert Vignola.

Ryan's Daughter
GB 1970 206m col F
d David Lean *w* Robert Bolt *ph* Freddie Young *m* Maurice Jarre
Sarah Miles, Robert Mitchum, Chris Jones, John Mills, Trevor Howard, Leo McKern, Niall Toibín.

A Sense of Loss
USA/Switz 1972 132m b/w D
wd Marcel Ophuls *ph* Simon Edelstein *m* various

Shake Hands with the Devil
GB 1959 110m b/w F
d Michael Anderson *w* Ivan Goff, Ben Roberts *n* Rearden Connor *ph* Erwin Hollier *m* William Alwyn
James Cagney, Dana Wynter, Glynis Johns, Cyril Cusack, Don Murray, Michael Redgrave, Sybil Thorndike, Noel Purcell, Niall McGinnis, Richard Harris, Ray McAnally.

The Shamrock Handicap
USA 1926 6 reels 5685' silent b/w F
d John Ford *w* John Stone *s* Peter Barnard Kyne *ph* George Schneiderman

Janet Gaynor, Leslie Fenton, J Farrell MacDonald, Louis Payne.

The Shaughraun
USA 1912 3 reels 3000' silent b/w F
d Sidney Olcott *w* Gene Gauntier *pl* Dion Boucicault
Sidney Olcott, Jack Clark, Robert Melville, Gene Gauntier.

Song o' My Heart
USA 1930 85m b/w F
d Frank Borzage *w* Tom Barry, J J McCarthy *ph* Chester Lyons, Al Brick *m* various
John McCormack, Maureen O'Sullivan, John Garrick, J M Kerrigan, Alice Joyce.

Stage Irishman
UK 1968 15m col D
prod BAC Films *d* Kieran Hickey *w* Des Hickey *ph* Bestick Williams, Sean Corcoran
Cyril Cusack, Donal McCann.

A Terrible Beauty
aka: Night Fighters
GB 1960 90m b/w F
d Tay Garnett *w* Robert Wright Campbell *n* Arthur J Roth *ph* Stephen Dade *m* Cedric Thorpe Davie
Robert Mitchum, Anne Heywood, Dan O'Herlihy, Cyril Cusack, Richard Harris.

Traveller
GB 1982 80m col F
d Joe Comerford *w* Neil Jordan *ph* Thaddeus O'Sullivan *m* Davy Spillane and others
Judy Donovan, Davy Spillane, Alan Devlin, Johnny Choil Mhaidhc, Paddy Donovan, Joe Pilkington.

Ulysses
GB 1967 132m b/w F
d Joseph Strick *w* Joseph Strick, Fred Haines *n* James Joyce *ph* Wolfgang Suschitzky bsc *m* Stanley Myers
Maurice Roeves, Milo O'Shea, Barbara Jefford, T P McKenna, Anna Manahan, Maureen Potter, Martin Dempsey, Joe Lynch.

The Violent Enemy
GB 1968 98m col F
d Don Sharp *w* Edmund Ward *n* Hugh Marlowe *ph* Alan Hume *m* John Scott
Tom Bell, Ed Begley, Owen Sullivan, Susan Hampshire, Noel Purcell, Michael Standing.

Wings of the Morning
GB 1937 89m col F
d Harold Schuster *w* Tom Geraghty *s* Donn Byrne *ph* Ray Rennahan, Jack Cardiff *m* Arthur Benjamin *songs* John McCormack
Henry Fonda, Annabella, Stewart Rome, John McCormack, Leslie Banks, Irene Vanbrugh.

The Writing on the Wall
orig title: Nous étions tous des noms d'arbres
Fr/Belg 1982 114m col D
wd Armand Gatti *ph* Armand Marco *m* Philippe Hemon-Tamie, The Demons
John Deehan, Brendan "Archie" Deeney, Paddy Doherty, Nigel Haggan, John Keegan.

You'll Remember Ellen
USA 1911 silent b/w F
d Sidney Olcott *poem* Thomas Moore
Gene Gauntier, Jack Clark.

Young Cassidy
GB 1964 110m col F
d Jack Cardiff, John Ford *w* John Whiting from the writings of Sean O'Casey *ph* Ted Scaife *m* Sean O Riada
Rod Taylor, Maggie Smith, Edith Evans, Flora Robson, Michael Redgrave, Julie Christie, Jack McGowran, Sian Phillips, T P McKenna.

Bibliography of Irish cinema

The following bibliography, consisting of books, booklets and articles in journals, magazines and newspapers, is arranged chronologically. Where possible, authorship has been established. In general, articles in Irish film journals, such as *Film Directions* (1975-) and *The Irish Limelight* (1917-18) are excluded. # denotes an item from the "cinema" section of *Manuscripts Sources for the History of Irish Civilisation* Ed. Richard J Hayes. Boston: G K Hall & Co, 1965.

Books, pamphlets and articles in books

Nicholl, William. "Synopsis of a lecture on electric cinematograph". *Belfast Natural History and Philosophical Society Proceedings*, 1897: 62-65.

The Classic Cinema, Castle Lane, Belfast (souvenir programme). December 1923. (Public Record Office of Northern Ireland D3573/2/4).

Gauntier, Gene. *Blazing the Trail*. (Unpublished manuscript dated 16 December 1928, lodged at the Museum of Modern Art).

Mullen, Pat. *Man of Aran*. Cambridge, Mass: MIT Press, 1935; 1970.

Devane S J, Father Richard/Oliver Bell Eds. *Irish Cinema Handbook*. Dublin: The Parkside Press, 1943.

O'Leary, Liam. *An Invitation to the Film*. Tralee: The Kerryman, 1945.

Cinema and Theatre Annual Review and Directory of Ireland 1947. Dublin: The Parkside Press, 1947.

Ó Conluain, Proinsias. *Scéal Na Scannán*. Dublin: Oifig an tSolathair, 1953.

Ó Conluain, Proinsias. *Ar Scannain Fein*. Dublin: Foilseachain Naisiunta Teoranta, 1954.

Marcus, Louis. *The Irish Film Industry*. Dublin: *Irish Times* 1967.

Report of the Film Industry Committee. Dublin: The Stationery Office, 1968.

Maclochlainn, Alfred. "Cinema." *Encyclopaedia of Ireland*. Dublin: Allen Figgis, 1968: 383-385.

Film Industry Bill 1970. Dublin: The Stationery Office, 1970.

The Irish on Film. Toronto: Toronto Film Society, 1970.

Baxter, John. *The Cinema of John Ford*. New York: A S Barnes & Co, 1971: 52-57.

Hickey, Kieran. *The Light of Other Days: Irish Life at the Turn of the Century in the Photographs of Robert French*. Boston: David Godine, 1975.

Watters, Eugene and Matthew Murtagh. *Infinite Variety: Dan Lowrey's Music Hall 1879-97*. Dublin: Gill and Macmillan, 1975: 165-170.

De Felice, James. *Filmguide to Odd Man Out*. Bloomington and London: Indiana University Press, 1975.

Richards, J M. *Provision for the Arts*. Dublin: The Arts Council and the Calouste Gulbenkian Foundation, 1976.

O'Leary, Liam. *Cinema Ireland 1896-1976*. Dublin Arts Festival, 1976.

Directory of Irish Production Companies and Documentary Films. Dublin: Irish Film Workers' Association, 1976.

Report of Investigations by the Examiner of Restrictive Practices into the Distribution of Cinema Films. Dublin: Department of Industry and Commerce, 1977.

Farrell, Michael. The Cinema Industry and the Nation: Ireland. PhD University of Southern California, 1977.

Slide, Anthony. "The O'Kalems." Aspects of American Film History Prior to 1920. Metuchen, N J: The Scarecrow Press, 1978: 87-97.

Gray, John. Theatres and Cinemas in Belfast: a retrospective view: catalogue of an exhibition (at Belfast Central Library) 12-30 May, 1979. Belfast: Irish and Local Studies Department, Central Library, 1979 (9 leaves).

Gray, John. Checklist of Belfast Cinemas. Belfast: Irish and Local Studies Department, 1979 (5 leaves).

Gray, John. Summary of ephemeral and archival material relating to Belfast theatres and cinemas held by agencies in Belfast. Belfast: Irish and Local Studies Department, Central Library, 1979 (9 leaves).

Cine Irlandes. Barcelona: Filmoteca National de Espana, 1979.

Dolan, Martin. The Irish National Cinema and its Relationship to Irish Nationalism. PhD University of Wisconsin-Madison, 1979; published Ann Arbor, Michigan: Xerox University Microfilms.

Clarke, Thomas J. "On Tone Memorial" and "The Bodenstown Film." Letters to John Devoy, 18 and 25 June 1913. Devoy's Post Bag: 1871-1928 vol 2 1880-1928. Eds. William O'Brien and Desmond Ryan. Dublin: The Academy Press, 1979: 410-11.

O'Leary, Liam. Rex Ingram: Master of the Silent Cinema. Dublin: The Academy Press, 1980.

Rockett, Kevin. Film and Ireland: A Chronicle. Dublin: A Sense of Ireland, 1980.

The Collected Screenplays of Bernard Shaw. Edited with an introduction by Bernard F Dukore. London: George Prior Publishers, 1980.

Morrison, George. "Film-Making." Integrating Tradition: The Achievement of Sean O Riada. Eds. Bernard Harris and Grattan Freyer. Irish Humanities Centre, Ballina, and Keohanes, Ballina and Sligo, and Dufour Editions Inc., Chester Springs, Pennsylvania, 1981: 64-71.

Morrison, George. The Irish Civil War: An Illustrated History. Dublin: Gill and Macmillan, 1981.

Ellmann, Richard. James Joyce. New York: Oxford University Press, 1982.

Proceedings of the Public Hearing of Bord Scannán na hÉireann/Irish Film Board. Dublin: Irish Film Board, 1982.

Morrison, George. "Cinema." Ireland: A Cultural Encyclopedia. Ed. Brian de Breffny. London: Thames and Hudson, 1983: 64.

Standúin, Pádraic. Súil le Breith. Clo Chonamara, 1983.

Shaw-Smith, David. Ireland's Traditional Crafts. London: Thames and Hudson, 1984.

Irish Films. Dublin: Irish Film Board, 1984.

McLoone, Martin and John MacMahon. *Television and Irish Society: 21 Years of Irish Television*. RTE-Irish Film Institute, 1984.

Cathcart, Rex. *The Most Contrary Region: The BBC in Northern Ireland 1924-84*. Belfast: The Blackstaff Press, 1984.

O'Leary, Liam and George Fleeton. *A Seat Among the Stars: The Cinema and Ireland*. Belfast: Ulster Television, 1984.

Kavanagh, David, Kieran Hickey, Luke Gibbons and Kevin Rockett. *The Green on the Screen: A Celebration of Film & Ireland* Dublin: Irish Film Institute, 1984.

Open, Michael. *Fading Lights and Silver Screens: A History of Belfast Cinemas*. Antrim, N Ireland: Greystone Books, 1985.

Robertson, James. "Ireland." *The British Board of Film Censors: Film Censorship in Britain, 1896-1950*. London: Croom Helm, 1985: 86-89.

Woodman, Kieran. *Media Control in Ireland*. Galway: Galway University Press, 1985.

Dunn, Joseph. *No Tigers in Africa! Recollections and Reflections on 25 Years of Radharc*. Dublin: The Columba Press, 1986.

Hammond, David. Ed. *Steel Chest, Nail in the Boot and the Barking Dog: The Belfast Shipyard — a story of the people told by the people*. Belfast: Flying Fox Films, 1986.

Hurst, Brian Desmond. *Hurst*. Unpublished autobiography. British Film Institute (donated by Astrid Frank, 1986).

Morrison, George. *An Irish Camera*. London: Pan Books, 1979.

Jordan, Neil and David Leland. *Mona Lisa*. London: Faber and Faber, 1986.

Quinn, Bob. *Atlantean*. London: Quartet Books, 1986.

Films in Focus (publication of Bord Scannán na hÉireann/Irish Film Board). Autumn 1986 and Spring 1987.

Cinema Irlandais February 1987 (programme booklet of Irish film season at the Cinémathèque Française, Pompidou Centre, Paris).

Woll, Allen L and Randall M Miller. "Irish." *Ethnic and Racial Images in American Film and Television: Historical Essays and Bibliography*. New York: Garland, 1987: 261-274.

Rockett, Kevin, Luke Gibbons and John Hill. *Cinema and Ireland*. London: Croom Helm, 1987.

Filmscan '87: The ACTT Film and Video Directory for Ireland.

Sheehan, Helena. *Irish Television Drama: A Society and its Stories*. Dublin: RTE, 1987.

Kearney, Richard. "Nationalism and Irish Cinema." *Transitions: Narratives in Modern Irish Culture*. Manchester University Press, 1988: 173-192.

Jordan, Neil. *Angel*. London: Faber and Faber, 1988.

Catalogues from the International Festival of Film and Television in Celtic Countries 1980-1988.

General historical guides

Lyons, F S L. *Ireland Since the Famine.* London: Fontana, 1981.

Beckett, J C. *The Making of Modern Ireland 1603-1923.* London: Faber and Faber, 1985.

Brown, Terence. *Ireland: A Social and Cultural History 1922-85.* London: Fontana, 1985.

Articles in journals, magazines and newspapers

Anon. (announcement of International Cinematograph Society Volta) *The Bioscope* 23 December 1909: 37.

Anon. "A Kalem Girl in Ireland." *Moving Picture World* 15 July 1911: 31.

Bush, Stephen. "The Shaughraun." *Moving Picture World* 14 December 1912: 1065.

Blaisdell, George. "Irish History on the Screen." *Moving Picture World* 29 August 1914: 1245.

Belfast: Public Record Office of Northern Ireland. D.2587: Correspondence relating to Coleraine Picture Palace Ltd., 1915-1922.

Dublin: National Archives (formerly Dublin Public Records Office). M.5190: Memorandum and articles of association of the Film Company of Ireland, March 2 1916.

Laegh (pseud.) "Matters of the Moment." (references to the provision of the right kind of films for children) *Catholic Bulletin* April 1916: 193.

Anon. "Pictures in Ireland-Under-Arms." *The Bioscope* 18 May 1916: 845.

Editorial. *Catholic Bulletin* January 1917: 5-6 (mentions former Irish MP appointment as Chairman of the British Board of Film Censors in England).

Drennan, Max. "The cinema and its dangers." *Irish Monthly* February 1917: 74-82.

National Library of Ireland, Dublin, Ms. 18,543: Typescript letter of Robert V Justice, Secretary of the Film Company of Ireland Ltd., Dublin to the assistant Provost Marshall, Dublin Castle, requesting permission to use a gun in a scene from *Knocknagow*, with indication of approval, 29 June 1917.

Ryan, John. "The Cinema Peril." *Studies* March 1918: 112-126.

Anon. "Knocknagow." *The Bioscope* 16 October 1919: 58.

Anon. (on landmine explosion) *Irish Times* 19 March 1923: 9.

Anon. "Duller Dublin: Theatres and Cinemas Closed." *Irish Times* 18 June 1923: 5.

Lawrence, W J. "The Moving Pictures of Other Days." *Irish Monthly* October 1923: 496-500.

Majolier, Christine. "The Art of Raquel Meller." *Dublin Magazine* May 1925: 672-674.

McMahon, Charles A. "The American Public and the Motion Picture." *Studies* March 1926: 47-64.

Price, Mona. "The Aesthetic of the Film: a review of *Films of the Year 1927-28* by Robert Herring." *Dublin Magazine* April-June 1928: 48-52.

Reardon, John P. "The Cinema and the Child." *Studies* September 1929: 431-442.

Martindale, Reverend Cyril Charles S.J. "The Cinema and the Adult." *Studies* September 1929: 443-448.

M.S.P. Review of *Star-dust in Hollywood* by Jan and Cara Gordon. *Dublin Magazine* April-June 1931: 72-73.

Montgomery, Niall. Review of *Film* by Rudolf Arnheim. Translated by L M Sieveking and Ian F D Morrow. *Dublin Magazine* October-December 1933: 77-80.

'John' (pseud.). "When the Fianna Raided a British Propaganda Film." *An Phoblacht* 22 December 1934: 8.

Power, Joseph A. "Fine All-Irish Amateur Film." *Irish Independent* 21 January 1935: 7.

Anon. "National Film Institute for I.F.S." *Sight and Sound* Summer 1935: 51-2.

Beere, T J. *Cinema Statistics in Saorstát Éireann*. Statistical and Social Inquiry Society of Ireland Journal, 89th Session, 1935-36.

Ó Faracháin, Riobárd. "Everyman Talks to a Cinema Manager." *Irish Monthly* March 1936: 153-160.

Sheridan, John Desmond. "The Flight from Leisure." *Irish Monthly* May 1936: 287-292.

Bodkin, A P. "The Time and Tide: Contemporary Cuttings on the Cinema, with a Commentary." *Irish Monthly* May 1936: 293-304.

Anon. "The IRA on the Screen." (on *Ourselves Alone*). *Irish Times* 7 July 1936: 4.

P.M.L. "The Voice of the Irish Public." (an article on *The Informer*) *Irish Monthly* August 1936: 540-547.

Dalton, G F "The Irish Film." *Ireland Today* September 1936: 64-65.

Bodkin, A P. "Dublin Documentary Film Unit." *Irish Monthly* October 1936: 682-93.

Anon. "Building Battle Starts in Northern Ireland" and "Running Time in Irish Kinemas: Films Hacked' by Censors." *Kinematograph Weekly* 15 October 1936: 37.

O'Cahill, Donal. "And so we made *The Dawn*." *The Capuchin Annual* (1937): 119-22.

MacManus, Francis. "The Shape of Nonsense to Come." *Irish Monthly* March 1937: 181-185.

Dalton, G. F. "Films: Discontinuity". *Ireland Today* August 1937: 73-74.

Bodkin, A P. "Countryside Cinemas Un-Ltd." *Irish Monthly* October 1937: 689-700.

Fallon, Gabriel et al. "Celluloid Menace." *The Capuchin Annual* (1938): 248-271.

O'Leary, Liam. "Films." *Ireland Today* vols 1-3 June 1936-March 1938.

Hughes, Emily. "A Timid Suggestion: put forward by one who knows nothing of film technique." *Irish Monthly* April 1938: 273-278.

O'Mahony, N. "Fact and Film." *Irish Monthly* May 1938: 331-338.

Anon. "Hollywood: Land of Make Believe." *Irish Monthly* September 1939: 640-645.

Hutchins, Patricia. "The Mountain and the Swan." *Sight and Sound* Autumn 1939: 107-8.

O'Leary, Liam. "Dublin to Killarney." *Sight and Sound* Autumn 1940: 52.

Dowling, John. "Meditations on the Movies." *Ulster Parade* no 2 (1941): 34-37.

The Bellman (pseud.). "Meet Dr Hayes or The Genial Censor." *The Bell* November 1941: 106-114.

MacCarthy, Henry. "Children and the Cinema." *The Bell* November 1942: 83-9.

Montgomery, James. "The Menace of Hollywood." *Studies* December 1942: 420-428.

O'Leary, Liam. "Developments in Éire." *Sight and Sound* Summer 1943: 12.

Brennan, Marion. "The Fourpenny Flicks." *The Bell* December 1943: 244-248.

National Library of Ireland, Dublin, Ms. 17,984: Dr Michael Quane Papers: Miscellaneous Items, including report of Inter-Departmental Committee on Educational Films (1944).

Sinkins, Melchior A A "In the Land of the Gaels." *Kinematograph Weekly* 13 January 1944: 79-90.

MacCarthy, Bridget G et al. "The Cinema as a Social Factor." *Studies* March 1944: 45-67.

Parsons, Reverend Wilfrid S J. "The Focus is on Faith." *Irish Monthly* October 1944: 412-423.

Sherry, Peter. "Production in Éire." *Sight and Sound* October 1944: 72-73.

Glazebrook, Lucy. "A Tour of Films." *The Bell* (series) April 1945-February 1946.

Hogg, Edward. "Hollywood Grows Up." *The Bell* July 1945: 319-329.

Mac Gall, Rex (pseud. i.e. Deasún Breatnach). "How Your Films Are Censored." *The Bell* September 1945: 493-501.

Sheehy, Tom. "Rank Clears Way to Éire Market." *Motion Picture Herald* 10 November 1945: 28.

Anon. "J A Rank Acquires Big Irish Cinema Interest." *Irish Times* 19 January 1946: 1.

Hogg, Edward. "Hollywood's New Departure." *The Bell* May 1946: 155-162.

Mac Gall, Rex (pseud. i.e. Deasún Breatnach). "Towards an Irish Film Industry." *The Bell* June 1946: 234-241.

Murtagh, Reverend James G. "Hollywood is a Myth." *Irish Monthly* June 1946: 257-64.

O'Dwyer, Kevin. "The Child and the Cinema in Éire." *Sight and Sound* Summer 1946: 68.

O'Donnell, Donat (pseud. ie Conor Cruise O'Brien). "Beauty and Belfast. A Note on *Odd Man Out* by F L Green." *The Bell* May 1947: 55-62.

Hutchins, Patricia. "News From Ireland." *Sight and Sound* Summer 1947: 50-51.

O'Keefe, C. "Catholic Film Developments." *Irish Monthly* October 1947: 437-40.

O'Leary, Liam. "*Captain Boycott*." *The Bell* November 1947: 64-67.

O'Leary, Liam. "The Film Society Movement." *The Bell* December 1947: 56-64.

O'Leary, Liam. "Theatre and Film." *The Bell* February 1948: 52-57.

O'Leary, Liam. "Theatre and Films." *The Bell* March 1948: 57-60.

Gerrard, John. "A History of Irish Production." *Sight and Sound* Spring 1948: 20-23.

Grierson, John. "A Film Policy for Ireland." *Studies* September 1948: 283-291.

Sheehy, T J M. "Towards an Irish Film Industry." *Irish Monthly* September 1948: 417-20.

Fallon, Gabriel. "The Film called Hamlet." *Irish Monthly* November 1948: 495-501.

Boland, Barney. "Hollywood Irish." *Irish Bookman* December 1948: 73.

O'Shea, Brendan. "Documentaries Need Sponsors." *Irish Cinema Quarterly* Winter 1948: 21-23.

Gerrard, John. "Ireland and the Documentary." *Sight and Sound* Winter 1948-9: 164-165.

O'Leary, Liam. "Initiation." *Irish Cinema Quarterly* 1948/49: 8-9.

Gerrard, John. "Irish Documentaries." *Sight and Sound* Autumn 1948: 133-134.

Gerrard, John. "Film Societies in Ireland." *Sight and Sound* Spring 1949: 134.

Gerrard, John. "Irish Censorship — Or Fighting for a Cleaner Cinema." *Sight and Sound* Summer 1949: 81-82.

O'Shea, Brendan. "Irish Cinema Roundabout." *International Film Review* 5 (1950): 72-74.

O'Leary, Liam. "Films, directors and scripts." *Irish Monthly* November 1950: 504-513.

MacBride, Seán. "A Native Film Industry." *National Film Quarterly* Winter 1950: 26.

Hutchins, Patricia. "James Joyce and the Cinema." *Sight and Sound* August-September 1951: 9-12.

Anon. "Hopes For An Irish Film Industry Are Increasing." *Daily Film Rental* 7 May 1952: 8.

Anon. "Ireland Import £1,799 Worth of Equipment from Britain." *Daily Film Renter* 24 July 1952: 14.

Anon. "Old Failing, being amusing tales about the early days of the cinema in Carlow." *Carloviana* December 1952: 15.

Edwards, Hilton. "An Irish Film Industry?" *The Bell* January 1953: 456-463.

Anon. "Seat Prices 'decontrolled' in Ireland." *Today's Cinema* 26 January 1953: 7.

Anon. "Irish Union Urged: Bar Royal Film." *Today's Cinema* 29 April 1953: 9.

Jameson, Storm. "The Death of the Novel." *Irish Writing* June 1953: 55-59.

Anon. "The Irish (33%) and the Cinema." *Today's Cinema* 9 June 1953: 3,5.

Anon. "Ireland's Coronation Decision." *Kinematograph Weekly* 18 June 1953: 26.

Ó Conluain, Proinsias. "Ireland's First Films." *Sight and Sound* October-December 1953: 96-98.

Mulhern, Bernard. "The Power of the Cinema." *Irish Monthly* November 1953: 431-435.

Mitchell, George. "Sidney Olcott." *Films in Review* April 1954: 175-181.

Anon. "Éire Kinema Survey." *Kinematograph Weekly* 27 January 1955: 7.

Redmond, Brigid. "Films and Children." *Studies* Summer 1956: 227-233.

Hurst, Brian Desmond. "The Director." *Films and Filming* February 1957: 27, 32.

Dooley, Roger B. "The Irish on the Screen I and II." *Films in Review* May 1957: 211-217; June-July 1957: 259-270.

Charman, Bernard. "Ireland's First Studio." *Daily Cinema* 17 December 1958: 9-14.

Neeson, Sean. "Cork Film Festival." *Threshold* Autumn 1959: 76-80.

McCaffrey, John. "James Joyce Managed Ireland's First Cinema." *Ireland's Own* 19 December 1959: 9.

Neeson, Sean. "Cork Film Festival." *Threshold* Autumn-Winter 1960: 82-90.

Fanning, David. "Sidney Olcott in Ireland." *Irish Times* 19 June 1961: 8.

Anon. "Cinemas Should Show Irish Language Programmes." *Kinematograph Weekly* 23 January 1964: 7.

O'Leary, Colm. "The Mystique of Robert Flaherty." *The Dubliner* Summer 1964: 26-34.

Kelly, Reverend John C S J. "Cinematic." *Studies* Winter 1964: 420-438.

O'Connor, Seamus. "A National Need: An Irish Film Archive." *Studies* Spring 1965: 83-90.

Marcus, Louis. "Production: Film Scripting and Direction." *Vision* Summer 1965: 14-15.

Sheridan, John D. "Writing Film Scripts." *Vision* Autumn 1965: 14-15.

Anon. "Renters Ask Minister to Intervene in Ireland." *Daily Cinema* 20 December 1965: 1, 6.

Morrison, George. "An Irish National Film Archive." *Éire-Ireland* 1:4 (1966): 39-62.

Slide, Anthony. *"The Colleen Bawn."* *Vision* Spring 1967: 22-23.

Sheehy, T J M. "The Tourist Film." *Vision* Summer 1967: 4-5.

Slide, Anthony. "The Silent Cinema and Ireland." *Vision* Autumn 1967: 20.

Sheehy, T J M. "Huston Urges Ireland Develop Film Industry." *Motion Picture Herald* 11 October 1967: 12, 14.

Slide, Anthony. "A British Film Pioneer in Ireland." *Vision* Winter 1967: 5-6.

Linehan, Fergus. "The shortage of good shorts in our cinemas." *Vision* Spring 1968: 12-14.

Anon. "Irish John Huston Blasts John Lehners." *Variety* 3 April 1968: 1, 11.

Miller, Liam. "Patrick Carey and the making of *Yeats Country*." *Ireland of the Welcomes* August-September 1968: 19-30.

Codelli, L. "Entretien avec Marcel Ophuls sur *A Sense of Loss*." *Positif* June 1973: 60-67.

Chase, Richard. "How *No Go!* was Filmed." *American Cinematographer* August 1973: 1017, 1053-1059, 1014-1017.

"Politics and Autobiography: An Interview with Marcel Ophuls by Daniel Yergin." *Sight and Sound* Winter 1973/74: 20-22.

O'Leary, Liam. "Ireland's Film Culture Past and Present." *Hibernia* 7 February 1975: 23.

Sweeney, Conor. "O'Leary: Search for a Film Heritage." *Hibernia* 5 September 1975: 11, 12.

"Fergus Linehan Talks to Joseph Strick." *Irish Times* 27 February 1976: 10.

Sweeney, Conor. "Cinema: The Irish Experience." *Hibernia* 12 March 1976: 21.

Morrison, George. "Film Making in Ireland — Time for New Directions?" *Hibernia* 7 May 1976: 32.

Anon. "Bungling That Led to Strike in RTE." *Sunday Independent* 23 May 1976: 4.

Cusack, Jacqueline. "Ireland at Cannes." *Irish Times* 2 June 1976: 8.

Falk, Quentin. "Ireland? No Threat to Us, says Sapper." *Screen International* 5 June 1976: 1.

Carty, Ciaran. "Studios Seek Private Finance For Movies." *Sunday Independent* 10 October 1976: 2.

Carty, Ciaran. "Why I'll always be a foreigner in Connemara." (interview with Bob Quinn) *Sunday Independent* 7 November 1976: 2.

Denieffe, Michael. "Ghost Walks Again for Film Makers." *Sunday Independent* 7 November 1976: 7.

Danker, Trevor. "Shaw's Offer Ignored — So We Missed Millions." *Sunday Independent* 21 November 1976: 15.

Anon. "Little Hope for State Subsidy for Irish Film Industry Next Year." *Irish Times* 14 December 1976: 5.

Rushe, Desmond. "The Problems Regarding Uris's Film." *Irish Independent* 21 December 1976: 6.

Gleeson, John. "Irish Film Industry Needs Reform." *Sunday Independent* (letter to the editor) 2 January 1977: 25.

Linehan, Fergus. "The Irish Film Theatre." *Irish Times* 12 January 1977: 8.

Anon. "Arts Council to set up new Irish Film Theatre." *Irish Times* 12 January 1977: 11.

Mayer, P M. "Celtic Twilight at Cannes." *Irish Times* 25 May 1977: 8.

Anon. "Film Trade to Have Public Enquiry." *Irish Times* 3 June 1977: 11.

Anon. "Film Bill Coming, Says Studio Boss." *Sunday Independent* 12 June 1977: 2.

Younge, Deidre. "False Start for a Film Industry." *Hibernia* 24 June 1977: 23.

MacGiolla Cearr, Peadar. "RTE Censorship Allegations." *Irish Times* 1 July 1977: 10.

Anon. "Operation of Cinema Cartel is denied by Century Fox." *Irish Independent* 9 July 1977: 3.

Anon. "Film Cartel Claim Denied by Irish Distributor." *Irish Times* 9 July 1977: 8.

O'Fearail, Padraig. "When Films Were Made in Bray." *Irish Times* 16 August 1977: 8.

Lewis, Frank. "When the Movie Makers First Came to Killarney." *The Irish Press* 28 October 1977: 9.

Carty, Ciaran. "The First Flicker of Irish Cinema." *Sunday Independent* 1 January 1978: 21.

"Ireland's Film Industry" (letter by film-makers). *Irish Times* 3 June 1978: 15.

Hayes, Tom. "Native Film Industry: Twenty Years Aborting." *Irish Times* 13 June 1978: 8.

Cullen, Brian. "An Extra in the Great Train Robbery." *Irish Times* 15 July 1978: 9.

Wall, Joseph. "The Public in Relation to Cinema in Ireland Today." *Studies* Winter 1978: 343-346.

Downing, Taylor. "The Film Company of Ireland." *Sight and Sound* Winter 1979/80: 42-45.

Rockett, Kevin. "Irish Cinema: Notes on Some Nationalist Fictions." *Screen* Winter 1979/80: 115-123.

Rockett, Kevin. "Film Censorship and the State." *Film Directions* 3:9 (1980): 11-15.

O'Leary, Liam. "A Very Private Archive: Cinema in Ireland." *Historical Journal of Film, Radio and Television* vol 1: 2 (1981): 183-187.

Johnston, Claire. "*Maeve*: Interview with Pat Murphy." *Screen* 22:4 (1981): 54-71.

Lowery, Robert G. "The Silver Screen and The Emerald Isle." *Aisi-Eiri, the magazine of Irish-America*. Fall 1981: 18-23.

Kearney, Richard. "Avenging *Angel*: An Analysis of Neil Jordan's First Feature Film." *Studies* Autumn 1982: 297-302.

Fernett, Gene. "The Historic Film Studios: The Kalem Story." *Classic Images* December 1982: 10-12.

Gibbons, Luke. "'Lies That Tell the Truth': *Maeve*, History and Irish Cinema." *The Crane Bag* 7:2 (1983): 148-155.

Rockett, Kevin. "Stars Get in Your Eyes." *Framework* 25 (1984): 28-41.

O'Connor, Barbara. "Aspects of Representation of Women in Irish Film." *The Crane Bag* 8:2 (1984): 79-83.

Feeney, Peter. "Censorship and RTE." *The Crane Bag* 8:2 (1984): 61-64.

Kearney, Richard. "Film Notes: The Iphigeneia Complex in Recent Irish Cinema." *Studies* Spring 1984: 67-69.

Burns, Walter. "10 Questions and 9 Answers about Film Culture in Northern Ireland." *Film Directions* 6:24 (1984): 3-5.

Mackillop, James. "Ireland and the Movies: From the Volta Cinema to RTE." *Éire-Ireland* Summer 1984: 7-22.

Birchard, Robert. "Kalem Company: Manufacturers of Moving Picture Films." *American Cinematographer* August/September 1984: 34-38.

Harvey, Sylvia. "'Those Other Voices': An Interview with Platform Films." *Screen* November-December 1984: 31-48.

Moran, Dermot. "Irish Film: Neil Jordan and Angela Carter." *Irish Literary Supplement* Spring 1985: 5.

Banville, John, Thaddeus O'Sullivan and Andrew Pattman. "Birchwood: Extracts from the screenplay." *The Irish Review* 1 (1986): 65-73.

Gibbons, Luke. "The Politics of Silence: *Anne Devlin*, Women and Irish Cinema." *Framework* 30-31 (1986): 2-15.

Kythreotis, Anna. (on Neil Jordan) *The Times* 6 September 1986: 16.

Casey, Daniel. "Irish Films and Film Making." *The Recorder* Winter 1986.

de Burca, Seamus. "Ireland — A Nation." Unpublished MSS (3 pp.) 8 July 1982; another version (2 pp.) 13 February 1987.

Anon. "Irish Eyes." *Stills* February 1987: 15-16.

Gibbons, Luke. "Word and Image: The Resistance to Vision." *Graph: Irish Literary Review* Spring 1987: 2-3.

O'Leary, Liam. "Why We Need a National Film Archive." *Irish Times* 30 April 1987: 12.

Marcus, Louis. "Facts and Fantasies of 20 Years of Irish Film." *Irish Times* 29 July 1987: 8.

Taylor, Doreen. "Death brings mountains of mourning" (on demise of IFB). *The Guardian* 17 August 1987: 7.

Gibbons, Luke. "Romanticism in Ruins: Developments in Recent Irish Cinema." *The Irish Review* 2 (1987): 59-63.

Johnston, Pat. "Ireland — A Nation." *Dublin Historical Record* September 1987: 145-147.

Comiskey, Ray. "Liam O'Leary: Lifetime Fighter for Film." *Irish Times* 6 February 1988: Weekend II.

Muldoon, Paul. "The Irish at the Odeon." Review of *Cinema and Ireland* by Kevin Rockett, Luke Gibbons and John Hill. *Times Literary Supplement* March 25-31, 1988: 325-326.

Arden, John. "A Potential Natural Cultural Voice." *Krino* Spring 1988: 63-69.

Hattendorf, Manfred. "Journey in a Buoyant Haze (six months in Irish film, 1987)." *Krino* Spring 1988: 70-77.

McIlroy, Brian. "The Past of Irish Film-Making." Review of *Cinema and Ireland* by Kevin Rockett, Luke Gibbons and John Hill. *Irish Literary Supplement* Spring 1988: 8.

Battersby, Eileen. "Irish films down by the Riverside." *Irish Times* 18 May 1988: 14.

Finlan, Michael. "Script to screen — how *Reefer* got made." *Irish Times* 29 July 1988: 10.

Index

Italic type indicates still.

208

.